M000198888

Out of the Shadows

African American Baseball
from the Cuban Giants
to Jackie Robinson

The Best of *NINE*

Edited and
with an introduction by
Bill Kirwin

University of Nebraska Press : Lincoln and London

Library of Congress Cataloging-in-Publication Data
Out of the shadows: African American baseball from
the Cuban Giants to Jackie Robinson / [edited by]
Bill Kirwin.   p.   cm.   Includes index.
ISBN-13: 978-0-8032-7825-7 (paperback: alkaline paper)
ISBN-10: 0-8032-7825-x (paperback: alkaline paper)
1. African American baseball players — History.
2. Negro leagues — History. 3. Discrimination in
sports — United States — History. I. Kirwin, Bill, 1937–
GV863.A1058   2005
796.357′64′08996073–dc22   2005004661

Contents

Introduction

No moment in baseball history is more important than the April day in 1947 when Jackie Robinson stepped onto Ebbets Field, ending a ban that had extended back to 1882 prohibiting African Americans from fully participating in the National Pastime. "Cap" Anson's dictum, in 1882, of "Get that nigger off the field," referring to the presence of black player Moses Fleetwood Walker on a Major League ground, merely reflected the overwhelming social attitude of the day. But in 1947 baseball no longer followed custom, but changed it. Branch Rickey and Jackie Robinson's integration plans went beyond challenging Major League baseball's apartheid policies, their actions set in motion and preceded, by a decade, the actions of the courts and government to rectify the injustice of segregation throughout society in general.

The road to Robinson's appearance at Ebbets Field on April 15, 1947, was a long, often crooked, and dark one. Partially hidden and ignored by the general population, black baseball emerged as a parallel version of the National Pastime subsisting on the margins of society. Black ball differed from Major League ball in many different ways. The game as played by African American players relied on speed and offered entertainment as a bonus. Rather than the static dependence that Major League baseball placed on power hitting, Negro baseball utilized speed, bunting, and hit-and-run tactics. Attempts to organize various Negro leagues met with limited success. Andrew "Rube" Foster organized the National Negro League (NNL)in 1919. In 1923, the Eastern Colored League (ECL) was formed, resulting in the playing of the first Colored World Series in 1924. The Kansas City Monarchs of the NNL defeated the ECL representative Hillsdale Club of Philadelphia five games to four with one tie. But scheduling was erratic, finances weak, white newspapers ignored game results, and teams were required to continually barnstorm, resulting in fan apathy.[1]

With the onset of the Depression, the lifeblood of black teams depended more and more on owners scheduling barnstorming games against local white nines. Black teams found money and a sort of once-a-year racial acceptance if they came into a town, played the local team, won or lost graciously, and then left town with a promise to come back and entertain once again the next year. This annual diversion might afford some whites the opportunity to see blacks for the only time in a year; for others it was a rare chance to see black men compete with whites. But the barnstorming exercise was severely constrained. Negro teams were allowed to play and interact in a very proscriptivefashion for the two hours or so that it took to play the game with the local team. No scrappy John McGraw hyperaggressive play would be allowed, just an apparent laid back "we-are-here-to-have-fun" sort of game. After the game they were back on the road. They were not usually allowed to stay or eat in local hotels; rather they were consigned to sleep in a bus or a ghetto flophouse. The money, however, was good, for the owners both of the Negro team and the local team. The attendance for the annual game was often the highest of the year.

*

Parallel with serious Negro ball were the black clown teams, such as the Zulu Cannibal Giants, the Indianapolis Clowns, or the Florida Colored Hoboes. White fans would come out and watch a game featuring the Ethiopian Clowns and the Satchel Paige All-Stars one night and be oblivious of a game featuring the Homestead Grays or the Cuban Giants the next. Clown ball conveniently fit the stereotype that much of the white population had about Negro ball and about African Americans in general. As clowns or entertainers they were welcomed; as serious competitors they were to stay in their place. Entertainment superseded winning. Barnstorming, in the final analysis, significantly contributed to the notion that baseball as played by blacks could not, indeed should not, be taken seriously. It was a ruse, a minstrel show that everyone could go along with, because it was, first and foremost, entertainment.

Barnstorming also weakened attempts by the various Negro teams to be regarded by both the white and black populations as serious competition. The Depression of the 1930s paved the way for the ownership of most Negro professional clubs by numbers bankers. It was difficult for the average fan, white or black, to take a game seriously that appeared to concern itself primarily with entertainment and had such dubious ownership. Serious owners like Cumberland "Cum" Posey of the Homestead Grays might fret that clown ball in effect was ridiculing black players' serious attempts at competitive play. But the reality was that, for the majority of white fans at least, the only role for blacks on the playing field was that of a clown. Exploding cigars, oversize equipment, midgets, female players, phantom routines, and disappearing-ball acts were all part of the circus atmosphere that white audiences expected of a black barnstorming club.

It was perhaps because of this clowning perception most white fans had about Negro baseball that Branch Rickey would come to choose Jackie Robinson. Many serious black players like Buck Leonard believed that Robinson was not, by a long stretch, the best choice to integrate baseball. Leonard claimed that "we had a whole lot better ballplayers than Jackie, but Jackie was chosen 'cause he had played with white boys." [2] Undoubtedly Rickey took that into consideration, but it seems evident that he also was impressed by Robinson's religious background, his non-drinking, noncarousing, independence, and aloofness. Robinson was not one of the guys on the Kansas City Monarchs – he was very much his own man. If Baseball's "Great Experiment," as Jules Tygiel called it, was to succeed, Rickey reasoned that recruiting the player with the most ability was not as important as recruiting a strong-willed individual who would be able to withstand the immense strain that was surely to become part of his life.

*

When I founded NINE in 1992 one of my principle motivations was to offer an opportunity to explore the historical and social implications of black baseball and its impact on the game and greater society in general. When I was a bat boy for the local town team I remember being fascinated by the annual visit of a black barnstorming club. I especially remember some player comments about how good some of the barnstormers were, especially those players who did little clowning or grandstanding. Comments like "that Jigger-boo can hit," or "if you walk that shine it's as good as giving him a double" continue to resonate in my mind, more than a half-century after the fact. Or my father saying to me "Let's go see the blacks play" when the Dodgers were in Boston. (Of course he did not call them "blacks"!) As offensive as these terms are to our ears now, it is worth noting that, within the obvious racist content, there was admiration of the skills of black players. This recognition of baseball skills served as a societal first step out of the subhuman quagmire in which African Americans were immersed. And that was the genius of Rickey's plan. He knew that, given the opportunity to seriously compete, the good black player could hold his own on an integrated diamond. He also had the foresight to realize that once a player or a fan recognized that a player could compete there was a good chance that racist feelings would abate, for, above all, both the white player and the white fan wanted a winning team.[3]

It is obvious that any book about the emergence of black baseball would involve the roles played by Jackie Robinson and Branch Rickey. Thus the articles by Anthony Pratkanis and Marlene Turner lay out the affirmative action model Rickey and Robinson have given advocates of social change. Lee Lowenfish's work about Rickey and Robinson stresses the power of faith. Steve Wisendale's article about Robinson's life outside of the baseball lines and the independent road that Robinson chose illuminates this exceptional individual.

Don Newcombe, like Robinson, was also a pioneer. For Newcombe represented not the first black man on the mound (that honor went to Dan Bankhead), but rather the first truly successful black pitcher in the Majors when he posted a 17–8 record in 1951 and was named the NL Rookie of the Year.[4] Guy Waterman's article outlines the new dimension brought about when suddenly the baseball was in the hands of a huge black man and consequently, as Newcombe recalled, "Nobody was going to bother me."[5]

The initial constraints that Rickey placed on Robinson must have been extremely difficult for a player as fiery as Jackie Robinson. Rickey was looking for the player with "the guts not to fight back." It somehow seems appropriate that this volume offers William Kashatus's article about Dick Allen, for here is someone who was ready to fight at the first opportunity. Less than twenty years after Robinson first stepped on a Major League playing field, Dick Allen's career illustrated how radically the role of black players had changed. Allen was brash, talented, and ever ready to remind people that, although baseball players were well paid, in the end the game was merely another form of slavery.

*

The late Jerry Malloy wrote about the fascinating, often forgotten world of black baseball's first historian, Sol. White. Baseball history owes much to the efforts of Sol. White and to Malloy himself. In his essay "The Birth of the Cuban Giants" Malloy reveals a singular example of how a team of color could maintain its dignity and distinctiveness and demonstrate to the dominant community that, despite the disheartening circumstances, not only could it compete but often better white competition. The Cuban Giants, black professional baseball's first truly professional team, owed much of their existence to the dreams of a Florida hotel entrepreneur who wanted to lavish conspicuous leisure onto his northern winter guests. From such beginnings the Cuban Giants expanded to take on all teams, including Major League teams (often successfully) and offered a model for the numerous teams that were required to play in a segregated society. The black game combined talent and entertainment and served as a source of pride within the African American community. Black ball served notice that, despite all the constraints placed on black ballplayers, they could hold their own if given the opportunity.

*

Baseball can provide a sense of community and power, Rob Ruck tells us, even if people are constricted by poverty and nearly hopeless economic opportunity. To the African American community in Pittsburgh, baseball as played by the Grays and the Crawfords offered such an example, while in San Pedro de Macoris of the Dominican Republic, it offered another. When Branch Rickey claimed that the greatest untapped source of talent was the black race, few thought he was referring beyond the borders of the United States. Today one in six Major League players comes from Latin America; the majority of these come from the southeastern coast of the Dominican Republic. Sammy Sosa, Pedro Martinez, Albert Pujols, Manny Ramirez, Vladimir Guererro – the list goes on and on. It sometimes seems that every Major League organization has a shortstop from either Bani or San Pedro de Macoris.

Effa Manley was an owner like no other. Called the "queen of black baseball," she had players like Larry Doby, Don Newcombe, and Monte Irvin, all of whom went on to play in the Majors.[6] Unlike other Negro League managers she received compensation when Doby, the first black player to play in the American League, was signed by Bill Veeck to play for the Cleveland Indians. Gai Ingham Berlage writes about this tireless civil rights advocate who lent to Negro League owners a well-needed touch of respectability.

Jean Hastings Ardell's essay about Mamie "Peanut" Johnson is as much about the end of the Negro Leagues as it is about another untapped resource – a resource that waits to be developed as soon as given the opportunity. Perhaps in fifty years a volume similar to this one will be compiled citing the achievements and exploits, on and off the field, of the so-called weaker sex.

NOTES

1. See B. Chadwick, *When the Game Was Black and White* (New York: Abbeville, 1985), 23–60.

2. Quoted in D. Rogosin, *Invisible Men: Life in Baseball's Negro Leagues* (New York: Atheneum, 1983), 203.

3. Of course commentators today who on the one hand praise a player for his athleticism yet on the other complain about his lack of knowledge of the game often seem to be speaking in code, especially if the player is of color. During the 2002 season, listening almost daily for two months to a variety of baseball games carried on the MLB Audio network I kept informal data on such comments. I noted that of the nineteen times I heard the "athleticism/lack of knowledge" comment, sixteen times the player in question was black. Thus the obvious hypothesis.

4. Fans of Satchel Paige might argue that Paige, compiling a 6–1 record and 2.48 ERA in his "rookie" Major League season at the age of forty-two, should have been deemed a star player for the 1948 world champion Indians.

5. When as a boy I saw Newcombe play – at least twice – it was not so much his pitching that impressed me, but rather his hitting. For as long as I can remember, I have had a fascination with pitchers who can also hit, and I believe that this interest had its genesis with him hitting the ball all over Braves Field.

6. P. Debono, *The Indianapolis ABCs* (Jefferson NC: McFarland and Co., 1997), 101.

Out of the Shadows

JERRY MALLOY

The Birth of the Cuban Giants

The Origins of Black Professional Baseball

The Cuban Giants, the great colored base ball nine, whose appearance [in Boston] created such interest and enthusiasm, and whose magnificent playing called forth vociferous plaudits, has an interesting and creditable history which shall be known of all colored and white lovers of the national sport. – New York Age, October 15, 1887

THE CUBAN GIANTS, born in 1885, enriched a wide range of communities across the sprawling province of nineteenth-century baseball. They set a standard for black baseball excellence that would be unequalled, though not unchallenged, for ten years. And in the process, they built a foundation for black professional baseball that would survive sixty years of racial exclusion from organized baseball.

White baseball had long abandoned its origins as a gentlemen's social romp, little more than a good excuse for a smashing buffet. A muscular professionalism had propelled the game to new heights of national prestige – and commercial reward. Now, in the mid-1880s, African American baseball took a similar plunge into professionalism. Black baseball established itself as a viable economic entity when the Cuban Giants were born.

The Cuban Giants played a key role in nineteenth-century baseball's halting, uncertain drift toward the color line. The impenetrable veil of racial exclusion that ultimately prevailed obliterated memories of a more hopeful time, a time when the African American role in baseball's future was uncertain and fluid – even appeared promising. The Cuban Giants came into existence at just such a time and prepared black baseball for the harsh realities that were to follow.

Yet surprisingly little has been written about this pioneering team. Those familiar with the Cuban Giants at all probably have two vivid images of them. Image number one is the ball-playing waiters from Babylon, New York. Image number two is of these players jabbering inarticulate gibberish, hoping it sounded enough like Spanish to convince whites that they were Cubans, not black Americans. These two colorful images dominate virtually everything written about the Cuban Giants. And both of them originate in one man: Sol. White.

Solomon (Sol.) White achieved distinction as a player, manager, promoter, journalist, and historian of the black game. But is his portrayal of the Cuban Giants, as ball-playing waiters in linguistic and ethnic disguise, accurate? Or, could it be that Sol. White has, as Samuel Johnson said of Shakespeare's histories, every virtue except that of being right?

A close examination of the Cuban Giants' first year will address these matters and reveal much about the nature of African American baseball and its uneasy relationship with white baseball . . . and white America.

Neither Giants Nor Cubans

The Cuban Giants, who by the way, are neither giants nor Cubans, but thick-set and brawny colored men, make about as stunning an exhibition of ball playing as any team in the country. – New York Sun (quoted in *Sporting Life*, September 5, 1888)

In 1907, Sol. White wrote black baseball's first history: *Sol. White's Official Guide: History of Colored Base Ball*. According to White, Frank P. Thompson, headwaiter at the Argyle Hotel in the Long Island resort community of Babylon, formed a baseball team from among his waiters, whose play amused the hotel's patrons. [1] Encouraged by the makeshift team's popularity, Thompson took them on the road, and signed three key players from the Orions, a prominent black semi-pro team from Philadelphia. "This move," wrote White, " . . . was one of the most valuable acts in the history of colored baseball. It made the boys from Babylon the strongest independent team in the East, and the novelty of a team of colored players with that distinction made them a valuable asset." By the following spring, Walter Cook (white), of Trenton, New Jersey, was their owner, S. K. Govern (black) was their manager, and "Cuban Giants" was their name. [2]

Sol. White played for the Cuban Giants just a few years after these events, and knew many of the people involved. He was well positioned, historically. Plus, the tale has an appealing whimsy to it. Lucky Frank!

It just so happened that his crew of waiters included some of the best African American baseball players in the country.

A more plausible account of the birth of the Cuban Giants appeared twenty years earlier in the *New York Age*, a prominent African American newspaper, in its coverage of a trip the Cuban Giants made to Boston. On October 15, 1887 their Boston correspondent wrote:

> Mr. F. P. Thompson, formerly of Philadelphia, but now of the Hotel Vendome [in Boston], organized in May 1885, in Philadelphia, the Keystone Athletics. On July 1, they were transferred to Babylon, L.I. During the month of August a consolidation of the Keystone Athletics, the Manhattans of Washington, D.C., and the Orions of Philadelphia, took place, under the name of the Cuban Giants. The proprietors were Messrs. F. P. Thompson, L.[*sic*] K. Govern and C. S. Massey.

This account of a tripartite merger probably was based upon an interview with Frank Thompson himself. It indicates that even in an embryonic stage, the Cuban Giants were athletic entertainers in the resort hotel industry. Thompson, a hotelman by trade, had carved a niche for himself with the curiosity of an all-black baseball team. The players may have supplemented their incomes by working as waiters, bellhops, porters, and the like, but these occupations were incidental to their employment as professional baseball players.

The owner of the Orions played no role after the team was formed. The key to the early history of the Cuban Giants is in the careers of Thompson and Govern. But first, let's consider the moniker: why were they called the "Cuban Giants"? The "Giants" part seems easy enough, in view of the National League's powerful and popular New York team. But why "Cuban"?

Again, the prevailing explanation derives from Sol. White. Not, that is, in his 1907 *Guide*, but rather in an article that appeared in *Esquire Magazine* in September 1938:

> Most old-timers today are vague as to the origin of [the name, "Cuban Giants"], but Sol. White – who joined the club four years later . . . – says that the version which came to him is that when that first team began playing away from home, they passed as foreigners – Cubans, as they finally decided – hoping to conceal the fact that they were just American Negro hotel waiters, and talked a gibberish to each other on the field which, they hoped, sounded like Spanish.[3]

As we shall see, several players had played in Havana even prior to the merger that created the Cuban Giants, and some may have learned some rudimentary Spanish. But this exotic linguistic experiment of chattering mock-Spanish must surely have been quickly abandoned (if indeed it was attempted at all). No contemporary accounts reported it, nor did White include it in his 1907 *Guide*. In fact, no one is known to have mentioned it prior to the *Esquire* article in 1938.

Still, avoiding the opprobrium of hostile white Americans by "passing" as Cubans may have been a factor in naming the team, even though such a ruse would hardly have deceived informed baseball fans, who already were accustomed to such euphemisms as "Cuban," "Spanish," and even "Arabian" being applied to black ballplayers by the sporting press. The rationale behind the name may be irretrievably lost, but it seems possible that "Cuban Giants" was chosen, in part, because in the first winter of its existence, that of 1885–1886, the team did play in Cuba.

Establishing a beachhead in Havana was most likely due to S. K. Govern. On July 2, 1886, the *Trenton Times* reported that the team had agreed to play in Cuba from mid-December 1886 through mid-January 1887 and tells of prior winter tours in Havana, probably Govern's Manhattans, dating back to 1882. The best guess is that S. K. Govern, a native of St. Croix, Virgin Islands,[4] was responsible for exploiting (indeed, recognizing) the commercial possibilities of Caribbean winter baseball. Govern was certainly aware that baseball fever in the 1880s was an epidemic of Pan-American dimensions. And nowhere was this more evident than in Cuba, which had a professional baseball league as early as 1878.[5]

Sol. White once wrote that Govern "was a smart fellow and a shrewd baseball man."[6] He could have described Frank Thompson as a smart fellow and a shrewd hotel man. Together, they devised a strategy for the survival of the Cuban Giants that would serve as a paradigm for the future of African American baseball. The key was to play all year. Govern's bookings in Cuba ended in time for the team to repair to St. Augustine, Florida, for the peak of the resort hotels' festive winter season. That a black baseball team should be a part of these festivities was due to Thompson, who put the Cuban Giants into the annual winter employment of Henry Morrison Flagler, whose hotel-and-railroad empire brought Florida into the modern era.

The Colored Employees of the Hotel Ponce de Leon

The colored employees of the Hotel Ponce de Leon will play a game today at the fort grounds with a picked nine from the Alcazar. As both teams possess some of the best colored baseball talent in the United States [,] being largely composed of the famous Cuban Giants, the game is likely to be an interesting one. – St. Augustine Weekly News, January 17, 1889

In fact, at the time the Cuban Giants were born, so was Florida. In the same summer, that of 1885, that the Cuban Giants appeared, Flagler made the momentous decision to build the fabulous Hotel Ponce de Leon in St. Augustine, an unlikely place for such an undertaking. Florida was widely viewed as a swamp-laden wilderness, suitable mainly for alligators and mosquitoes, despite a climate salutary for consumptives. Flagler wondered what St. Augustine could be if a first-rate luxury hotel were available, one with opulent trappings and a variety of amusements, one where he and his wealthy friends could find princely shelter from the harsh winters of the North. Flagler's new vision of St. Augustine was as a place not for the sick to restore health, but for the rich to squander wealth. St. Augustine, he decided, would become the Newport of the South.[7]

The centerpiece would be the Ponce de Leon, which immediately was recognized as one of the country's most luxurious inns.[8] Flagler bought a nearby hotel, then built the Hotel Alcazar and an immensely popular Casino. It was Flagler's determination to provide his wealthy clientele with an extravagant array of first-class amusements that brought Frank Thompson and the Cuban Giants into this unlikely world of lavish, conspicuous leisure.

Flagler hired Osborn D. Seavey, a second-generation Yankee innkeeper, to manage his St. Augustine hotel empire. Somewhere along the way, the careers of Osborn Seavey and Frank Thompson intersected and the two had entered into a long professional alliance. The link between them was the Cuban Giants.

During the team's St. Augustine years, Thompson also formed an organization called the Progressive Association of the United States. The *New York Age,* on February 23, 1889, printed a special correspondence from St. Augustine written by none other than S. K. Govern. He reported that Thompson had called a meeting "to inaugurate a course of annual sermons to the hotel men that come to St. Augustine each winter, and the citizens in general, upon our progress [during] the past twenty-five years." Thompson was named president of the organization and Govern secretary, and at least two players were charter members.

Although nothing is known of the fate of this cadre, it got off to a promising start. At one time, Thompson addressed his crew of employees for forty-five minutes in the dining room of the Ponce de Leon "on the unpardonable sins of race prejudice in the South: "His eloquence [wrote Govern] brought forth many rounds of applause. At the close he invited the men to name any day on which they would speak on the subject and he would arrange for the occasion from time to time as they desired."⁹

Flagler was wrong about St. Augustine. It would become a way-station en route to Palm Beach, the eventual "Newport of the South."¹⁰ There, in 1894, he built the majestic Royal Poinciana Hotel, and later The Breakers. Flagler's St. Augustine hotel manager, Osborn Seavey, did not accompany him to Palm Beach, but African American baseball certainly did. Two decades into the twentieth century, well into the heyday of Rube Foster's Chicago American Giants, the Royal Poinciana and the Breakers were still providing their distinguished guests with the highest caliber of American baseball.¹¹

The Cuban Giants (and black baseball) benefited greatly by this association with Henry Flagler. The late 1880s would prove to be relatively prosperous years for African American baseball, but bleakness loomed ahead. For entire seasons, the Cuban Giants would be the only viable black professional team in the East, due to the increasingly toxic atmosphere of the 1890s and beyond. Many factors contributed to this dark, painful time, a time when black baseball (indeed black America) struggled merely to survive. In large part, the Cuban Giants were successful because of this commerce between wealthy whites and ball-playing blacks, this mixture of America's most and least favored classes. An unlikely alliance between the class most blessed and the one most oppressed was the lasting legacy of African American baseball's headwaiter, Frank Thompson.

The Happiest Set of Men in the World

When Mr. Cook signed his men for . . . 1886, they were the happiest set of men in the world. As one of them told the writer, not one would have changed his position with the President of the United States. – Sol. White's Official Base Ball Guide, 13

When the Cuban Giants headed north from St. Augustine for their first full season of summer baseball in 1886, they had not yet made arrangements for a home base. The journey, during which they won forty straight games, eventually took them to Trenton, New Jersey.[12] Trenton had been active at the origin of what we now call Minor League baseball in 1883, but in 1885, the team moved to Jersey City.[13] Now, thanks to businessman Walter E. Simpson, a town without a team found a team without a town, and the Cuban Giants ended up at Trenton's Chambersburg Grounds. Less than two months later, Simpson sold the team to Walter I. Cook, whose impact on the Cuban Giants would be far more notable.[14]

Cook was a scion of one of the oldest and wealthiest families on the Eastern shore. "Unlike the more straitlaced members of his household," according to one report, "Walter idolized sporting life and spent his money generously on the team."[15] Cook's ballplayers appreciated his generosity, particularly when it came to illnesses and injuries. In gratitude, they played a benefit game in August, donating their pay to him.[16]

Box scores of more than forty games printed in Trenton's two daily newspapers, the *Times* and the *True American,* reveal a team with a potent and diversified offensive attack. The Cuban Giants had long ball hitters, line drive hitters, and crafty base runners. At the heart of the offense was the speed of second baseman (and captain) George Williams, and center fielder Ben Boyd, followed by the power of catcher Clarence Williams, first baseman Arthur Thomas, and shortstop Abe Harrison. Defensively, they were strong up the middle and had a terrific third baseman in Ben Holmes.

Shep Trusty, Billy T. Whyte, and George Parago divvied up the pitching and outfielding chores. The local press called the tall, lean Trusty, with his assortment of hard breaking pitches, "the best colored pitcher in the country,"[17] and he may have been so, had it not been for George Stovey. But we'll get to Stovey later.

How good were these players? The *New York Sun* wrote in 1888 that "[o]ld time ball players . . . will have a revival of old memories if they go to see the Cuban Giants when they are really loaded for bear. . . . [I]t is one of the best teams in the city to see." The same year, New York's correspondent for the *Sporting News* wrote that "[T]here are players among these colored men that are equal to any white players on the ballfield. If you don't think so, go and see the Cuban Giants play. This club, with its strongest players on the field could play a favorable game against such clubs as the New Yorks or Chicagos."[18]

According to Sol. White, "Their games attracted the attention of base ball writers all over the country, and the 'Cuban Giants' were heralded everywhere as marvels of the base ball world. . . . [T]hey were classified as men of talent." He believed that George Williams, Clarence Williams, Billy Whyte, Ben Boyd, Ben Holmes, and Arthur Thomas were players of National League caliber.[19] White had a special fondness for Arthur Thomas, and apparently the Philadelphia Athletics agreed: in June 1886 they offered Thomas a Major League contract, but he declined the offer.[20]

Auspicious Conditions

The Cuban Giants were recognized as a full-fledged professional team in 1886. . . . With the backing of Mr. Walter Cook, a capitalist of Trenton, N.J., and a ground well equipped and adequate for all purposes, the Cuban Giants started their new career under the most auspicious conditions. – Sol. White, *Amsterdam News*, December 18, 1930

Sol. White called the first six years of the Cuban Giants' era "the money period" for nineteenth-century black baseball.[21] Right from the start, the "Cubes" had little difficulty scheduling games against white ball clubs. Even Major League teams. Within weeks of the team's birth, in the fall of 1885, they played both the New York Metropolitans and the Philadelphia Athletics.[22]

On May 28, 1886, in their forty-first game, they suffered their first loss of the season, and it took a Major League team to beat them.[23] Shep Trusty lost to the St. Louis Browns, 9–3, before two thousand Trenton fans. A week-and-a-half later, an exhibition game against the Athletics was rained out after four innings, with the Cuban Giants trailing, 3–0, despite Trusty's working on a no-hitter. On July 21, Trusty pitched them to a 9–4 win over Cincinnati (of the American Association). Five days later, he beat Kansas City's National League Cowboys, 3–2. Valor got the better part of Trusty's discretion, though, when he requested to pitch against the same team the next day and failed to survive the first inning en route to a 13–4 shellacking.

Yet it was a satisfying season with regard to Major League exhibition games for Trenton's thousands of baseball "Kranks." The following year, this same St. Louis Browns team staged a well-publicized boycott in an exhibition game scheduled against the Cuban Giants.[24] Nevertheless, for several years to come, the Cuban Giants continued to play many lucrative games against Major League teams.

Of far greater moment to the Cuban Giants and their Trenton fans, though, was another league: the Eastern League. Cook's goal was to gain admission to a league, preferably the Eastern League. Besides enhanced prestige, Eastern League membership could provide certain safeguards. The Cuban Giants' independence incurred certain vulnerabilities, which were clearly illustrated in the George Stovey affair.

George Washington Stovey, an ill-tempered, left-handed flame-thrower, is generally regarded as the greatest black pitcher of the nine-teenth century. A native of Williamsport, Pennsylvania, the twenty-year-old Stovey was pitching for a white team that was playing in Canada when S. K. Govern signed him to a Cuban Giants contract in June 1886.[25] In his first game, on June 25, he struck out eleven in a 4–3 loss to Bridgeport, of the Eastern League. But before the Cuban Giants had time to use him again, Stovey was literally stolen from them by Jersey City's Eastern League team.

Jersey City manager Pat Powers was in need of pitching, so he returned to his hometown of Trenton for a midnight raid. Years later he told the story to an African American newspaper, the *Cleveland Gazette*:

> By luck I happened to think of a colored pitcher named Stovey in Trenton, a fellow with a very light skin, who was playing on the Trenton team. It was my game to get him to Jersey City the next day in time for the game. I telegraphed a friend to meet me in Trenton at midnight, and went to Stovey's house, roused him up, and got his consent to sign with Jersey City.
>
> Meanwhile some Trenton people got onto the scheme and notified the police to prevent Stovey from leaving town. I became desperate. I worked a member of "Trenton's finest" all right, and finally hired a carriage, and, amid a shower of missiles, drove Stovey to a station below, where we boarded a train for Jersey City.
>
> I gave Stovey $20 to keep up his courage, and dressed him in a new suit of clothes as soon as the stores opened in the morning. I then put him to bed and waited for the game . . .
>
> When I marched my men on the field the public was surprised, [New-ark's players] gave me a laugh . . . Stovey was put in to pitch for the home team, and dropped the Newarks out in one, two, three order.
>
> The game ended with the score 1–0 in Jersey City's favor, and Stovey owned the town.[26]

Powers went on to state that later that year the New York Giants negotiated to buy Stovey from Jersey City so he could be "sent to Chicago to pitch the last four decisive games . . . Stovey had his grip packed and awaited the word," but the call never came, due, no doubt, to Cap Anson's notorious disdain for black players.

Powers then presented Trenton with a Hobson's choice: the Eastern League would forbid its teams from playing exhibition games with the Cuban Giants if Cook attempted to enforce his contract with Stovey. Cook could ill-afford to lose these lucrative bookings, and had no choice but to acquiesce in this extortion.[27] In this case, independence, for the Cuban Giants, amounted to perilous isolation.

The solution, of course was to gain admission to the Eastern League – and it almost happened in mid-season when Meriden, Connecticut, dropped out of the League. Rumors circulated that the Cuban Giants would replace them, but the *Newark News* saw it differently. "While the dusky team is classed among the first-class clubs," they wrote, "there is little prospect of its being admitted, as the color-line will be drawn tight." And they were right. The League chose to resume the season in an unwieldy five-team format rather than admit the Cuban Giants, leading the *Meriden Journal* to speculate that "the dread of being beaten by the Africans had something to do with the rejection of the application of the Cuban Giants. . . . Meriden," they added, "is glad that it is out of a League in which a race prejudice is so strong that a first-class club is refused admission simply because its players are black."[28]

Finally, the 1886 season saw the inauguration of what would prove to be a long rivalry between the Cuban Giants and another black team, the Gorhams of New York City. The Gorhams, owned by an African American named Ambrose Davis, was little more than an accomplished semi-pro team in 1886. The first meeting between these two black teams occurred on August 13, and the Cuban Giants left little doubt as to which team was superior, defeating the Gorhams by a resounding margin of 25–4.

Undeterred, Davis would accumulate capable players, many of whom later played for the Cuban Giants, including Sol. White. Occasionally the Gorhams would reach a level close to parity with the Cuban Giants. As early as 1888, the Gorhams defeated their haughty rivals, 4–3, in a thrilling game in Newburgh, New York.[29] Davis's finest hour would come in 1891 when the heart of the Cuban Giants team, then owned by J. M.

Bright, jumped to the Gorhams, then managed by S. K. Govern, in mid-season. Sol. White rated the resultant coalition, called the Big Gorhams, the greatest African American baseball team in the nineteenth century.[30]

Esteem and Respect for the Race

One fact cannot be doubted, and that is their extremely large following, by no means [all] colored, who flock in hundreds to see them. For the last two seasons the residents of the old Dutch town owe much to the Cuban Giants for the amount of life they have given the place and the interest stimulated in this national sport. If any one doubts the popularity of this colored team, let him stand at 14th Street Ferry upon a Saturday afternoon and hear the comments and see the immense crowds flocking to their games. . . . This is another way of cultivating esteem and respect for the race, and it is a good way, judging from appearances. – New York Age, July 28, 1888

J. M. Bright bought the Cuban Giants from Walter Cook in June 1887 and led them through several tumultuous years. Bright's business acumen would be most valuable for the team, and he was able to place them in the Middle States League in 1889, the team's last year in Trenton. But penurious dealings with his players stood in sharp contrast with Walter Cook's largesse and Bright frequently had to contend with renegade players. Sometimes they fled en masse, as in 1890, when the entire team played as the Colored Monarchs of York, Pennsylvania (see Jerry Jaye Wright's essay elsewhere in this volume); and sometimes in mid-season, as in 1891, when the Big Gorhams played a memorable half-year. Bright was able to reassemble the dissident players annually until they finally found an owner to their liking: E. B. Lamar Jr. of Brooklyn.

In 1896, Lamar signed them all, and called his team of ex-Cuban Giants the "Cuban X Giants."[31] Thereafter, Bright's team, usually inferior to the X's, often was called the "Genuine Cuban Giants" or "Original Cuban Giants." The nominal similarity, which occasioned legal contretemps, was the source of no end of confusion to contemporary fans no less than future historians. Both teams played well past the turn of the century, and Lamar's Cuban X Giants fashioned a successful ten-year run as one of the premier African American teams in the East.

But by the turn of the century, they no longer dominated African American baseball as they once had. That dominance was a victim of the team's own success, which encouraged spirited imitation. Within thirty years of the team's birth, Sol. White identified nine African American professional baseball teams within one hundred miles of Philadelphia alone.[32] Plus, powerful black teams had also been assembled in the midwest.

By then, an iron-clad veil of race had descended across the world of baseball as it had elsewhere. The Cuban Giants played a singular role in providing refuge for African American players victimized by the erratic, though inexorable, march of Jim Crow into the national game, players such as Jack Frye, George Stovey, and the great Frank Grant. Even more importantly, the Cuban Giants, salaried, year-round professionals, proved their mettle by surviving the ineffably difficult times of the 1890s. This great black baseball team is a case study of the broader theme of black America's struggle to respond to an increasingly hostile and predatory environment.

The creation of the Cuban Giants meant the birth of an entire black subculture of baseball, developing simultaneously with its white counterpart, while retaining its own distinctive identity. Similar dynamics were at work across the entire spectrum of the African American experience – in religion, entertainment, journalism, the arts, fraternal societies, business associations, and countless other realms. All would react to exclusion by creating institutions that imitated the standards of the white community that rejected them, while maintaining the unique African American heritage that was the root cause of that exclusion. In the birth of the Cuban Giants, we witness the emergence of this development in baseball.

African American baseball survived sixty years of oppression in a way that demonstrated its ingenuity in making the best of the most disheartening of circumstances – and in doing so it fashioned an exuberant, energetic, entertaining legacy, one that bespeaks the resourcefulness, persistence, and artistry of African American society and culture.

If the past is prologue, black professional baseball's past starts in 1885, with the creation of the Cuban Giants.

NOTES

This essay was first presented as a paper given at the Cooperstown Symposium for Baseball and American Culture, Cooperstown NY, 1992.

1. For an account of the Argyle Hotel, see S. M. Aldrich, "The Argyle Hotel, Babylon, New York, 1881–1904," typescript, Babylon Public Library.

2. S. White, *Sol. White's Official Base Ball Guide: History of Colored Base Ball* (Philadelphia: H. Walter Schlichter, 1907), 11, 13.

3. A. F. Harlow, "Unrecognized Starts," *Esquire Magazine*, September 1938, 75.

4. *New York Age*, October 15, 1887. Govern had managed the Manhattans as early as 1881. See *Trenton Times*, June 8, 1886.

5. A. Torres, *La Historia del Beisbol Cubano, 1878–1976* (Los Angeles: n.p., 1976), 7. R. Ruck, *The Tropic of Baseball: Baseball in the Dominican Republic* (Westport CT: Meckler, 1991), 1–2.

6. *Amsterdam News*, December 18, 1930.

7. E. N. Akin, *Flagler: Rockefeller Partner and Florida Baron* (Kent OH: Kent State University Press, 1988), 116. S. W. Martin, *Flagler's Florida* (Athens GA: University of Georgia Press, 1949), 94–95. D. L. Chandler, *Henry Morrison Flagler: The Astonishing Life and Times of the Visionary Robber Baron Who Founded Florida* (New York: Macmillan, 1986), 88, 94.

8. Chandler, *Astonishing Life*, 103–4.

9. *New York Age*, February 23, 1889.

10. T. Graham, *Flagler's Magnificent Hotel Ponce de Leon* (St. Augustine FL: St. Augustine Historical Society, 1990), 20. Originally printed in the *Florida Historical Quarterly* 54 (July 1975).

11. Black baseball's prolonged engagement with Flagler's resort system was based on the sheer entertainment they unfailingly provided. See Chandler, *Astonishing Life*, 205, for an eyewitness account of the rollicking atmosphere of a Cuban Giant game in Palm Beach in 1907: "The crowd would yell themselves hoarse, stand up in their seats, bang each other over the head, and even the girls would go into a perfect frenzy as if they were in a Methodist camp meeting."

12. *New York Age*, October 15, 1887. According to the *New York Age*, they played "in every large city from St. Augustine to Philadelphia."

13. J. M. DiClerico and B. J. Pavelec, *The Jersey Game: The History of Modern Baseball from its Birth to the Big Leagues in the Garden State* (New Brunswick NJ: Rutgers University Press, 1991), 66, 75.

14. *Trenton True American*, April 5, 1886. *Trenton Times*, May 12, 1886.

15. F. B. Lee, ed., *Genealogical and Personal Memoirs of Mercer County, New Jersey* (Chicago: Lewis Publishing Company, 1908), 1:107. [Trenton] *Sunday Times Advertiser*, March 31, 1929, September 27, 1936.

16. *Trenton Times*, August 19, 1886.

17. *Trenton Times*, May 10, 1886. *Trenton True American*, May 12, 1886.

18. *New York Sun* quoted in *Sporting Life*, September 5, 1888; *Sporting News* in R. Peterson, *Only the Ball Was White: A History of Legendary Black Players and All-Black Professional Teams before Black Men Played in the Major Leagues* (Englewood Cliffs NJ: Prentice Hall, 1970), 35.

19. White, *Guide*, 15, 177.

20. White praised Thomas in a recollection that appears in the *New York Age*, December 27, 1930. On Philadelphia's offer to sign Thomas, see *Trenton True American*, June 29, 1886. This was the first known attempt of a Major League club to sign a African American player since Fleet and Welday Walker had played for Toledo of the American Association in 1884.

21. White, *Guide*, 25.

22. [Babylon NY] *South Side Signal*, October 10, 1885, cited in Peterson, *Only the Ball*, 35–36. Also found in Babylon Public Library. The Cuban Giants lost both games, 11–3 to the Mets and 13–7 to the A's. According to the *Trenton Times*, May 10, 1886, Trusty pitched both games.

23. All 1886 game accounts are from Trenton's two daily newspapers, the *Times* and the *True American*.

24. *Sporting Life*, September 21, 1887. Nonetheless, within a month after the Browns' boycott, the Cuban Giants played two other Major League teams, Boston of the (NL) and Cincinnati of the (AA) See *New York Freeman*, October 7, and (its successor) *New York Age*, October 15, 1887.

25. On Stovey's background, *The* [Williamsport PA] *Grit*, March 29, 1936, November 4, 1945. On Govern's signing him, *Trenton Times*, June 17, 1886.

26. *Cleveland Gazette*, May 13, 1892.

27. *Trenton Times*, June 24, 26, *Trenton True American*, June 26, 1886. Stovey had a terrific season for Jersey City, though the team finished third, behind Newark and Waterbury. According to the *Reach Guide*, Stovey held opposing batters to an average of .167, second best in the league. White, in his *Guide* (59), says Stovey had twenty-two strikeouts against Bridgeport (CT) – and lost the game. Powers, incidentally, later became long-time president of the International League.

28. *Newark News* appears in *Trenton True American*, July 19, 1886. *Meriden Journal* in *Trenton Times*, July 23, 1886. With the demise of the Meriden franchise, their one African American player, Frank Grant, went on to Buffalo, where his star shone brightly through the 1888 season.

29. White, *Guide*, 41.

30. White, *Guide*, 95.

31. *Sporting Life*, April 11, 1896. White, *Guide*, 21. White misstates the year as 1895 in "The Grand Old Game," *Amsterdam News*, December 18, 1930.

32. White, *Guide*, 35. All nine teams had "Giants" in their name.

LEE LOWENFISH

When All Heaven Rejoiced

Branch Rickey and the Origins of
the Breaking of the Color Line

*He really leads a double life – one with his conscience and the other with the
employer who pays him one of the top salaries in baseball. . . . Perhaps the most
moral man in private life in the sports field, Rickey is an ardent churchman, a
volunteer, non-professional missionary.* – Stanley Frank, *New York Post*

*If our aim is to make Brooklyn the baseball capital of America, by Judas Priest,
we'll do it! The Yankees made New York the capital of the American League and
they didn't do that by any chance or any luck. They did it by personnel, industry
and program. They have been winning not because God has been smiling on them
and on no one else. They toiled and they sweated to get something and they got it.*

I T WAS A VINTAGE Branch Rickey speech, extolling the virtues of
hard work and competition on this earth while never forgetting to
mention that there was a God above overseeing it all.[1] Rickey was
addressing one of his favorite audiences, a Rotary Club in Brooklyn,
shortly before the beginning of the 1943 baseball season, which would
be Rickey's first as president and general manager of the local heroes, the
Brooklyn Dodgers.

The great orator was just getting warmed up. "Brooklyn has more industries than New York, but most of the executive offices are in Manhattan. What happens then?" Rickey asked rhetorically. "The Brooklynites
resent Manhattan getting all the credit. They have a real pride in their
own and refuse to become parasitical. When anything comes along dis-
tinctly Brooklyn, they rally behind it because it is an expression of themselves, even an entity as lowly as a baseball club."[2]

Rickey professed to understand the Brooklynites' hatred of their fat cat
rivals across the East River. "'Poo on the Giants,' they [the Dodger fans]
say, and they are right," he exclaimed. "It is the pooling of support behind
the team, by George, which makes it successful." He concluded with a

folksy story that was as much a trademark of a Rickey presentation as the highs and lows of his dramatic cadences and the waving of his ever-present cigar.

> I can remember once a superannuated minister in a town where Mc-Kendry College is located in Illinois [a school that had granted Rickey's first honorary degree in 1928]. When his wife died he had her buried in the cemetery near the college. I'll never forget the inscription on the tombstone. It said, "She was more to me than I expected." I never was able to figure out exactly what he did expect, but I can echo his sentiments in so far as Brooklyn is concerned.[3]

While Branch Rickey did admire the special, defiant quality of Brooklyn's fans, in fact he had moved east at age sixty-two with a certain reluctance and trepidation. He was a lifelong midwesterner, a genuinely religious farm boy who grew up in straitened circumstances in Scioto County, a "particularly bleak" region of southern Ohio, to quote Lee Allen, one of baseball's first and best historians.[4] Rickey had gotten used to living the life of a country gentleman twenty miles outside of St. Louis, where he and his immensely supportive wife, Jane, his mother-in-law, a sister-in-law, and the six Rickey children had resided since 1929 on a twenty-three-acre estate that Rickey grandly named Country Life Acres. It featured a mansion-sized house, a smaller guest house, horses, farm animals, numerous dogs and cats, fruit orchards and, in the vivid description of Murray Polner, author of the most recent Rickey biography (1982), "Jane's vegetable garden guarded by a possessive bantam hen; . . . and especially for the children, a lake with an island that could be reached by a small bridge."[5] In addition, there was enough room on the estate for Rickey, a man who made his living carefully breeding ballplayers, to engage in the serious hobby of breeding turkeys and chickens.[6]

Branch Rickey had earned this comfortable lifestyle because, for the prior quarter century, he had built the St. Louis Cardinals into a National League powerhouse. He was field manager from 1919 to 1925 and, most importantly, was the architect of the revolutionary farm system of player development that between 1926 and 1942 brought the city of St. Louis six National League pennants and four World Series titles. The triumph of the Cardinals, in a St. Louis metropolitan area with one-tenth the population of New York City, had made Branch Rickey a household name nationally, giving hope to underdogs and little guys everywhere that with brains and pluck they could compete successfully with the rich big-city guys and their fat wallets.

Greatest Triumph

Rickey's last Cardinals team in 1942, dubbed the "St. Louis Swifties" by local sportswriters, was perhaps his greatest triumph. With a squad almost totally bred on Rickey farm clubs, including an unparalleled five rookies on a championship team, the "Swifties" trailed the Dodgers by 10 games in August, then roared down the stretch, winning an astounding 37 of their last 43 games, including 5 of their final 6 head-to-head meetings with the Dodgers. They beat out Brooklyn for the pennant by 2 games, amassing a total of 106 wins, and then capped a wondrous year by beating the haughty Yankees in 5 games in the World Series. Third baseman Whitey Kurowski hit a clinching two-run homer in the ninth inning of the last game at Yankee Stadium, and, rubbing salt in the Yankee wounds, catcher Walker Cooper picked Joe Gordon off second base to squelch a bottom-of-the-ninth rally. [7]

But it had long been an open secret in baseball that Rickey was out in St. Louis after the 1942 season, win or lose. Rickey's longtime boss Sam Breadon, the president and chief stockholder of the Cardinals, had been retired from his lucrative St. Louis automobile dealership for several years, and it became increasingly evident that Breadon thought he could run the team without the assistance of the assertive, loquacious Rickey and his very expensive contract, which at the time made Rickey the highest-paid man in baseball.

The beginning of the end in St. Louis for Rickey started in March 1938 when baseball commissioner Kenesaw Mountain Landis, a longtime opponent of the farm system, freed more than ninety Cardinal farm hands whom he declared Rickey had covered up in the minors, stifling their advancement. Rickey vigorously denied any wrongdoing and argued that he had saved many minor leaguers while providing baseball jobs for players during a period of economic depression. But Breadon refused Rickey's pleas to sue Landis for illegally seizing Cardinal player property. Then, in 1939, Breadon fired Columbus, Ohio, farm club auditor Donald Beach, Rickey's college fraternity brother and a Florida banker whom Rickey had employed when Beach's bank failed during the first years of the Great Depression in the early 1930s. [8] A blow against a member of

Rickey's baseball family was like a blow against a member of his blood family.

Breadon escalated the internal warfare during the mid-1940s by firing manager Ray Blades without telling Rickey of his decision. Blades was one of Rickey's favorites, whom he had signed as a fleet outfielder out of one of his tryout camps in the early 1920s. Shortly thereafter, Sam Breadon informed the Cardinal board of directors that he was entering more of an austerity mode than usual and that he didn't think the organization should take on major expenditures as the United States entered an uncertain period of world war. It was a thinly veiled allusion that Branch Rickey should not expect an offer of another long-term contract.[9]

Branch Rickey would turn sixty-two on December 20, 1942, but he was in good health and proudly possessed a prodigious work ethic. The word *retirement* was not in his vocabulary. "I expect my funeral cortege to move at a stately pace," he observed wryly.[10] Rickey pondered new career choices. Friends and admirers in the Missouri Republican party wanted him to run for either governor or U.S. senator. His vigorous campaigning in the rural districts of Missouri for Republican gubernatorial candidate Forrest Donnell had helped the G.O.P. win the governor's mansion in a close 1940 election.[11]

Rickey considered himself a Republican in the tradition of Abraham Lincoln, the martyred first Republican U.S. president, whose famous photograph taken by Matthew Brady hung prominently on Rickey's Cardinal office wall. He enjoyed more than a passing acquaintance with ex-president Herbert Hoover, whom he felt had been unfairly blamed for the disasters of the Depression. Rickey vigorously opposed the New Deal government programs of President Franklin D. Roosevelt as the ominous growth of a welfare state that would stifle individual enterprise and initiative, character traits that Rickey considered the cornerstone of the republic.

But the brilliant baseball executive did agree with Roosevelt's foreign policy of quarantining the fascist aggressors in Europe. "I much prefer an adventurous freedom to a peaceful slavery," Rickey declared not long before the Japanese bombing of Pearl Harbor precipitated American entry into the Second World War.[12] Rickey and Governor Donnell spearheaded a war-bond drive in Missouri that raised more money for the war per capita than did any other state in the union.[13] But it is quite likely that

Rickey's prowar, antifascist position doomed any support for high office he might have garnered from the isolationist wing of his party.

Work as an insurance-business executive loomed as another new career possibility for Rickey. Insurance mogul Carroll B. Otto, his good friend and next-door neighbor at Country Life Acres, encouraged him to think about entering the insurance field because of his great gift for salesmanship and optimistic oratory.[14] Rickey even traveled to New Jersey for a meeting with the insurance company Mutual Benefit Life, only to discover that the company president was reluctant to hire a man like Rickey, who was sure to dominate any enterprise he joined.[15]

*

In hindsight, it is hard to imagine that Branch Rickey ever seriously considered leaving baseball. With God and family, baseball was a vital part of the trinity of his life. The game, the competition, the chance to excel, and the camaraderie all entranced Branch Rickey. As the clock ran down on his Cardinal career, he was gratified to receive feelers from two American League teams, the Tigers and the Browns. Detroit was interested because the club wanted Rickey to fortify its recently started farm system, even though Commissioner Landis had recently freed scores of Detroit farm hands for the same reason he had cracked down on Rickey.[16] The crosstown St. Louis Browns, purchased in 1937 by local businessman Donald Barnes, were a more intriguing possibility because, if hired, Rickey would not have to uproot his family from Country Life Acres. The Browns were operated by William Orville DeWitt, a good friend and Rickey protégé who started in baseball as a teenage Cardinals vendor and office boy. But neither the Tigers nor the Browns offered the kind of money and perks that Rickey had become used to and felt unquestionably that he deserved.[17]

Only the Dodgers

Only the Brooklyn Dodgers provided the kind of opportunity and salary to which Branch Rickey was accustomed. The team had been interested in hiring Rickey in 1937, and National League president Ford Frick had highly recommended him to the Dodger board of directors, but Sam Breadon, then, would not allow Rickey to negotiate with Brooklyn. Now, in 1942, the Dodgers came calling again because Larry MacPhail, the onetime Rickey protégé who had built the Dodgers into a contender, had resigned after the 1942 season to accept a lieutenant colonelcy in the supply division of the U.S. Army in Europe. Dodger management offered Rickey a contract almost identical to the one Breadon had refused: five years at approximately $50,000 per year during wartime to rise closer to $100,000 after the war plus a percentage of all player sales, for both the Major and Minor Leagues. Rickey also was enticed by a promised chance to buy into ownership, which indeed happened in 1945 and 1946.[18]

Two other factors entered into Rickey's decision to move east. He told his close friend J. G. Taylor Spink, editor of the St. Louis–based weekly the *Sporting News*, that he resented the Yankees beating him out of many prospects by telling the players and their parents that he was cheap. He wanted the challenge of beating the Yankee dynasty on its home turf in New York.[19]

A second, probably clinching factor in Rickey's accepting the Brooklyn job was a chance to work with his only son, Branch Rickey Jr., who since 1939 had been working in MacPhail's Dodger farm system in what Senior called a "semi-executive" capacity.[20] As the rift with Breadon had grown irreparable, Rickey had not wanted his son to work for the Cardinals and had welcomed MacPhail's offer to his son. But by 1942, Rickey was worried that working under the turbulent MacPhail, whose alcohol-induced rages could be terrifying, had sapped Junior's enthusiasm for baseball. In Rickey's only book, *The American Diamond: A Documentary of the Game of Baseball*, published shortly before his death in 1965, the executive, in his characteristically Victorian style, called his agreeing to Junior's working with MacPhail "the most grievous decision I have ever faced."[21] Rickey could now look forward to working with his son and likely one day grooming him as a successor.

In his memoir, *1947: When All Hell Broke Loose in Baseball*, Red Barber, the Dodgers radio broadcaster, reflected fondly about his friend Branch Rickey, whom Barber said "never got in a situation he didn't think his way out of." Barber concluded perceptively about Rickey's decision, "He had to save his pride and he had to find a suitable position where his superb skills could continue to work."[22]

In coming to Brooklyn, Rickey was also to be reunited with Dodger player-manager Leo Durocher, the fiery shortstop who had led Rickey's Gashouse Gang 1934 world champions in St. Louis but who was always getting into serious scrapes and confrontations off the field. Leo's high-stakes card games with his own players during the height of the 1942 pennant race, for instance, wereEcircumflexconsidered by some observers a key factor in why the Dodgers lost their big lead to the Cardinals. [23] Branch Rickey Jr. often called Durocher "Dad's favorite reclamation project," and many a time Rickey Sr. sighed, "Leo has an infinite capacity for taking a bad situation and making it worse."[24] During 1943, Rickey wrote Robert Clements, one of his assistants in St. Louis who was now serving in the Pacific theater of the war, "Mrs. Durocher is divorcing Leo, and I have more reason for a divorce than she has."[25]

Durocher

At bottom, though, Rickey hated to fire anybody, and in his scheme of baseball organization, the field manager was a less important cog than the scouts, the developers, and of course, the players. And Rickey had an abiding belief in Durocher's special abilities. "I don't think there's anyone in America who understands baseball as well as Leo," Rickey insisted, adding a characteristic country example to buttress his point. "He's like a turkey in a tobacco patch," said the gentleman turkey farmer, "that sees the worm and knocks down 20 stalks to get it."[26]

So Durocher stayed in Brooklyn as Rickey planned the overhaul of his new team. Perhaps in the back of the executive's mind, too, he sensed that Leo Durocher would be an ideal manager once a Negro player joined the team. Rickey understood intuitively and correctly that Durocher would fight for one of his own guys on the field, regardless of color, creed, or anything else extraneous to the winning of ball games.

Secure with his long-term contract and the support of the Dodger board of directors, Rickey planned the overhaul of a ball club that may have won the pennant in 1941 and 104 games in 1942 but was getting dangerously old. In one of his first interviews upon taking the Dodger job, Rickey told *Brooklyn Eagle* sportswriter Harold Parrott, "We are sitting on a volcano of complete andEcircumflexsudden disintegration here in Brooklyn."[27] (In 1944, Parrott would join the Rickey organization as Dodger traveling secretary.)

To compound problems, the Second World War draft was soon to take the Dodgers' best young players: shortstop Harold "Pee Wee" Reese, whom MacPhail had purchased from the Boston Red Sox farm system, and outfielder Pete Reiser, a product of the St. Louis sandlots and the best of the Minor Leaguers freed by Commissioner Landis in 1938, a player who, in Rickey's uncharacteristically terse but lovely phrase, had been born "with the gift of speed and the urge to run."[28]

Dead Weight

To overcome the dead weight of what he called his excessively "veteranized" roster, Rickey established a master plan to scour the country looking for prospects. While his rivals in the baseball business were cutting back on scouting as the Second World War raged on, Rickey doubled the Dodger scouting and development budget. Unlike many of his cautious and fearful fellow baseball owners and operators, who cut expenses during wartime, Branch Rickey never doubted that the United States would win the war. Rickey had four sons-in-law in the military serving in responsible positions, and he was a genuine patriot; at age thirty-six, in the First World War, Rickey himself had gone to France to serve in the American Chemical Warfare Service.[29]

Rickey was thrilled when the Dodgers were able to use the facilities of the United States Military Academy, at West Point, New York, for his first Brooklyn spring training in 1943; Commissioner Landis had ruled that as long as the war continued no teams could train in the South. Rickey became as active in the war-bond drive in New York as he had been in St. Louis. In late April 1943, he made a rare Sabbath Sunday appearance at a ballpark to support a fund-raising war-bond drive during an unusual round-robin exhibition game at Ebbets Field that featured the three New York teams: the Yankees, the Giants, and the Dodgers.[30]

Meanwhile, just as he had done in painstakingly building the farm system in St. Louis, Rickey was implementing a comprehensive program of scouting and development. He drafted a letter that was sent to thousands of high school coaches and hundreds of college coaches asking for the names of prospects. He solicited tips on promising players from his wide circle of friends in all walks of life. He placed advertisements in the popular young men's monthly magazine *Argosy* announcing tryouts in all corners of the country as much as wartime restrictions allowed.[31] Rickey enticed George Sisler, perhaps his greatest conversion (from southpaw pitcher to Hall-of-Fame first baseman), into heading his scouting and development department. Sisler was another midwesterner initially reluctant to move east, but he could not turn down the offer from his mentor and dear friend.[32] The fruits of the Rickey-supervised talent search turned up in the first year alone such postwar Dodger stars as Ralph Branca, from Mount Vernon, just north of New York City; Carl Erskine, from Anderson, Indiana; Carl Furillo, from northeastern Pennsylvania; and Edwin "Duke" Snider, from Southern California.[33]

One of Rickey's operating principles was "trade a player a year too soon instead of a year too late." Having no pennant hopes for his first Dodger team, in early August 1943 Rickey dealt left fielder Joe "Ducky" (or "Muscles") Medwick, a onetime star of the Gashouse Gang, and first baseman Dolph Camilli to the hated Giants in separate deals. Although Rickey had evaluated correctly that Medwick and Camilli were near the end of their careers, the executive was stunned by the virulence of the Dodger fan reaction. The Camilli trade drove the Allied invasion of Sicily in the Second World War to a subordinate front-page role in many local newspapers.[34] "Leave Us Have MacPhail" and "Leave Us Have Camilli" signs were draped on Ebbets Field walls, and Rickey was hung in effigy at Brooklyn's Borough Hall.[35] Jane Rickey Jones, the second oldest of his five daughters, recalled being afraid of cab drivers' reactions if they discovered they were driving a Rickey.[36]

Rickey, no doubt, had feared what might happen when the sportswriters on the nine competing daily newspapers in the city took aim at him in print. With these unpopular trades, Jimmy Powers, sports editor of the prominent tabloid the *New York Daily News*, accelerated his attacks on Rickey as "El Cheapo" (a campaign that by the postwar period so enraged Rickey that he seriously contemplated suing the journalist for libel).[37] But the executive stuck to his guns. "I am trying to bring a pennant to Brooklyn," he told the writers. "I do not propose to deviate from such calculations . . . to help the club."[38]

In the first weeks on the job in Brooklyn, Branch Rickey also got the approval of the club directors to scout the hitherto untapped reservoir of American Negro baseball talent. He proposed this plan at a special meeting of the board held at the exclusive New York Athletic Club (NYAC) on Central Park South in Manhattan. The NYAC was as establishment and conservative an institution as there was in the United States; by the early 1940s, it had not even considered accepting Negro or Jewish members. Not surprisingly, no minutes were taken at the secret meeting of the Dodger board of directors, but it was learned years afterward that George McLaughlin, president of the Brooklyn Trust Company bank and a key member of the Dodger board, gave Rickey the go-ahead. "You might find something," McLaughlin said but quickly added, "My God, Rickey, you've got to know you're doing this not to solve any great sociological problem!"[39] Branch Rickey doubtless nodded vigorous agreement because he himself was outspokenly opposed to leftist agitation for racial justice that, he felt, only turned race against race in the United States.

Rickey fully realized that scouting Negro talent to augment the traditional Caucasian supply of players had to be a delicate, secret, and even conspiratorial operation. The midwestern mastermind relished the opportunity for this kind of behind-the-scenes work. By spring 1943, Rickey already had sent scout Tom Greenwade in Mexico City to check on the progress of a twenty-eight-year-old Cuban shortstop, Silvio Garcia, who had recently played for the New York Cubans in the American Negro Leagues. "I hope you will be able to work quietly without any newspaper publicity whatever," Rickey wrote Greenwade (who in 1945 would move to the Yankees and later gain fame as the man who signed Mickey Mantle out of Commerce, Oklahoma). Rickey added, "If you run into anything especially good, . . . I might even come myself."[40] As it turned out, Greenwade thought Garcia was both too much of an opposite-field hitter and too much of a showboat, on and off the field, to be considered a real prospect for the Major Leagues. Garcia also was slated soon for induction into the Cuban Army.[41] But Rickey instructed Greenwade and such other trusted Dodger scouts as Clyde Sukeforth and Wid Matthews to continue to file reports on promising players of color in the American Negro Leagues. Rickey also enlisted the services of two university friends, political science professor Robert Haig (another Ohio Wesleyan fraternity brother), of Columbia, and physical education graduate student Jose Seda, of Puerto Rico and New York University, in scouting the Caribbean countries.[42]

Charles Thomas

So it is clear that as soon as Branch Rickey went to work in Brooklyn, he had already set the wheels in motion for his second and most profound baseball revolution – racial integration. While no hard evidence exists, there is considerable anecdotal evidence that he had begun to consider breaking the color line while still in St. Louis. The Rickey children and several of their friends have remembered stirring conversations at the Rickey dinner table at Country Life Acres about Abraham Lincoln, the Civil War, and the unfortunate, continuing effects of slavery on American Negro life.[43] St. Louis associates also recall that when Rickey entertained a visit from Charles Thomas, a Negro dentist from Albuquerque, New Mexico, who had been the catcher on Rickey's 1904 Ohio Wesleyan College team, the executive would remain in his Cardinals office during a game rather than send Thomas to watch the action from the segregated bleachers of Sportsman's Park.[44]

It was Thomas who had been denied a hotel room because of his color when Rickey's Ohio Wesleyan team went to play Notre Dame in South Bend, Indiana. Rickey insisted that the player stay in his room, and decades later, once the Jackie Robinson signing had been announced, Rickey often cited the early discrimination against Thomas as his motive for pushing baseball integration.

While in St. Louis, though, Rickey could do little to change matters. A local ordinance restricting Negro seating to the bleachers at Sportsman's Park did not end until May 1944, more than eighteen months after Rickey left for Brooklyn. The lifting of the ban did not noticeably boost Negro attendance, the lack of which was cited candidly by Rickey in an interview the next year with Taylor Spink of the *Sporting News*. Rickey accurately foretold that St. Louis, the most southern of the Major League cities, could not support two franchises, and indeed the Browns were moved to Baltimore after the 1953 season.[45]

Rickey clearly understood that polyglot-proud Brooklyn was a better place to try integration, but he also knew that he had to act cautiously and surreptitiously because the social mores against integration were so ingrained. So Rickey held his tongue when, in December 1943, singer-actor-social activist Paul Robeson gave an impassioned plea for racial integration of Major League Baseball to the owners' annual meeting in New York City. "They said that America never would stand for my playing Othello with a white cast," Robeson declared, "but it is the triumph of my life."[46] Commissioner Landis had instructed his colleagues not to ask any questions of Robeson, a restriction on speech that normally might have irked the loquacious Rickey, but Rickey certainly did not want to even hint of his secret plans already under way. While he despised Robeson's communist politics, he knew this was not the right place to challenge Robeson's political leftism. After the owners meeting concluded, Landis reiterated for the press what he had been saying for years: "There is no rule, written or unwritten, barring Negroes from playing in the Major Leagues. It is up to the owners of the clubs to say whom they want to hire."[47]

As Rickey's scouts continued their secret search, the Dodger leader addressed the issue of racial integration in general terms at a Brooklyn Rotary Club meeting in 1944. With his characteristic passion, he warned that integrating baseball with the wrong kind of player might set the cause of true integration back generations, just as the alcohol prohibition movement had hurt the temperance movement.[48] While Rickey was often caricatured as a puritanical, teetotaling "dry," he was, quite to the contrary, a political and psychological realist who understood what drove people to drink and who realized that after the violent, ineffective history of legal prohibition, the temperance movement had taken a serious step backward. Similarly, Rickey understood the deep-seated fears of white men about racial equality and was concerned about too precipitous a move for racial integration.

The Numbers Business

It is hard to determine when, precisely, Rickey came up with the idea of an ostensible third Negro league that would compete with the existing, loosely organized Negro American and Negro National Leagues but whose purpose would really be to camouflage his intention to integrate his mainstream Dodgers franchise. Rickey understood that the status quo served owners like Clark Griffith, of the Washington Senators, and William Benswanger, of the Pittsburgh Pirates, who were getting sizable rental fees from the owners of the existing Negro League franchises.[49] Whenever the idea first came up in his fertile and sometimes Machiavellian brain, we know that he made it public on May 8, 1945, at a press conference at the Dodger offices in Brooklyn. A five-team United States League was to start play that summer, with the Brooklyn Brown Dodgers as one of the franchises along with teams in Toledo, Detroit, Pittsburgh, and Chicago. Rickey dismissed the existing Negro Leagues as "organizations in the zone of a racket," deriding the booking agents whom he said wanted outrageous fees to book the teams and the Negro League owners who were often in the numbers business and other disreputable enterprises.[50]

It is certainly ironic, or some might say hypocritical, that Rickey dismissed the existing Negro Leagues while joining with similar bookers and gamblers in his own short-lived Negro league. "I spent $30,000 of Brooklyn money and lost it all," Rickey told Jackie Robinson in 1963 in an interview for Robinson's book about civil rights progress, *Baseball Has Done It.* "We organized that racket colored league – and that's what it was, pure racket."[51]

But sensing baseball's traditional conservative, if not reactionary, attitudes toward change, especially such major racial change, Rickey obviously felt some chicanery was necessary to mask his intentions. Rickey's United States League certainly fooled many journalists in the Negro press who would have been very sympathetic if they had known what Rickey was secretly planning. Ludlow Werner, of the *New York Age*, called Rickey's formation of a new Negro league the action of a "pompous ass," and A. S. "Doc" Young, one of the most eloquent of the Negro sportswriters, railed, "Rickey is no Abe Lincoln or FDR and we won't accept him as a dictator of Negro baseball. Hitler and Mussolini are no longer! We need no American dictator!"[52] Rickey must have chortled at the Negro activists' uninformed attacks on him, just as he must have been amused at the ignorance of his unsuspecting partners and competitors in the mainstream baseball business.

In actuality, two months before his announcement of the camouflage league, Rickey had been thrilled when the New York state legislature, on March 12, 1945, passed the Ives-Quinn Act, the first state law in American history aimed at "eliminating discrimination in employment because of race, creed, color or national origin."[53] Jane Rickey Jones remembers her father reading the news of the Ives-Quinn passage at the breakfast table and bouncing up, chortling, "They can't stop me now!"[54] And off he went to work in the most buoyant of spirits.

Red Barber recalled a private lunch with Rickey in March 1945 at Joe's Restaurant, a favorite Dodger personnel hangout, in which the executive enlisted the support of his southern-born broadcaster in the dramatic step he was planning. "I don't know who he is or where he is, but, he is coming," Rickey whispered to Barber.[55]

Another vivid moment early in the critical year 1945 has been recalled by Rickey's eldest daughter, Mary Rickey Eckler. Her father was a close friend of Lowell Thomas, the world traveler and internationally known radio broadcaster. When Rickey confided to Thomas what he intended to do about integrating baseball, Mary Eckler remembers Lowell Thomas's warning, "Branch, all hell will break loose." Rickey replied, "No, Lowell. All heaven will rejoice."[56]

*

In conclusion, the question I get asked the most when I tell people I am writing a new biography of Branch Rickey is, Were his motives economic or humanitarian in breaking the color line? I think it is an easy question to answer. Both. Branch Rickey was proud to be a professional baseball man and was always unapologetic about his goal of running a baseball business for profit. But in spite of his wheeling and dealing and trading, which usually kept him one step ahead of the befuddled baseball establishment, Branch Rickey was also a genuinely humanitarian, charitable, and religious man.

In breaking the color line, Rickey wouldn't deny the economic intent in the ditty about Robinson that circulated in the Negro press: "Jackie's nimble / Jackie's quick / Jackie makes the turnstiles click."[57] But there is no doubt that Branch Rickey was genuinely happy to have opened up baseball for the deserving, previously neglected Negro players. It was not an accident that hanging on the wall of Branch Rickey's baseball offices from St. Louis to Brooklyn to Pittsburgh was an epigram that I believe comes from Henry Drummond, the late nineteenth-century Scottish philosopher who became world renowned for his writings reconciling science and religion: "He who will not reason is a bigot; he who cannot reason is a fool; he who dares not to reason is a slave."[58]

NOTES

1. A. Daley, "Sports of the Times: The Dodger Deacon Discourses," *New York Times*, February 12, 1943, 26.

2. Daley, "Sports of the Times," 26.

3. Daley, "Sports of the Times," 26.

4. L. Allen, *The National League Story* (New York: Hill and Wang, 1961), 179.

5. M. Polner, *Branch Rickey: A Biography* (New York: Atheneum, 1982), 96.

6. E-mail from William G. Turner, St. Louis friend of the Rickey family and later employee of Rickey organizations in Pittsburgh and Brooklyn, March 2000.

7. W. Sheed, *My Life As a Fan* (New York: Simon and Schuster, 1993), 102.

8. Polner, *Branch Rickey*, 102.

9. D. Farrington, *Sporting News*, November 26, 1941, 5.

10. E. Griswold, "Mr. Rickey Starts in the Cellar," *American Magazine*, May 1951, 78.

11. F. Graham, "Rickey Fighter against Odds All His Career," *New York Journal American*, July 12, 1961; see also G. Holland, "Mr. Rickey and the Game," in D. Halberstam, ed., *The Best American Sports Writing of the Century* (New York: Houghton Mifflin, 1999), 222 (article originally published in *Sports Illustrated*, March 7, 1955).

12. Polner, *Branch Rickey*, 116.

13. *Brooklyn Eagle*, June 24, 1943.

14. D. Kaegel, *Sporting News*, March 5, 1966.

15. Polner, *Branch Rickey*, 116–17.

16. J. G. Taylor Spink, *Judge Landis and 25 Years of Baseball* (St. Louis: Sporting News Company, 1974), 205.

17. L. Lowenfish, "The Two Titans and the Mystery Man," in J. Dorinson and J. Warmund, eds., *Race, Sports, and the American Dream* (Armonk NY: Sharpe, 1999), 170.

18. See R. Rennie, "Branch Rickey Gets Around," *New York Herald Tribune*, October 22, 1942; and A. E. Patterson, "MacPhail's Successor Likely to Receive $80,000 Annually," *New York Herald Tribune*, October 30, 1942.

19. J. G. Taylor Spink, "'Exclusive' – Rickey's departure from St. Louis," *Sporting News*, November 26, 1942.

20. "Lawyer, Churchman, Politician – That Is Rickey, Boss of Cardinals," Associated Press wire story in *Milwaukee Journal*, March 31, 1940.

21. B. Rickey and R. Riger, *The American Diamond: A Documentary of the Game of Baseball* (New York: Simon and Schuster, 1965), 166.

22. R. Barber, *1947: When All Hell Broke Loose in Baseball* (Garden City NY: Doubleday, 1982), 7, 27.

23. P. Golenbock, *Bums: An Oral History of the Brooklyn Dodgers* (Chicago: Contemporary Books, 2000), 58; see also Tommy Holmes, *Dodger Daze and Knights* (New York: McKay, 1953), 169–72.

24. Holmes, *Dodger Daze and Knights*, 169.

25. Branch Rickey to Robert Clements, October 23, 1943, "Correspondence C" box, Branch Rickey Papers, Library of Congress.

26. R. Shaplen, "The Nine Lives of Leo Durocher," *Sports Illustrated*, May 30, 1955, 57.

27. H. Parrott, reprinted in *Sporting News*, November 26, 1942.

28. Parrott, *Sporting News*, November 26, 1942.

29. Polner, *Branch Rickey*, 76–78.

30. *New York Times*, April 30, 1943.

31. C. Dexter, "Brooklyn's Sturdy Branch," *Collier's*, September 15, 1945, 48; L. Allen, *The Giants and The Dodgers* (New York: Hill and Wang, 1964), 85.

32. Interview with Dave Sisler, youngest son of George Sisler, St. Louis, Missouri, August 2000.

33. Polner, *Branch Rickey*, 145.

34. See, for instance, *New York Journal American*, August 1, 1943.

35. J. Tygiel, *Baseball's Great Experiment: Jackie Robinson and His Legacy* (New York: Oxford University Press, 1983), 51.

36. Interview with Jane Rickey Jones, Elmira, New York, July 1998.

37. Polner, *Branch Rickey*, 128–30.

38. *New York Times*, August 10, 1943, 24; *New York Post*, August 10, 1943, 24.

39. Golenbock, *Bums*, 153; J. Robinson, *Baseball Has Done It*, ed. C. Dexter (Philadelphia: Lippincott, 1964), 41.

40. Communication of Branch Rickey to Tom Greenwade, May 10, 1943, courtesy of Jim Kreuz.

41. Polner, *Branch Rickey*, 146–47.

42. Polner, *Branch Rickey*, 146–47.

43. E-mail from Bill Turner, March 2000; interview with Elizabeth Louis, Rickey's granddaughter, St. Louis, August 2000.

44. Letter from Gene Karst, Cardinals publicity director (1931–34), August 1999.

45. J. G. Taylor Spink, "Big Major Map Changes Coming, Says Rickey," *Sporting News*, August 23, 1945, front page.

46. Tygiel, *Baseball's Great Experiment*, 41.

47. *New York Times*, December 4, 1943, 37; see also D. Burley, "Negroes in the Major Leagues?" *Inter-Racial Review: A Journal of Christian Democracy* 17, no. 7 (1944): 102.

48. A. Mann, *Branch Rickey: American in Action* (Boston: Houghton Mifflin, 1957), 224.

49. Tygiel, *Baseball's Great Experiment*, 84–85.

50. Polner, *Branch Rickey*, 158–60.

51. Robinson, *Baseball Has Done It*, 42.

52. L. Werner, *New York Age*, May 8, 1945, quoted in Polner, *Branch Rickey*, 159; A. S. "Doc" Young, *Chicago Defender*, May 26, 1945, 7.

53. *New York Times*, March 13, 1945, 38.

54. Quoted in S. Roberts, *New York Times*, April 13, 1997, sec. 4, p. 7.

55. Barber, *1947*, 52.

56. Roberts, *New York Times*, April 13, 1997; interview with Mary Rickey Eckler, Sebastopol, California, August 2000.

57. Tygiel, *Baseball's Great Experiment*, 189.

58. Polner, *Branch Rickey*, introductory flyleaf.

ANTHONY R. PRATKANIS & MARLENE E. TURNER

The Year "Cool Papa" Bell Lost the Batting Title

Mr. Branch Rickey and Mr. Jackie Robinson's Plea for Affirmative Action

I N THE EYES OF MANY BASEBALL FANS, James "Cool Papa" Bell was the headiest and fastest base runner of his or any other time. In 1933 (his best season), he stole 175 bases in 180 or so games with the Pittsburgh Crawfords. He would often score from first on a single or reach third on a sacrifice. In his 29 seasons, Bell compiled a .339 lifetime batting average in the Negro Major Leagues. (He hit .392 against white pitching in 54 exhibition games and stole 15 bases in the 35 games where records were kept.) He played on at least five Negro Major league All-Star teams and was named to the *Pittsburgh Courier*'s All-Time All-Star team as a center fielder.[1]

Ironically, many fans remember him for what he didn't achieve on the playing field – the year he purposely lost the batting title. In 1946, at age 43, Bell was hitting .411 and locked in a race for the batting title of the Negro Major League with the younger Monte Irvin. Bell, always the competitor, this time pulled himself out of the line-up for the last games. Irvin went on to win the title with a .389 average. (Bell lacked the needed number of at-bats to qualify for the crown). When asked why he had deliberately lost the title, Mr. Bell responded: "For the first time the Major Leagues were serious about taking in blacks. I was too old, but Monte was young and had a chance for a future. It was important he be noticed, important he get that chance." When a player as competitive as Bell deliberately comes up short on the playing field, it behooves us to try to understand why. The answer lies in the actions taken by two men – Mr. Branch Rickey and Mr. Jackie Robinson – just one year earlier in 1945. To appreciate the significance of their actions, we must go back in time to the middle of the nineteenth century and to the origins of baseball's exclusion of black Americans.

For the most part, blacks' participation in organized baseball paralleled their treatment in white society in general.[2] During the antebellum period, there is some evidence that a few black Americans played organized ball. Just after the Civil War, about two dozen black Americans began to star in baseball including pitcher/second baseman Bud Fowler, second baseman Frank Grant, and bare-handed catcher Moses Fleetwood Walker. Their treatment was characteristic of the ambivalent racial attitudes of the Reconstruction period – black players were subjected to a mixture of blatant racism and half-hearted acceptance by whites. As Reconstruction was drawing to a close, however, even this half-hearted acceptance was withdrawn. Many leagues began banning blacks from play and adopted "gentlemen's agreements" preventing the hiring of black Americans. Cap Anson, manager of the Chicago White Stockings, hastened the end. In 1887 during a game against the Toledo Blue Stockings of the American Association, Anson yelled across the field at Moses Fleetwood Walker, "Get that nigger off the field." His words rang true; at the end of the season, Fleet Walker was not rehired and no black American played in the white Major Leagues until 1947. (Some continued in the Minor Leagues until the turn of the century.)

Throughout the later nineteenth century, Cap Anson continued to lead efforts to erect barriers to prevent black Americans from playing organized baseball – efforts that mirrored the Jim Crow laws being adopted in parts of the United States. In the 1920s, Anson's cause was picked up by baseball Commissioner Kenesaw Mountain Landis. Landis (a former judge) was hired by Major League baseball to lend a "clean image" to the sport after the Black Sox scandal of 1919. Officially, Landis claimed that the leagues did not bar blacks from playing. Unofficially, he did everything he could to maintain the barriers.

One story involving Leo "The Lip" Durocher should make the point. In 1942, Durocher told newspapers, "I'll play the colored boys on my team if the big shots give the OK. Hell, I've seen a million good ones. Only a subterranean rule was keeping them out."[3] Durocher was ushered into Landis's office and the next day Landis issued a statement saying that Durocher never made the remark and that there was no rule, "subterranean" or otherwise, excluding blacks. Given what we know about "The Lip's" outspoken nature, this was probably Durocher's way of compromising (you go ahead and withdraw my words) to make his point (the big shots do have a rule, don't you see). Five years later Durocher would be managing the Brooklyn Dodgers and overseeing the integration of baseball.

Women were also excluded from playing baseball (and, for the most part, still are). After a few years of operation, the All-American Girls Professional Baseball League, dramatized in the film, "A League of Their Own," began to produce high-caliber women baseball players who were invited to try out for all-men professional teams. In 1948, when Minor League contracts were offered to Dorothy Kamenshek and Elenor Engle, baseball barred the signing of women to Major League contracts.[4]

Excluded from the white leagues, black ballplayers began to form their own teams and leagues.[5] Teams such as the Cuban X Giants, the Norfolk Red Stockings, and the Chicago Unions began barnstorming across the country playing an entertaining form of baseball. In 1920, Andrew Rube Foster – one of baseball's great administrators – formed these teams into what became known as the Negro National League. One objective of this league was to develop a pool of talent for integrating the white leagues. In many cities, such as Pittsburgh and New York, the Negro League clubs began rivaling the white clubs for attendance and talent. Except, however, for a few interleague scrimmages, baseball remained segregated.

Black American exclusion from baseball in the first half of the twentieth century mirrored the conditions of blacks in American society.[6] Many communities erected laws to prevent blacks from voting. Black Americans were often terrorized by white violence in the form of lynchings and race riots. Many states required separate and unequal schools. Demagogues such as "Pitchfork Ben" Tillman, Cole Blease, and Theodore Bilbo toured the nation and received thunderous applause for hatemongering speeches advocating lynching as a means to protect the virtue of white women, proclaiming the unfitness of "niggers" for American life, and seeking the deportation of black Americans to Africa. In a survey of white Americans in the 1940s, over 70 percent of whites believed black Americans were intellectually inferior, with heredity as the major cause of the supposed deficit. Black Americans were at the lower end of the socioeconomic spectrum. In 1930, 58.2 percent of black male employees were either servants or unskilled laborers versus 15 percent of whites. In the 1940 U.S. census, black Americans were three times as likely to be unemployed as were whites.

While many resignedly accepted or even applauded the status of black

Americans in baseball (and in American society), a few were determined to change dramatically and forever baseball's apartheid segregation policy. Mr. Branch Rickey and Mr. Jack Robinson were two such reformers. In the 1940s, they would start on a course that would bring organized baseball's first affirmative action effort.

The First Affirmative Action Program

Branch Rickey and Jackie Robinson were raised in a segregated world. Rickey, born in 1881 on a southern Ohio farm, was raised a devout Christian. He spent part of his youth as a school teacher, a college coach, and then a lawyer. Rickey played four seasons of pro ball as a catcher, batting .239. His mother, a Christian, was not fond of his playing baseball because she did not want her son going to the ballpark on Sunday; Rickey promised her that he would never go to the park on Sunday – a promise that he would keep for the rest of his life. In 1916, Rickey began his general manager career with the St. Louis Cardinals, where he created baseball's first farm system and put together the famed Cardinal club known as the "Gashouse Gang." In 1942, he joined the Brooklyn Dodgers as their general manager.

Jackie Robinson was born on January 31, 1919, in Georgia. His grandfather had been a slave. When Jackie was one year old, he and his family moved to Pasadena, California, hoping to avoid the intensity of racism found in the South. After high school, Robinson starred in track at Pasadena Junior College (winning the national junior broad jump championship). He later went to UCLA where he starred in football (averaging 12.2 yards per carry), basketball (led the Pacific Coast Conference in scoring), and track (winning NCAA championships). Ironically, he did not star on UCLA's baseball team. During the Second World War, Robinson served his country in the army as a second lieutenant. Robinson quickly became disturbed by the racism he encountered in the army and brought matters to a head by refusing to take a seat in the back of a bus. In response, the army began court-martial proceedings against Robinson, which were later dropped; Robinson received an honorable discharge in 1944. In 1945, he signed to play baseball with the Kansas City Monarchs of the Negro Major Leagues.

Events of the 1940s would bring Mr. Rickey and Mr. Robinson together. After the 1944 season, Judge Landis died, removing a formidable obstacle to integration. He was replaced by a Kentuckian named Happy

Chandler, who would prove to be much more supportive of blacks in baseball. Rickey, having shown himself to be a winner with the St. Louis Cardinals, had the position and influence to attempt his experiment. The end of Second World War brought a renewed interest in improving race relations in America. Fifty-four Negro Major League baseball players served during the war and some began to feel that "if they are good enough to fight, they are good enough for baseball". [7] Politicians began setting up committees to investigate the color barrier in baseball. In response, blacks began receiving "try-outs" with various clubs. These efforts, however, are best viewed as having been little more than publicity stunts as opposed to a real effort at integration.

Despite these changes, there was still considerable opposition to breaking the color barrier. For example, in the spring of 1945 at an owners' meeting, a secret vote was taken on whether to bring blacks into baseball. The result was 15–1 against, with Mr. Rickey's representing the lone vote in favor.

Something was about to happen, however, that would capture the attention of "Cool Papa" Bell and the nation. [8] For the last year or so, Mr. Rickey had been scouting top Negro League players with the intention of bringing a black American to play for his Dodgers. Because of potential opposition, Rickey had shrouded his efforts in secrecy using the ruse that he was interested in starting the Brown Dodgers in a new Negro League he was forming. On August 28, 1945, Mr. Rickey met with Jackie Robinson in his Brooklyn office. At the end of the meeting, both men agreed that Robinson would play for Brooklyn's top farm club in Montreal in the International League for the 1946 season – the year Bell would forsake the batting title. The contract was announced on October 23, 1945.

After a successful year with the Montreal Royals, Jackie Robinson was called up to play for the Brooklyn Dodgers on April 10, 1947. Five days later, Robinson donned Brooklyn Dodger uniform number 42 for his first regular season game against the visiting Boston Braves. A crowd of 26,623 (including many black Americans) applauded and cheered each time Robinson came to bat or touched the ball. Among those in attendance were Rachel Robinson, Jackie's wife, and their newborn son, Jackie Jr. In the top of the first, Jackie Jr.'s dad took his position at first base. Although a natural second baseman, Robinson learned the new position because that is where the Dodgers needed him to play. He played nine innings of errorless ball, making eleven put-outs. In the bottom of the first inning, batting second, Robinson faced the Boston pitcher, Johnny Sain. In his first at-bat, Robinson grounded to short. In his third at-bat, Robinson reached base for the first time via a sacrifice and a throwing error; he turned the error into his first run. On April 17, Robinson collected his first Major League hit – a perfect bunt down the third base line that caught the Boston third baseman, Bob Elliot, playing deep. The next day, at the Polo Grounds, Jackie drove a shot into the left-field stands for his first home run. The Dodgers went on to win eight of their first ten games.

Red Barber, the Brooklyn Dodger sportscaster, famously described 1947 – the year Robinson and Rickey broke the color barrier – as the year "all hell broke loose" in baseball. Despite Robinson's and the Dodger's early successes on the field, there remained considerable opposition to Mr. Rickey's hiring of Jackie Robinson. Throughout the season, both Robinson and Rickey routinely received death threats. In his first thirty-seven at-bats, Robinson was hit by a pitch six times. (Seven beanings in an entire 162 game season is usually considered high.) In one town, a black cat was sent onto the field and someone screamed out, "It's your brother, Jackie." Some fans and players taunted Robinson with racial slurs of "nigger" and "watermelon eater"; other players tried to spike him, perhaps with an eye toward ending his career. Still other players attempted to organize petition drives and walk-outs to prevent Robinson from playing. Throughout it all, Mr. Jackie Robinson batted .297, with 12 home runs, 48 RBIs, and a league-leading 29 stolen bases. He was voted *Sporting News* Rookie of the Year. And the Brooklyn Dodgers fans realized their dreams of going to the World Series (which they lost in 7 games to the New York Yankees)

When Branch Rickey hired Jackie Robinson he began what we view as the first, largely successful affirmative action program in human history. There are other candidates for the honor of first affirmative action effort. After the Civil War, there were attempts in the South at integration with blacks and whites sometimes sharing restaurants, hotels, and train cars.[9] These attempts at affirmative action, however, came to a close around 1877 with the end of Reconstruction and the rise of segregation. In the early part of the twentieth century, black Americans were "admitted" into the U.S. military; however, they were segregated from the rest of the military (for example, the Tuskegee Airmen) and treated as second-class employees.[10] It was not until 1949, when President Truman initiated Executive Order 9981, that the military began a policy of equal opportunity for black Americans.

But what do we mean by "affirmative action"? Although the basis for stigmatization can vary, every culture has its out-groups – socially defined categories of people who are perceived by others as less qualified, less clean, less talented, or less of something of value. [11] Typically, cultures deal with stigmatized out-groups through some form of exclusion, subjugation, segregation, or forced change of identity. When Mr. Rickey hired Jackie Robinson, he introduced a new strategy of "affirmative action," or the proactive removal of discriminatory barriers and the promotion of institutions leading to integration of in- and out-groups. Our definition of affirmative action may strike some as odd. In common parlance, affirmative action has come to mean a "quota" system. This confuses one possible tactic (among many) with what should be an overall objective of integration.

Our view of affirmative action is based on the observation that genuine racial integration is a necessary condition for the eradication of racism and prejudice. [12] Integration is not mere desegregation (in-groups and out-groups share the same space); neither is it assimilation (the out-group is subsumed by the in-group). Integration refers to inclusion processes for an out-group that has a history of exclusion and the promotion of positive relations between the members of the groups. In 1946, black Americans still served as baseball's principal out-group.

In our essay elsewhere in this volume we describe how Mr. Rickey and Mr. Robinson designed and implemented the first affirmative action program. [13] For the present we would like to address the question, why did they do it? The potential costs to both men were high. At the time he hired Jackie Robinson, Mr. Rickey was entering the end of his career. His family, noting his age and his long years of service to baseball, urged him not to do it. It was time to sit back and enjoy life; he did not need the trouble that hiring a black player for the Dodgers would bring. Although still in his youth, Mr. Robinson had already intensely experienced the sting of prejudice and knew firsthand the pain and trouble that inevitably came when a black man attempted to cross the color barrier. Why Mr. Rickey and Mr. Robinson did it can teach us a lot about why we need affirmative action today.

Mr. Rickey's Two Metaphors for Affirmative Action

Branch Rickey often gave two reasons why he hired Robinson: (a) morality demanded it; and (b) it was good for baseball (profits). [14]

To illustrate the moral imperative of integration, Branch Rickey told the story of Charley Thomas, and he told it often – to anyone who would listen. According to legend, it was 1904 and Branch Rickey was in his third year as the young coach of the Ohio Wesleyan University baseball team. The team's catcher was a black man named Charley Thomas, whom Rickey described as "a fine young man, fine family, good student, and my best player." (Charley Thomas would later become Dr. Thomas, a successful St. Louis dentist.) On a trip to South Bend, Indiana, Thomas attempted to register at the team hotel when a loud voice boomed, "We don't allow Negroes here." After much argument, Mr. Rickey finally got the manager to place a cot in his room for Thomas to sleep on, as they would do for an accompanying black servant. That night Thomas cried in bed pulling at his skin, "It's my black skin, Mr. Rickey – it's my skin. If I could pull it off I'd be like everybody else – it's my skin, Mr. Rickey."

Rickey's first full dose of racism left a lasting impression. For over forty years, Rickey heard that young man's voice crying and he vowed to do whatever he could to see that other Americans did not have to face the bitter humiliation heaped on Charley Thomas. Rickey believed strongly in the American creed of equality and the Judeo-Christian belief of love for one's neighbor. For him, racism was wrong. As he once put it, "I could not face my maker any longer knowing that his black children were held separate and distinct from his white children in a game that has given me all I own."

Rickey's second reason for hiring Robinson was for the good of his team, the Dodgers. As Rickey told an aide, "The greatest untapped reservoir of raw material in the history of the game is the black race! The Negroes will make us winners for years to come, and for that I will happily bear being called a bleeding heart and a do-gooder and all that humanitarian rot." [15] Rickey was right in his analysis. With Robinson and other black players, the Dodgers were perennial contenders, Rickey had a steady supply of great players, and the gates swelled as many black Americans came to see Robinson and his team.

In arguing to Bill Veeck (owner of the Cleveland Indians) that he should hire Larry Doby (a black American), Rickey confessed his one regret about hiring Robinson: there were not enough seats at Ebbets Field for all those wanting to buy tickets. On July 5, 1947, Veeck hired Doby, who became the first black American to play in the American league. [16] At the time, Clyde Sukeforth was scouting Doby for the Dodgers. True, however, to the Charley Thomas story, Mr. Rickey told him to back off and "let him go over to the other league. It will help the movement."

One of the ironies of the view that affirmative action amounts to a "quota system" is that it assumes that integration is bad for business and the bottom line. Such was not the case in 1947 (and still isn't). Those who were quickest to break the color barrier were the owners and managers looking for a competitive advantage. Branch Rickey was a self-described cheapskate who devoted his career to finding the best talent at the lowest cost. Bill Veeck was the last of the nonmillionaire owners and struggled financially with his franchise. Leo Durocher – the sixth-winningest Major League manager of all time – had one goal in mind: winning. He once said that "I'll play an elephant if he can do the job, and to make room for him I'll send my own brother home." Seeing Robinson in a couple of exhibition games was all the convincing Durocher needed.

Rickey's two reasons for affirmative action may strike some as odd; after all, you can't serve God and mammon. Perhaps owing to his Methodist theology, Rickey didn't see the contradiction and would give both reasons in the same paragraph. As he told Arthur Mann, "I didn't mean to be a crusader. My only purpose is to be fair to all people and my selfish objective is to win baseball games."

Interestingly, Rickey's two reasons for hiring Robinson map neatly onto metaphors for affirmative action used today. In 1965, President Lyndon Johnson gave a commencement address at Howard University where he said, "Is it reasonable to start a race between two runners, one of whose legs are shackled at the beginning of the race and unshackled halfway into the contest and declare a fair ending without adjusting for the handicap?" In other words, discrimination is unfair, un-American, and morally wrong. The second metaphor is based on Coretta Scott King's observation that "while we may have come over on different ships, right now we are in the same boat." In other words, we share a common fate; when any person is prevented from fully contributing to the common good, we all suffer. In the 1992 U.S. presidential election, Bill Clinton made use of this metaphor by arguing for affirmative action on the grounds that "we don't have a mind to waste in this country." Business and the country both will benefit when we all live up to our human potential.

Both of these metaphors have advantages and pitfalls. The "footrace" metaphor has the advantage of establishing an objective standard for eliminating discrimination – the American creed of equality. It has the disadvantages of implying that the recipient of affirmative action has a handicap requiring preferential treatment, and the policy relies on the benevolence of the in-group in serving as "helpers" of the disadvantaged out-group. [17] Our research and that of other social psychologists documents the negative consequences that can occur when a person is placed in the role of "a recipient of help."[18]

The "teamwork" metaphor has the advantage of not relying on the benevolence of the in-group to live up to its moral creed before integration can begin. It can, however, place an undue burden on the out-group member to achieve at superhuman levels. Durocher often told the white Dodgers that "Robinson will put money in your pockets," meaning that their chances of going to the World Series were much improved with him. Such expectations undoubtedly placed undue pressure on Robinson to perform. Further, some may not recognize the economic advantages of integration. Many owners in 1945 felt that Rickey's hiring of a black man would send baseball into financial ruin: the opposite happened. Branch Rickey, a master at persuasion, used both metaphors to his advantage to win support for the cause of integration.

The True Costs of Exclusion

Not all black Americans greeted Mr. Rickey's overtures with enthusiasm. For example, baseball great Wilmur Fields turned down many offers to play for white teams and continued to play in the Negro Major Leagues until 1958. [19] The teams of the Negro Major Leagues were generally profitable enterprises for many black owners. After 1947, white clubs made wholesale raids on the black talent on these ball clubs. Owners were frequently not reimbursed for their players and, if they were, the payment was typically below the market rate. For example, Mr. Rickey never paid J. L. Wilkerson, owner of the Kansas City Monarchs, a penny for Robinson's contract. Effa Manley, co-owner of the Newark Eagles, lost Larry Doby, Monte Irvin, and Don Newcombe and was a particularly strong critic of the raids. [20] Although she eventually received some compensation, however in 1960 the Negro Major Leagues went defunct; the black community lost a source of revenue, pride, and entertainment.

Black Americans as a whole rooted for Jackie Robinson and other blacks to make it, however. Jackie Robinson understood why they cheered so loud. A few days after his first game as a Brooklyn Dodger, he telephoned his sister, Willa Mae, and told her quite frankly, "I did it for my people." It should be noted, though, that Robinson went through periods of his life where he despaired over the pace of racial progress; at such times he would withdraw from baseball. The demise of the Negro Major Leagues and the despair of Robinson offer a lesson for the in-group: the process of integration has its costs for the out-group and, given a long history of previous exclusion and rejection, the in-group member should not be surprised to find that the out-group member does not suddenly gush with appreciation at a small step forward.

Nevertheless, the actions of "Cool Papa" Bell and the support of black Americans for Robinson does show the commitment of most black Americans to integration. One reason for this support is that black Americans know better than most the true costs of segregation. [21] Today, a black child is twice as likely to die in infancy than a white child. The life expectancy of a black American is 5.6 years shorter than that of the population as a whole. Blacks, on average, make about half as much income as whites. The unemployment rate for blacks is consistently twice as much as the rate for whites. A black male born in California is three times more likely to be killed in his neighborhood than to attend the University of California. Segregation and the forced exclusion from the mainstream can have painful psychological consequences. [22]

Black Americans must often face subtle forms of racism even from those professing nonprejudicial attitudes. For example, recent studies find that whites are less likely to help blacks in a casual social setting, less likely to want to follow the directions of a black leader, and more likely to use inadmissible testimony in a court case to convict black (as opposed to white) defendants. [23] And the effects of racism can be observed in the strangest places. One study found that the rookie baseball cards for black Hall of Fame baseball players were worth considerably less on the open market than the comparable cards of white Hall of Famers. [24] The Los Angeles riots of the early 1990s should serve as a painful reminder of the costs of separation for all Americans. The strategy of exclusion just doesn't work.

The cost of segregation for baseball fans is straightforward: some of the game's greatest moments are now lost to history, never to be played. How would Satchel Paige, with a smokin' fastball early in his career and curve after '38, have pitched to Lou Gehrig or Babe Ruth? [25] Could the arms of Dizzy Dean or Lefty Gomez have stopped the home runs of Josh Gibson – greatest home run hitter of all times? [26] What would have happened if the '35 Pittsburgh Crawfords – arguably one of the best teams (if not the best) to play on a diamond, with five Hall of Famers in their prime (Paige, Gibson, Oscar Charleston, William "Judy" Johnson, and "Cool Papa" Bell) – suddenly showed up in the National League? It is doubtful that the Detroit Tigers would have won the Series that year. [27]

Some may consider all of this to be the silly daydreams of hopeless baseball fans. But the same question can be asked of many segments of American society even today. How many Satchel Paiges of science, Josh Gibsons of top management, "Judy" Johnsons of higher education, "Cool Papa" Bells of industry, Oscar Charlestons of law, and Rachel Robinsons of business have been lost to wasteful racial barriers? [28]

It would be wrong to conclude that Mr. Rickey and Mr. Robinson eliminated racism from baseball. In his autobiography, Hank Aaron recounts many racial incidents, some of a recent vintage. [29] Fans in the stands would refer to him as "nigger" and "jigaboo." When Aaron announced he might consider a managerial job, he received the following letter: "Dear Nigger: There are three things you can't give a nigger – a black eye, a puffed lip, and a job." [30] Aaron documents the exclusion of many black ballplayers from the ranks of managers and baseball's front offices. Such incidents are all the more remarkable when you realize that Hank Aaron went to the All-Star Game twenty-one years in a row.

Prophetically, just before his death, Mr. Robinson pointed to the next challenge for Major League baseball – breaking what has since come to be called the "glass ceiling." On October 15, 1972, Jackie Robinson threw out the first ball in a World Series game held at Cincinnati's Riverfront Stadium. He told a national television audience, "I'd like to live to see a black manager." He died of a heart attack nine days later. The first black manager, Frank Robinson, took the helm three years later in Cleveland. (Frank Robinson twice won the Manager of the Year award.) Baseball is in a unique position to shatter the glass ceiling – it was the first organization to employ affirmative action and as a consequence has developed a large pool of talented black Americans who know and love baseball.

"Cool Papa" Bell's Sacrifice at the Plate

James "Cool Papa" Bell's sacrifice was not in vain. In 1948, Monte Irvin signed with the New York Giants, becoming one of the first black Americans to play with the New York club. In 1951, he hit .312 with 24 homers, taking the Giants to the World Series (leading the National League in RBIS). In 1954, he took them back to the Series, hitting .329 with 21 homers. In seven seasons with the Giants and one with the Cubs, Irvin batted .293 with 99 home runs. He was twice named to the National League All-Star Team. Irvin had played the 1938–48 seasons with the Newark Eagles (minus a four-year stint in the military). He twice won the Negro Major League batting title with a career average of .373. In 1973, Monte Irvin was elected to the Baseball Hall of Fame. One year later, "Cool Papa" Bell became the seventh black American inducted into the Hall. When the phone call came, Bell, in typical fashion, asked, "Are any other Negro League players going in this year?" A disappointed Bell heard the voice on the other end of the phone reply: "No, they are only going to pick one."

Our sense of justice argues that it would have been more appropriate for Bell to have entered the Hall before Irvin – after all, those who place themselves last shall go first. Perhaps, Mr. James Bell would have wanted it this way. When asked what was his greatest thrill in life, Bell didn't hesitate for a minute, "But I've got to say my biggest thrill was when they opened the door to the Negro."[31] His delayed entrance into the Hall of Fame should forever remind us of the injustice black Americans experience. His voice joins with those of Mr. Branch Rickey and Mr. Jackie Robinson in an eternal plea for us to take affirmative action to dismantle discriminatory barriers and to promote racial integration.

NOTES

Portions of this paper were presented at the Baseball Hall of Fame's Fifth Cooperstown Symposium on Baseball and American Culture, June 10, 1993, in Cooperstown, New York. We thank Elliot Aronson, Susan Finnemore Brennan, Nancy Carlson, Jonathan Cobb, Ken Fuld, David Morishige, T. Douglass Wuggazer, and Dan Ziniuk for helpful comments and discussion.

1. For details on Bell's career see J. B. Holway, *Voices From the Great Black Baseball Leagues* (New York: Da Capo Press, 1992); R. Peterson, *Only the Ball Was White* (New York: Oxford University Press, 1970); A. Rust, *Get That Nigger*

Off the Field: The Oral History of the Negro Leagues (Brooklyn NY: Book Mail Services, 1992).

2. J. Tygiel, "Black Ball," in J. Thorn and P. Palmer, eds., *Total Baseball: The Ultimate Encyclopedia of Baseball* 3d ed. (New York: HarperCollins, 1993), 486–501. For a history of segregation see C. V. Woodward, *The Strange Career of Jim Crow* (New York: Oxford University Press, 1955) and idem, *Reunion and Reaction: The Compromise of 1877 and the End of Reconstruction* (New York: Oxford University Press, 1966).

3. J. B. Holway, *Black Diamonds* (New York: Stadium Books, 1991), 151.

4. S. Whitton, "The AAGPBL's Girls of Summer," NINE: *A Journal of Baseball History and Social Policy Perspectives* 1 (1993): 214–21.

5. For histories of the Negro Major Leagues see B. Chadwick, *When the Game was Black and White* (New York: Abbeville Press, 1992); P. Dixon and P. J. Hannigan, *The Negro Baseball Leagues: A Photographic History* (Mattituck NY: Amereon House, 1992); J. B. Holway, *Blackball Stars* (Westport CT: Meckler, 1988); Holway, *Black Diamonds*; Holway, *Voices From the Great Black Baseball Leagues*; Peterson, *Only the Ball Was White*; D. Rogosin, *Invisible Men* (New York: Atheneum, 1970); Rust, *Get That Nigger Off the Field*.

6. St. C. Drake and H. R. Cayton, *Black Metropolis* (Chicago: University of Chicago Press, 1993); C. M. Logue and H. Dorgan, *The Oratory of Southern Demagogues* (Baton Rouge: Louisiana State University Press, 1981).

7. G. I. Berlage, "Effa Manley, A Major Force in Negro Baseball in the 1930s and 1940s," NINE: *A Journal of Baseball History and Social Policy Perspectives* 1 (1993): 163–84.

8. We base our account on the following excellent descriptions of Robinson's introduction to the white Major Leagues: M. Allen, *Jackie Robinson: A Life Remembered* (New York: Franklin Watts, 1987); M. Alvarez, *The Official Baseball Hall of Fame Story of Jackie Robinson* (New York: Simon and Schuster, 1990); R. Barber, *1947: When All Hell Broke Loose in Baseball* (New York: De Capo, 1982); L. Durocher, *Nice Guys Finish Last* (New York: Pocket Books, 1976); G. Eskenazi, *The Lip: A Biography of Leo Durocher* (New York: William Morrow, 1993); H. Frommer, *Rickey and Robinson: The Men Who Broke Baseball's Color Barrier* (New York: Macmillan, 1982); P. Golenbock and P. Bacon, *Teammates* (San Diego: Harcourt Brace Jovanovich, 1990); A. E. Green (Director), *The Jackie Robinson Story Starring Jackie Robinson* [Film] (New York: Goodtimes Home Video Corp., 1950); R. Kahn, *The Boys of Summer* (New York: Harper and Row, 1972); A. Mann, *Branch Rickey: American in Action* (Boston: Houghton Mifflin, 1957); J. R. Robinson, *I Never Had It Made* (New York: G. P. Putnam and Sons, 1972); J. R. Robinson and C. Dexter, *Baseball Has Done It* (Philadelphia: J. B. Lippincott, 1964); F. Sabin, *Jackie Robinson* (Mahwah NJ: Troll, 1985); G.

Schoor, *The Leo Durocher Story* (New York: Julian Messner, 1955); R. Scott, *Jackie Robinson* (New York: Chelsea House, 1987); M. J. Shapiro, *Jackie Robinson of the Brooklyn Dodgers* (New York: Pocket Books, 1967); D. Snider, *The Duke of Flatbush* (New York: Zebra Books, 1988); J. Thorn and J. Tygiel, "Jackie Robinson's Signing: The Real, Untold Story," in J. Thorn and P. Palmer, eds., *Total Baseball: The Ultimate Encyclopedia of Baseball* 3d ed. (New York: HarperCollins, 1993), 148–53; and see especially J. Tygiel, *Baseball's Great Experiment: Jackie Robinson and His Legacy* (New York: Vintage, 1983).

9. Woodward, *Strange Career*; idem, *Reunion and Reaction*.

10. For a history see D. G. Mandelbaum, *Soldier Groups and Negro Soldiers* (Berkeley: University of California Press, 1952). For a personal account of the treatment of blacks in the military see B. O. Davis, *Benjamin O. Davis: American* (Washington DC: Smithsonian Institution Press, 1991).

11. S. C. Ainley, L. M. Coleman, and G. Becker, "Stigma reconsidered," in S. C. Ainley, G. Becker, and L. M. Coleman, eds., *The Dilemma of Difference* (New York: Plenum Press, 1986), 1–13; G. Becker and R. Arnold, "Stigma as a Social and Cultural Construct," in Ainley, Becker, and Coleman, *The Dilemma of Difference*, 39–57; D. E. Brown, *Human Universals* (Philadelphia: Temple University Press, 1991).

12. T. F. Pettigrew, *Racially Separate or Together?* (New York: McGraw-Hill, 1971).

13. A. R. Pratkanis and M. E. Turner, "Nine Principles of Successful Affirmative Action: Mr. Branch Rickey, Mr. Jackie Robinson, and the Integration of Baseball," *NINE: A Journal of Baseball History and Social Policy Perspectives* 3 (1994): 36–65 (reprinted elsewhere in the present volume).

14. M. L. King, *A Testament of Hope* (San Francisco, Harper and Row, 1986). (Observers often attributed a third, less flattering motivation: Branch Rickey was a pushy show-off trying to achieve personal fame; for a reply see the "drum major instinct" sermon of Martin Luther King.)

15. Quoted in Tygiel, *Baseball's Great Experiment*, 52.

16. J. T. Moore, *Pride Against Prejudice: The Biography of Larry Doby* (New York: Praeger, 1988).

17. J. E. Armstrong, "Forty Years of Affirmative Action: Where Are We Now?" Paper presented at the annual conference of the Western Psychological Association, San Francisco, California, April 1991.

18. For a review see M. E. Turner and A. R. Pratkanis, "Affirmative Action as Help: A Review of Recipient Reactions to Preferential Selection and Affirmative Action," *Basic and Applied Social Psychology* 15, 43–69.

19. W. Fields, *My Life in the Negro Leagues* (Westport CT: Meckler, 1992).

20. Berlage, "Effa Manley."

21. J. M. Jones, "Racism: A Cultural Analysis of the Problem," in J. F. Dovidio and S. L. Gaertner, eds., *Prejudice, Discrimination, and Racism* (San Diego: Academic Press, 1986), 279–314; idem, "Racism in Black and White: A Bicultural Model of Reaction and Evolution," in P. A. Katz and D. A. Taylor, eds., *Eliminating Racism* (New York: Plenum, 1988), 117–35; L. Sigelman and S. Welch, *Black American's Views of Racial Inequality: The Dream Deferred* (Cambridge: Cambridge University Press, 1991).

22. K. B. Clark and M. P. Clark, "Racial Identification and Preference in Negro Children," in T. M. Newcomb and E. L. Hartley, eds., *Readings in Social Psychology* (New York: Henry Holt, 1947), 531–41; K. B. Clark, *Dark Ghetto* (New York: Harper and Row, 1965).

23. S. L. Gaertner and J. F. Dovidio, "The Aversive Form of Racism," in Dovidio and Gaertner, *Prejudice, Discrimination, and Racism*, 61–89. See also Robinson, *I Never Had It Made*, 77.

24. J. N. De Bonis, J. D. Pincus, S. C. Wood, and J. B. Pincus, "Anomalies in the Baseball Card Values of Black vs. White Hall of Fame Players," Paper presented at the National Baseball Hall of Fame Fifth Cooperstown Symposium on Baseball and American Culture, Cooperstown NY, June 10, 1993.

25. For a hint see J. B. Holway, *Josh and Satch* (Westport CT: Meckler, 1991); S. Paige, *Pitchin' Man* (Westport CT: Meckler, 1948); S. Paige, *Maybe I'll Pitch Forever* (Lincoln NE: University of Nebraska Press, 1993).

26. Josh Gibson hit just under 800 home runs (according to his Hall of Fame plaque). Hank Aaron hit 755 home runs. Babe Ruth hit 714 homers. Both Gibson and Ruth have asterisks beside their totals since neither hit white or black (respectively) pitching. Aaron is the greatest home run hitter without an asterisk.

27. J. Bankes, *The Pittsburgh Crawfords* (Dubuque IA: William C. Brown, 1991); R. Ruck, *Sandlot Season* (Champaign-Urbana: University of Illinois Press, 1987). Bankes describes how the '35 Crawfords would match up against the '27 Yankees.

28. For a listing of the achievements of black Americans in science and technology see L. Haber, *Black Pioneers* (Orlando FL: Harcourt Brace Jovanovich, 1970). Rachel Robinson taught psychiatric nursing at Yale University and runs a real estate development business specializing in subsidized housing.

29. H. Aaron, *I Had a Hammer: The Hank Aaron Story* (New York: Harper-Paperbacks, 1991).

30. Aaron, *I Had a Hammer*, 385.

31. Quoted in Holway, *Voices*, 134.

ROB RUCK

Baseball and Community

From Pittsburgh's Hill to San Pedro's Canefields

W HAT IS IT about baseball that makes it so compelling, so meaningful to people? I've tried to address that question since I was a doctoral student at the University of Pittsburgh in the late 1970s. It still comes up just about every time I talk, write, or try to create something about the game. Why do I, and more importantly, why do you and so many other people care about baseball, investing it with emotion, studying it, and, as citizens, supporting it?[1]

For me, the answer has much to do with how baseball can engender a powerful sense of community – in those who play it and, more importantly, in a larger social sense, for those who identify with a team, whether they be from a neighborhood, city, or nation, or of a group denominated by race or nationality, and sometimes even class or gender. It's that often sociopsychological response to the sport that I see whenever I return to the game.

On an individual basis, belonging to a team gives someone an identity and a status. That belonging can bring forth strong emotions – elation or horror, satisfaction or humiliation, excitement or shame – and the intense connection with teammates whose success and failure you share. Almost anyone who has experienced being a member of a championship team at any level from Little League to professional baseball finds that an unforgettable experience. Even being a part of a good team can be exhilarating. And most ballplayers at any level share some affiliation to a fraternity in which they have been initiated.

Baseball is probably the most thrilling and meaningful to those who encounter it on that level, as players with nothing between them and the game – no mediating forces such as parents, coaches, and owners.

But even those who are not on a team can vicariously experience its emotional, psychological, and social ups and downs. I would like here to discuss the sport of baseball and how it has effected a sense of community in two venues to which I've kept returning since the late 1970s.

The first is the black community in Pittsburgh during the first half of the twentieth century, and the second the Dominican Republic, especially the West Indian migrants who became known as the Cocolos after their turn-of-the-century migrations to the island.

But I feel compelled to offer a few observations – not so much to reappraise my work or get me through a scholarly midlife crisis – but to help assess the degree to which community does result from baseball and sport more generally.

The first caveat is that I often wonder to what degree I'm projecting what I want to see onto the subjects I'm studying. I'm a product of the sixties and came of age in what many then simply called "the movement." That new left activism which shaped my personal sensibilities as well as my perceptions of society put a heavy emphasis on community. So did the labor history I pursued as a graduate student at Pitt with a group that coalesced around David Montgomery. It's fair to say that both activists and labor historians were attracted to groups acting in concert. I wonder if I might be finding what I find because that's what I've always wanted to find? Do these groups really stand for the often abstract and ideological notions I say they stand for? Or am I projecting that?

The second observation concerns the nature of the evidence regarding consciousness and a sense of community. Most of the time we're dealing with words as personal memories or as pronouncements in the press or for political ends. How much can they be trusted to tell us what is virtually impossible to prove, at least empirically? The historian's task is to try to find meaning in people's actions and behavior, but the direct linkages are often flimsier than we care to admit.

A third point. The further I get from the people and the locales I'm discussing, both geographically and temporally, the less I'm sure of what sport really meant to them. That suggests that the personal connections a researcher makes are critical. I recognize how much I'm swayed by the emotions and personae of the people I've used as my informants. I suspect that anthropologists deal with this dynamic all the time. I think that, to some extent, I'm absorbing my informants – their thoughts and feelings. This identification lessens over time, but even then, there is a powerful incentive to buy into your own conclusions and accept them uncritically after awhile. Over time, a scholar develops quite a stake in her or his interpretations.

Harold Tinker

But let's move from the abstract to the more empirical and look at the role that baseball played in the making of black Pittsburgh. I would like to do that by introducing Harold Tinker. [2] Harold Tinker was born in Birmingham, Alabama, in 1905. He turned 92 on March 23, 1997. His parents, William and Mamie Tinker, grew up in rural Alabama before coming to Birmingham, where his father worked as a barber, in real estate, and undertaking. Harold recalls riding around in the family's horse and buggy, a sign, he reflects, that the family was relatively well-to-do. Though his father had white clients as a barber, Harold grew up in a largely segregated world. He talks about sitting in the colored bleachers the first time he saw the Birmingham Barons play. His school was all black, as were his neighborhood and playmates. When the boys played ball in the street with their homemade bats and nickel rockets – canvas-covered balls they bought at the grocery store – it was among African Americans. Walking through white neighborhoods often meant rocks or words. But Harold does not recall lynchings or the Klan as a presence before he came north.

But in 1917, after William Tinker lost his undertaking business and the family lost their home, they joined what was becoming known as the Great Migration that had been reshaping America since before the First World War. Harold was twelve when the family left Birmingham for Pittsburgh.

His father had been in Pittsburgh for a year with the eldest son before sending for the rest of the family. William Tinker worked at Hornes Department Store as a shoeshine boy, then as a porter for the store, and eventually as a barber. They first lived atop Mt. Washington, the bluffs above the Monongahela River across from downtown. From there, Harold could see Exposition Park on the north side, across the Allegheny River where the Pirates had played until departing for Forbes Field in 1909. The family soon moved to the Hill, an integrated, multinational spot above the central business district that was, at the turn of the century, the traditional gathering spot for immigrants. "We were all mixed together: Jewish, Italians, and blacks," Harold remembers.

The family held together in its new city but never regained the standard of living they had known in Birmingham. Harold attended an integrated school but socialized and played mostly with people of his own race. He left school when he was in the eleventh grade after getting married. Leaving without a degree was a decision that he long regretted, and one that made the honorary degree he received at the age of ninety all the sweeter. Harold worked a variety of jobs and fathered three daughters before the Urban League, an institution that helped black migrants adjust to city life, gave him a letter of introduction to Path A films, where he was hired as a porter. Harold, only the second black porter in film row (as the motion picture shipping area was called) cleaned the company's offices for about a year and a half before becoming the first black man to get work as an assistant shipper. He worked for Path A and its successor companies until he retired after over fifty years with the company. Harold was one of the first workers to enlist in the union when the Congress of Industrial Organizations (cio) organized film row in the 1930s and he served on the union's executive board for over a decade. The union's pledge to end a discriminatory pay system was all he needed to hear.

Harold divorced but soon remarried and had six children with his second wife. He often worked a night job to make ends meet. Even then it was a frugal life. Looking at his material possessions and his work life, one might conclude that Harold Tinker lived a fairly drab existence without great accomplishments or glories. Think again. Let me now reintroduce Harold Tinker to you.

These are clips from "Kings on the Hill: Baseball's Forgotten Men," a documentary about the Negro Leagues and the role of sport in the black community [The clips introduced the Negro Leagues and feature Harold talking about his love for the game and his ambition of putting together a ball club that could beat the Homestead Grays, the best black club in the region.][3]

During the 1930s and 40s, Pittsburgh became to black sport what Harlem was to black literature and art in the 1920s, the center of a renaissance. You've just witnessed a bit about the two Negro League clubs that were the most developed and visible manifestation of that phenomena. But the Grays and Crawfords did not spring fully formed on to the sporting scene nor were they the only teams. They began on the sandlots in western Pennsylvania where, between the two world wars, 200 to 500 sandlot and semi-pro ball clubs played each year. Sandlot ball is little more than a remembrance in the United States these days. Its heyday was the first half of the century when self-organized, community, and workplace-based baseball (and football) thrived in almost every neighborhood in and around cities like Pittsburgh. In their prime in Pittsburgh, the sandlot teams collectively drew more fans and meant more to people on a day-to-day basis than did the Pirates.

Homestead Grays

The top black team, and maybe even the top team regardless of color, was the Grays of Homestead, a mill town across the river from Pittsburgh. The Grays began as the Blue Ribbon Nine, who were formed by African American steelworkers at the Homestead Works in 1900. They played ball simply because they enjoyed the game. By the time of the First World War, the Grays were one of the best sandlot clubs in the area and had a Homestead native, Cumberland ("Cum") Posey, playing in the outfield. Cum Posey's father, Captain Cumberland Willis Posey, was the most important black businessman in Pittsburgh. President of the prestigious Loendi Club and the *Pittsburgh Courier* newspaper, Posey owned the Diamond Coke and Coal Company, the largest black business in the region. His son, Cum, became renowned as one of the best basketball players in the nation. Cum Posey's Loendi and Monticello basketball clubs were often referred to as the informal national champions, but it was in baseball that he left his most enduring legacy.

Soon the manager and then the owner of the Grays, Posey not only made them the champions of the Negro Leagues by 1930 but established them on a more stable business footing. The Grays were a mainstay of League play during the 1930s and 40s. From 1937 through 1945, with Josh Gibson, Buck Leonard, Vic Harris, Luke Easter, and Bob Thurman on the squad, they won nine NNL pennants in a row. During the late 1930s and the Second World War, they played three games a week at Griffith Stadium in Washington DC as well as in Pittsburgh and parts between.

Harold Tinker grew up in neighborhood gyms and sandlots on the Hill, always aware of Posey, who was twelve years his elder. In the winter, Harold played basketball for the Bailey Big Five or the Courier Five. He even played once against Posey and his team. In the summer, Harold played for the WEMCO (Westinghouse Manufacturing Company) baseball team, then the Keystone Juniors, the Homewood Monarchs, and finally ET, the club representing the Edgar Thomson Steelworks, Andrew

Carnegie's first steel mill. Many steel mills sponsored ball clubs for their workers in the 1920s. Several of the ET players had played ball with Harold for years and followed his lead as to which club they should join. After a team called the Crawfords, which was formed in 1926 by James Dorsey, a community worker at the Crawford Bath House on the Hill, played ET in a close contest, Harold and his buddies switched their allegiances.

Tinker captained the Crawfords and played center field for them. His one ambition, as he explained in "Kings," was to put together a ball club that could beat the Homestead Grays. When Tinker added Josh Gibson, the Buena Vista, Georgia–born, Northside-bred teenager to the club, he took a giant step in that direction. By the time the Crawfords got their first game against the Homestead Grays, Cum Posey had recruited Josh Gibson away from them. While the Crawfords passed the hat at games and split the proceeds, they were strictly semi-pro compared to the Grays. Although Tinker was devastated to see Josh leave the team, he did not feel he could stand in his way. The Grays beat the Crawfords the first two times they played, but, as Harold explained, his team had two new forces on its side by their third encounter – Satchel Paige and Gus Greenlee. With Satchel coming out of the bullpen and throwing, Harold remembers, nothing but fastballs, the Crawfords rallied for their first victory. Harold Tinker soon left the squad, unable to support his family on what he then made from baseball. James "Cool Papa" Bell replaced him in center field. But Harold had fulfilled his sporting ambition. He did return to baseball after the Second World War as the manager of Terrace Village, the area's first integrated sandlot club, which represented the Terrace Village housing project.

Gus Greenlee, a numbers banker on the Hill, was another son of the Great Migration. Almost everyone in black Pittsburgh knew Gus. They played his numbers, drank and listened to jazz at his Crawford Grill, and cheered for the boxers and ballplayers he sponsored. Greenlee took the Crawfords on at the players' request and remade them into a world-class team. He built Greenlee Field, the finest black-owned ballpark in the country, on the Hill and soon had a lineup that included Paige, Oscar Charleston, William "Judy" Johnson, "Cool Papa" Bell, and Josh Gibson, whom he lured back to the Crawfords. Former Newark Eagle and Hall-of-Famer Monte Irvin compares them to the 1927 Yankees.

Migration

Now what does this have to do with community? During the early decades of this century, migration from the Deep South remade black Pittsburgh. The city had a black population of about 20,000 in 1900. Black Pittsburgh achieved a remarkable level of attainment given the multiple forms of discrimination that affected such urban areas at the time. It could boast of eighty-five black-owned businesses and a network of cultural and fraternal organizations that included a symphony orchestra and a string quartet. "They were go-getters and entrepreneurs," observes historian Laurence Glasco, "imbued with the ideology of the self-made man."[4]

But the migration swelled that population to over 50,000 by 1930, making Pittsburgh the fifth largest black community in the country. The migration introduced new elements of internal division from the First World War onwards. There was also tremendous turnover within black Pittsburgh as these early migrants found that secure work was hard to find, which contributed to the black community's sense of impermanence. An estimated two-thirds of all the African Americans living in Pittsburgh in 1920 were absent a decade later. The biggest source of division was due to the origins of the newer migrants. While the earlier black residents had come from Virginia and Maryland, the new arrivals were from the lower South.

By the 1920s, these newcomers had swamped black Pittsburgh, crowding into wards where housing and health were already the worst in the city. Against a backdrop of discrimination at work and in the community, black Pittsburgh also found itself divided internally along the lines of place of birth, skin color, and social class. The "Ops" or "Old Pittsburghers," as native-born black Pittsburghers were called, looked askance at their country cousins, with their darker skin, lesser education, and rural ways. Just as there was a tendency for the half dozen different nationalities on the Hill to cluster together, there was a marked clustering of migrant and Pittsburgh-born blacks.

In nearby Homestead, skilled black workers, professionals, and shopkeepers, mostly northern-born, lived in the Hilltop neighborhood while the southern migrants who labored in work gangs in the mills resided in crossed boarding houses in the ward along the river. They went to different churches on Sunday and returned to different neighborhoods afterwards, one a fairly pleasant residential section, the other a district with a reputation for honky-tonks, gambling dens, and whorehouses.

Class Division

The migration aggravated what was an already significant class division and led to two almost separate black communities based on place of birth and occupation. They lived apart, worked apart, and played apart amidst a fairly persistent discomfort that Old Pittsburghers felt over the new arrivals. On the one hand, the migrants were customers for the black business corridor that formed along Wylie Avenue on the Hill. But on the other, established northern-born black Pittsburghers feared that their position would be undermined by migrants who created greater demand for already scarce jobs, housing, and social services and would perhaps trigger a backlash against all African Americans in the area. This sense of unease over its own make-up was compounded by the material conditions facing blacks here. Life was harsh for most migrants to the region, which had attracted large numbers of Southern and Eastern Europeans from the 1880s through the First World War, but it was particularly grim for blacks. Pittsburgh might have been America's industrial epicenter, but it chewed up the workers who labored in its mills and made life in the shadows of the factory unrelentingly grim.

Housing was hard to come by and the Hill suffered the highest incidence of disease and public health problems in the city. Neither did the world of work offer much respite. While the prospects of steadier and better-paying jobs had induced many to migrate, only a small percentage escaped low-paying, unskilled labor. African Americans found work as porters, laundresses, teamsters, and day laborers, but not as clerks, teachers, or even, for the most part, in basic industry. Black men did not enter the mills in large numbers until after the Second World War.

One final factor undercutting black Pittsburgh's sense of self was that, unlike Chicago, New York, and Philadelphia, where there was a contiguous ghetto area, the black community here was split into one fairly large enclave on the Hill and a half dozen smaller neighborhoods. The absence of a consolidated black neighborhood undercut black business and political strength. Anybody who has ever been to Pittsburgh can probably see why the black community was so geographically fragmented. Much of that had to do with the topography of the city, which is sliced into smaller neighborhoods by the three rivers and the region's many hills and valleys. The creation of public housing projects in remote sections of the city after the Second World War deepened this sense of isolation and division.

What did this mean for sport? The relatively fragmented nature of the black community allowed external forces to intervene in the organization of its sporting life. These forces included settlement houses, the YMCA, the Urban League, the organized-play movement, and, most of all, local industry. Space doesn't allow me to discuss their agendas and how they sought to win the hearts and minds of black Pittsburgh. Instead, I would like to focus on the degree to which sport became a far more rewarding and positive sphere of activity than work, neighborhood, or politics in terms of the collective self-image of black Pittsburgh and its sense of cohesion.

Limited Fulfillment

For Harold Tinker and his peers, work offered limited fulfillment, neighborhoods were crowded and polluted, and politics off-limits. But in sport, these young and not-so-young men could revel in their own abilities to create, achieve, and win. The implications for individual self-esteem are fairly clear. But what about the collective sense of self-esteem and identity?

The Crawfords, the 18th Ward, the Homewood Monarchs, the Grays, and the dozen or so other black clubs were each a focus for their neighborhood. Their contests allowed neighborhoods to compete with each other and because their paladins in these matches were neighbors, workmates, and family, these games were something of an extension of the larger neighborhood as well as an affirmation of who they were. Sport transcended topography, social class, skin color, and place of birth. In playing against each other, players and spectators gained respect for each other. They shared something positive.

This shared experience of competition extended to their white opponents. Whatever else was occurring in their lives, when they played baseball against each other, the playing field was equal. That allowed sport to become, with the possible exception of the army, the most positive arena for racial interaction in the century.

As the Grays and the Crawfords developed into national and even international institutions, these teams allowed the entire black community to root for the same ball club and, in so doing, root for each other and themselves. With "Cool Papa" Bell flying around the basepaths, Josh

Gibson drawing accolades as the black Babe Ruth, and Satchel walking the bases loaded, telling his fielders to sit down, and striking out the side, black Pittsburgh celebrated its potential for self-organization, creativity, and competence. Baseball meant more than a dozen NNL titles and the chance to witness great athletes, including seven of the first eleven Negro Leaguers eventually selected to the Hall of Fame. Black Pittsburgh began to coalesce and overcome, at least temporarily, its internal divisions. It gained not only a pleasant cultural counterpoint to its less fulfilling experiences at work and socially, but also a bridge to white America.

*

I would like here to segue quickly to the Dominican Republic, where baseball has been played since Cubans brought the game there in the 1890s. I want to focus on one region of the country, the sugarcane mill towns in and around San Pedro de Macoris. About an hour's drive east of Santo Domingo, San Pedro has become baseball's Caribbean Mecca. San Pedro has sent more of its native sons to the majors on a per capita basis than any town in history.

If conditions for black migrants to Pittsburgh early in the last century were often horrendous, they were downright luxurious compared to those facing the men and women who came to San Pedro at the turn of the century to cut sugarcane. San Pedro's economy has revolved around sugar since Cubans fleeing the chaos of the Ten Years' War (1868–1878) began cultivating it on the plains around this port city. The sugarcane industry grew greatly as the island was incorporated into the United States' economic sphere in the early twentieth century, especially after the First World War. The biggest problem for the growers was the shortage of laborers willing to engage in this hot, dangerous, and low-paying work. It's still that way and most cane cutters today come from Haiti, where misery is the one commodity of which there is no shortage.

Because few Dominicans saw cutting cane or working in the toothed rollers that grind and refine the cane as desirable jobs, the industry began to recruit seasonal laborers from the down islands early in the century. These workers were men of African descent who came from St. Martin, Nevis, Tortola, Montserrat, and the other, mostly British, islands where the sugar industry had collapsed due to tariffs protecting the European sugar beet industry. At first, these men worked during the *zafra*, or harvest, and returned home afterwards. But gradually, thousands began to stay and brought their families. They were called the "English" and settled in a part of San Pedro called Miramar and in the sugar mill towns that encircled the city: Porvenir, Santa Fe, Quisqueya, Cristúbal Colún, Angelina, and Consuelo.

Scorned

As Roberto Caines, now almost seventy and recently pensioned from the Consuelo mill, explained to me several years ago: "They were brought to cut cane on the estates, but they were scorned. It was a great trial to go to another country. We lived in barracks, four families to a house, with plenty bugs, plenty sickness and vermin." Dominicans began calling them "Cocolos," a mispronunciation of the British Virgin Island, Tortola, where many were from. Calling someone a "Cocolo" was meant as an insult and often led to a fight. But this epithet would eventually become a term of pride as the English forged their own cultural definition of "Cocolo," one that transcended their different islands of origin and places of residence and emphasized discipline and self-organization at work and at play. Without these English-speaking, cricket-playing sojourners, Macorisano baseball never would have become the best in the Caribbean.

For these West Indian migrants, their children, and their grandchildren, sport fostered a spirit of self-celebration in which a sense of community and identity was forged. Sport provided the Cocolos a vehicle to assert a collective identity within a larger, frequently hostile society. That cultural role, even more than baseball later becoming a means of upward mobility, explains its extraordinary evolution and meaning to this group of people.

Like black Pittsburgh, San Pedro offered few social amenities or any real economic security. Divided into a half dozen mill towns and scores of *bateyes* (tiny clusters of primitive housing in the fields), the Cocolos were politically powerless – as was just about everybody else in this *caudillo*-led society – and socially scorned due to their immigrant status, Protestant religion, English language, and black skin. Their fragmentation along the lines of island of birth furthered this disorganization. Unlike black Pittsburgh, though, there were no serious divisions due to skin color or social class among the Cocolos.

These conditions lent sport a special significance as a force for cohesion and consciousness. "The only protection they have," argues Roberto Caines, "was to unificate [*sic*] with each other." This coming together took the form of a school for their children, which met under a tree in Consuelo, and mutual aid societies to care for the sick and pay the costs of a proper burial. These mutual aid societies were modeled after comparable British institutions. So, too, was their sense of sport.

"My father came from Antigua to cut cane," William Joseph, another retired Consuelo millworker explains. "They brought cricket with them from the islands and I learned the game from him." In Consuelo, the cutters and millworkers on the Ever Jolly and the Energetic cricket clubs pooled their money and sent for equipment from India. They made their own uniforms, all white of course, and wore white sneakers and a sash with the club's colors. And they played the game with a sense of discipline and propriety.

Cricket

Cricket developed within a context of fraternal societies and substantial race consciousness, with teams sometimes emerging from the societies. As Roberto Caines puts it, "The children had sport crafted in them. They were exposed to sport and taught they must try not to fail or that the color will fail, too, and the race will be beaten." Arguing that the Cocolos had no politics (for politics, especially in the era of dictator Rafael Trujillo, was a no-win proposition), Caines says "we did have the message of Marcus Garvey," the Jamaican-born leader of the Universal Negro Improvement Association (UNIA), the largest black nationalist movement of the twentieth century. "We always tried to maintain pride and heritage. We had a sense of discipline and organization with which we founded our clubs and societies, of good British discipline, of taking care of our people that have need." This approach carried over into the organization of their sporting life.

A network of cricket clubs emerged that represented the different mill towns and the Cocolo section of San Pedro. Like many of the sandlot clubs in Pittsburgh, these were self-organized teams. Unlike many black Pittsburgh teams, however, there was no company support. "We organized the teams," Antiguan native Coleridge Mayers explained. "We even made our own pitch, exclusively. Cricket was the sport of the English people and the sugar estates then."

Before the first match of the season, a cornet player and the young girls selected as the queens of the clubs led the players in a parade through the mill town. Holidays and weekends during the dead season were celebrated with matches. Twentieth-Century Fox played Miramar, Porvenir played Quisqueya, Santa Fe played the Ever Jolly. But gradually, cricket began to die out and baseball, as William Joseph remembers, became the English sport. By playing baseball, these immigrants' children gained acceptance and eventually some even gained a livelihood.

But cricket had helped to link a disparate group of immigrants together and contributed to their identity. Certainly, there are other elements to that Cocolo identity, but cricket was a special part of it. And when baseball became the sport of the sugarcane communities, it took on some of cricket's roles. Baseball became something that the Cocolos did well, better than anyone else on the island.

While the first generation of Cocolos born in San Pedro played cricket, their sons played cricket and baseball, and their grandsons just baseball. The third generation's names have become well known throughout baseball in America: Carty, Franco, Bell, Samuel, Guerrero, Duncan, Offerman, and Sosa. They have been joined by a substantial cohort of non-Cocolo San Pedro compadres. Though many of the ballplayers coming out of San Pedro today are not Cocolo in origin, the Cocolos led the way.

Overpowered

Baseball overpowered cricket by the 1930s. That reflected the Dominicanization of the children of the migrants. Baseball certainly eased that process just as it did for many in the United States. Baseball was by then the pan-Caribbean pastime. The 1936 and 1937 Championship Tournaments played in the Dominican Republic boasted the finest Cuban, Puerto Rican, Dominican, and African American players of the decade, including Martin Dihigo, Perucho Cepeda, Silvio Garcia, Horacio Martinez, Tetelo Vargas, "Cool Papa" Bell, Josh Gibson, and Satchel Paige. Indeed, that 1937 season, during which Paige, Gibson, Bell, and a half dozen other Crawfords jumped to play for Cuidad Trujillo, brought about the demise of the Crawfords.

By the 1950s, more and more Cocolos were becoming prominent in Dominican baseball and, after Rico Carty's breakthrough, in Major League baseball. Many Major Leaguers, such as Carty, Alfredo Griffin, and Nelson Norman, had fathers and grandfathers who started at cricket. Just as vital were the activists, men like Roberto Caines, who organized baseball teams in the *ingenios* and taught the craft of baseball with the same sense of discipline that had pervaded cricket.

The spectacular trajectory that San Pedro baseball has taken is not solely due to this Cocolo cultural legacy. Once a critical mass was achieved, including teachers, role models, scouts, and Major League academies, San Pedro baseball took on a life of its own. But much of its impetus had to do with the informal network of boys and men who built their own sporting life as part of the larger process of the Dominican English building a community. The Cocolos developed a sense of themselves as a people from the oppositional nature of the dominant Dominican culture. Just as in black Pittsburgh, sport loomed in importance because other avenues of expression and advancement were denied. As Janet Lever has demonstrated in her wonderful study of football in Brazil, *Soccer Madness*, the competition among clubs from the different estates created a larger, more inclusive sense of solidarity that transcended the emotions of a match.[5] Even though they played against each other, these teams and estates celebrated their sporting excellence together and forged a larger sense of identity in the process. For Janet Lever's Brazil, that became a national identity as Brazilians. In Pittsburgh and San Pedro, it was more of a sense of racial and national identity and community.

NOTES

This essay is drawn from remarks originally presented at the Fourth Annual NINE Conference, March 7, 1997, in Phoenix AZ.

1. This essay utilizes research conducted for *Sandlot Seasons: Sport in Black Pittsburgh* (Champaign–Urbana: University of Illinois Press, 1987) and *The Tropic of Baseball: Baseball in the Dominican Republic* (New York: Carroll and Graf, 1993).

2. Interviews with Harold Tinker were conducted during 1994 and 1995 in addition to those done for *Sandlot Seasons* and "Kings on the Hill."

3. "Kings on the Hill: Baseball's Forgotten Men" is a documentary first broadcast in 1993. I was the project director and writer for it.

4. R. Ruck and C. Fletcher, "Unequal Opportunity," *Pittsburgh Magazine*, September 1995, 88.

5. J. Lever, *Soccer Madness* (Chicago: University of Chicago Press, 1983). Lever's seminal study remains perhaps the best treatment of how sport can engender a sense of community.

JERRY MALLOY

The Strange Career of Sol. White

Black Baseball's First Historian

Life can only be understood backwards, but it must be lived forwards.
— Søren Kierkegaard

AFRICAN AMERICAN BASEBALL is the National Pastime's last historical frontier. In the past few decades, baseball history has widened its base of researchers, writers, and students. Having weathered the rigors of wars, depressions, and scandals, and basked in the warm glow of more prosperous times, baseball has a long, rich, diverse history. The game's tradition and lore are so deeply etched in American society and culture that historians recognize its value as an institutional lodestar, a fixed point of reference running through the nation's life relatively unchanged since the Civil War era. As such, historians have followed the muse Clio to the ballpark to help understand our nation's economics, social, and racial past.

The history of African American baseball has benefited greatly from this rising tide of scholarship, as well as from the recent surge in popular interest in the vibrant Negro Leagues of the 1920s–1940s. Since the publication of Robert Peterson's groundbreaking book *Only the Ball Was White* in 1970, accounts of twentieth-century African American baseball have awakened the echoes of a lost universe: a baseball world with far more roles for African Americans than exist in baseball today. For every Ty Cobb, Walter Johnson, or Lou Gehrig, African American baseball had an Oscar Charleston, Bullet Rogan, or Buck Leonard. But the world of black baseball also included African American managers, umpires, sportswriters,throngs of African American fans, executives, owners, and commissioners.

Baseball history's black component was long victimized by willful neglect. As early as 1895 *Sporting Life* remarked that "nothing is ever said or written about drawing the color line in the [National] League. It appears to be greatly understood that none but whites shall make up the League teams, and so it goes."[1] Black baseball's history has all the merits of the white game's, with the additional complexity of operating within a din of racial animosity. It is a wonder that African American baseball was able to survive and a tribute to the creativity and diligence of those who enabled it to do so. Negro League baseball, one of the most successful of black business ventures between the end of the First World War and the beginning of the Cold War, was a source of great pride within the African American community. The world of black baseball illustrates black America's ability to have created a vibrant subculture that fostered the standards and traditions of the same dominant counterpart that had dismissed them with scorn and hostility.

Those curious about the victories and vexations of African American baseball's early struggles to survive (much less thrive) in a harrowing racial environment are fortunate that a man of words, as well as deeds, was present to record black professional baseball's first twenty years. His name was Soloman White and by 1906 he had survived African American baseball's food chain most impressively. After a long career as a slugging infielder of considerable skill, he had succeeded in the more elevated realms of managing and owning the most powerful black team in the nation, the Philadelphia Giants.

In 1906 the Philadelphia Giants won 134 of the 155 games they played that year, fully 86 percent. They clinched a four-way battle for black baseball supremacy in the East before a crowd of ten thousand fans in the Major Leagues' Philadelphia Athletics' Columbia Park, "the largest crowd of spectators that ever attended a baseball game between colored teams," as White proudly recalled. Invigorated by the passions of triumph, White's partner in the ownership of the Giants challenged the winners of the white "World's Series" to "decide who can play baseball the best – the white or the black American."[2] But the White Sox's Hitless Wonders from the South Side of Chicago, champions of the white game in 1906, never locked horns with Sol. White's potent black squad.

At age 39 and at the apex of a distinguished career, White decided to promulgate an account of the origins of the black baseball empire he had recently conquered, recording his Olympian recollections of, and reflections on, the first twenty years of professional African American baseball. By the time the 1907 season commenced, *Sol. White's Official Base Ball Guide: History of Colored Base Ball* was published in Philadelphia by H. Walter Schlichter, a white sportswriter who was White's partner in the ownership of the Giants. White's engaging pastiche of history, lore, instruction, and even poetry chronicled the emergence of America's black sporting community and bestowed a unique glimpse into the world of the men and events that shaped black baseball's infancy. Sol. White's *Guide* is the Dead Sea Scrolls of black professional baseball's pioneering community.

Sol. White in Black Baseball

No colored ball player has had a wider experience in base ball than Sol., and no ball player has profited by experience greater than he has. – H. Walter Schlichter *in Sol. White's Official Base Ball Guide: History of Colored Base Ball*

Sol. White graced black baseball with his protean talents for an entire generation in a career played out at the highest elevation of the game. In his history of black baseball, his focus rarely drifted from the zenith of the game in his time and place – its greatest stars, its strongest teams, its storied rivalries. His career spanned forty years of the game at its fullest expression. Blessed with great ability during a period when ballplayers' careers (both black and white) often were peripatetic, White moved freely between the East and Midwest to play for the best black baseball teams of his era. A review of Sol. White's career as a ballplayer constitutes an overview of nineteenth-century black baseball.

Black baseball's first historian was also one of its earliest "lifers." Twenty years after he wrote his *Guide*, the *Pittsburgh Courier* wrote of White's long association with the game and noted that "he hardly talks about anything else."[3] Though White played briefly for a few white teams, his playing career was predominantly beyond the pale, within the world of African American baseball, which was gradually driven underground and became invisible to the white mainstream. Beginning with the tumultuous season of 1887, he traveled in black baseball's fastest lane for a quarter century.

Sol. White the ballplayer began his career in the midst of what Sol. White the historian later would call "the money period." "From 1885 until the close of 1890," he wrote, "colored base ball flourished."[4] In 1887 White, a nineteen-year-old infielder from the sandlots of Bellaire, Ohio (across the Ohio River from Wheeling, West Virginia), signed on with the Pittsburgh Keystones, a charter member of the nascent League of Colored Ball Players (often called the Colored or National Colored League). The

Cuban Giants, the country's first team of salaried black ballplayers, had attained "great prominence" since their formation two years earlier in 1885, wrote White, which "led some people to think that colored base ball, patterned after the National League, with a team in every big league city, would draw the same number of people."[5] Teams from Baltimore, Boston, Louisville, New York, Philadelphia, and Pittsburgh joined the league at a series of meetings in Baltimore.

Despite their moniker, the Cuban Giants of Trenton, New Jersey, were black Americans who supplemented their primary earnings as ballplayers by serving as waiters, porters, and bellhops at various resort hotels that hired them to play ball for the amusement of the guests. The *New York Sun* reported that the Cuban Giants "are neither giants nor Cubans, but thick-set and brawny colored men, [who] make about as stunning an exhibition of ball playing as any team in the country," adding that "it is one of the best teams in the city to see."[6] Investors in the new Colored League were disappointed that black baseball's most famous team declined to join the circuit. On the other hand, they were encouraged when, to the surprise of many, the fledgling league was granted admission into baseball's official family by being permitted to enter into the National Agreement, the pact that defined the polity of so-called organized baseball. *Sporting Life* remarked upon the pointlessness of this arrangement, explaining that signatories to the National Agreement benefit because "it guarantees a club undisturbed possession of its players. There is not likely to be much of a scramble for colored players [due to] the high standard of play required and to the popular prejudice against any considerable mixture of the races."[7]

The Colored League opened play on May 8, 1887, at Recreation Park in Pittsburgh, home grounds of Sol. White's Keystones. Following "a grand street parade and a brass band concert," 1,200 fans watched the home team lose to the Gorhams of New York City, a team that would soon employ White.[8] Ten days later, the Keystones lost to the Lord Baltimores in the unlucky league's thirteenth and final game.[9] Boston's Resolutes folded while the team was in Louisville, stranding its players. "At last accounts," reported the *Sporting News*, "most of the Colored Leaguers were working their way home doing little turns in barbershops and waiting tables in hotels."[10]

The Colored League was ahead of its time. The African American presence in baseball eventually followed a progression: from black players on white teams, to black teams in white leagues, to rivalry among strong, independent black teams, to the creation of cohesive black leagues, to post–Second World War desegregation. The Colored League was just the first of several failed attempts to form a strong black baseball association until Chicago's Rube Foster accomplished the Bismarckian task in 1920. Yet, despite the Colored League's quick demise, the mere fact that such an enterprise was undertaken indicates an atmosphere of optimism, a sentiment within the black sporting world that community prestige – and private profits – could be secured through the employment of men skilled enough to perfect America's favorite boyhood game. In this respect, African American baseball in the late 1880s was in tune with its white counterpart.

Twenty years later, Sol. White noted the boost the Colored League gave to black baseball despite its hasty dissolution. "[T]he short time of its existence served to bring out the fact that colored ball players of ability were numerous," he wrote. Indeed, White would play on several prominent African American teams with players he first met in the Colored League of 1887. Besides, most of the League's teams remained intact and "[w]ith reputations as clubs from the defunct Colored League, they proved to be very good drawing cards in different sections of the country."[11]

Meanwhile, events in white baseball's International League marked the traumatic 1887 season as a watershed year in nineteenth-century baseball's halting, uncertain drift toward racial exclusion. The color line that descended across baseball beginning in the 1890s remained in place for so long that memories of a previous acceptance of black ballplayers in the mainstream of the game were forgotten. But as the 1880s unfolded, white baseball's future policy of rigid racial discrimination seemed by no means inevitable.

In 1884 Moses Fleetwood Walker, a barehanded catcher, had become the first African American in Major League baseball when his Toledo team ascended to the American Association, an early rival of the National League. "Fleet" Walker's younger brother, Welday, played a handful of games for the same team. They would be the last African Americans in the Major Leagues until Jackie Robinson in 1947, and the last such black brothers until Mrs. Aaron's sons, Henry and Tommie, played in Milwaukee seventy-eight years later in 1962.

Just beneath the surface of the two Major Leagues, African American players began making a mark in baseball's sprawling Minor League province. Back in 1878 Bud Fowler, a twenty-year-old African American from Fort Plain, New York (near Cooperstown), became the first man of his race to play in the white minor leagues, playing three games in Lynn, Massachusetts. He went on to play ten scattered Minor League seasons as one of the finest second basemen in the country.

The stream of black players into the various white Minor Leagues widened in the mind-1880s. The zenith of this early experiment in interracial play, which was not altogether harmonious, occurred in 1887, "a banner year for colored talent in the white leagues," according to White.[12] Thirteen African Americans played that year on twelve white teams in five assorted Minor Leagues in the East and Midwest. Sol. White and Welday Walker were two of the four blacks in the Ohio State League that year, after having started the season as teammates on the all-black Pittsburgh Keystones.

But the most significant – and disquieting – events of 1887 occurred in the prestigious International League. Bud Fowler, Fleet Walker, George Stovey, Frank Grant, Robert Higgins, William Renfro, and Randolph Jackson played at one time or another for five International League teams that year. George Stovey won 34 games for Newark, setting an International League record that still stands. Buffalo's Frank Grant was one of the talent-laden circuit's finest players. A soft-spoken star at home and a great drawing card on the road, Grant was among his team and League leaders in several offensive categories and his fielding was often remarked upon as spectacular.

Yet troubling racial incidents, mostly fomented by white players, percolated throughout the season. Despite the obvious talent of black players, hostile teammates responded in a variety of ways, from refusing to sit for team portraits including black teammates to committing intentional errors behind black pitchers. In July Cap Anson, major domo of Chicago's swaggering National League champions, demanded that George Stovey be barred from pitching an exhibition game at Newark (Walker, Stovey's usual catcher, was not scheduled to play that game). On that same day, and probably not merely by coincidence, the directors of the International League announced that teams would not be allowed to sign African American players in the future.[13]

Sol. White, as well as most writers who followed him, probably exaggerated Anson's role in the origin of the color line in nineteenth-century baseball, yet Anson's commanding stature and widely reported antipathy toward blacks were considerable obstacles to the African American presence in organized baseball. Although the International League later retreated from its initial draconian position, allowing Fleet Walker to play through 1889, joined by Grant and Higgins in 1888, the writing was on the wall for African Americans in organized baseball. The wave of optimism had crested and a rip tide of prejudice set in. As Robert Peterson says, "Jim Crow was warming up."[14]

Yet despite the turmoil of 1887, three more seasons remained in what Sol. White the historian called "the money period," and the career of Sol. White the ballplayer quickly took off. In 1888 he returned to the Keystones of Pittsburgh, who played surprisingly well in a four-way tournament of African American teams in New York. So well that Gorhams of New York spirited away the Keystones' best player, Sol. White, for 1889.

For the next three seasons, White played for the Gorhams of New York, the Cuban Giants of Trenton, New Jersey, and the Colored Monarchs of York, Pennsylvania. All three teams were admitted to white baseball's Minor Leagues, with the latter having a League championship snatched away when a series of controversial rulings on forfeits during the League's postseason meetings altered records just enough to give the crown to the team from Harrisburg, Pennsylvania. More than 90 percent of the games White played in organized baseball's realm occurred in the first four years of his career, 1887 through 1890, the last of the six years of what Sol. White the historian termed "the money period."[15]

These seasons, with the abundant coverage the local and national sporting press accorded to teams with the Major Leagues' imprimatur, provided substantial statistical evidence of White's talent. Throughout his long career, White was one of the top four hitters in the lineup. Standing 5'9" and weighing 170 pounds, he eventually played all the infield positions, starting at third base and working his way around to first. He played in (at least parts of) five seasons in organized baseball. In his 159 Minor League games (roughly one season, in composite) White had 683 at bats and hit a robust .356, a career Minor League batting average second only to the Cuban Giants' George Williams among prominent black players in nineteenth-century Minor League ball. His 243 hits included 42 doubles, 12 triples, and 7 home runs. He scored 174 runs and stole 54 bases.[16] Ordinarily no shrinking violet, Sol. White the historian was surprisingly reticent about Sol. White the ballplayer's ability, which was clearly of Major League caliber.

The Cuban Giants entered the Connecticut State League in 1891, but White was one of the first renegade players in a midseason mass exodus to the Gorhams, the first black team owned by an African American, Ambrose Davis of New York. The resultant hybrid (which lasted only for the remainder of that one season) was called the Big Gorhams. Sol. White the historian called this the greatest black team of the 1890s. In 1896 he once again led a stampede from the Cuban Giants, this time to embrace the largesse of E. B. Lamar of Brooklyn. Unlike J. M. Bright, penurious owner of the Cuban Giants, Lamar, as Sol. White the historian said, "spent his time and mind making the game a lucrative calling for ballplayers." [17] Lamar called his team of ex-Cuban Giants the Cuban X Giants. Although Bright's team, thereafter known as the Original or Genuine Cuban Giants, survived for many years, it was the Cuban X Giants that became the dominant African American baseball team in the East until the turn of the century.

White remained in the East for most of his career, but he also played the inaugural seasons for a couple of the most interesting early black powerhouses in the Midwest: the Page Fence Giants of 1895 and the Chicago Columbia Giants of 1900. The Page Fence Giants, of Adrian, Michigan, some fifty miles southwest of Detroit, were the creation of two African American ballplayers, the ubiquitous Bud Fowler and Grant Johnson, the latter a rising star who would become the black game's premier shortstop by the turn of the century. Fowler and Johnson had been the only African Americans on a team from Johnson's hometown of Findlay, Ohio, the year before. Together they formed a black team to serve as an advertising medium for the Page Woven Wire Fence Company.

The Page Fence Giants had no home field, playing continuously on the road as a full-time barnstorming team. They traveled in an opulent, sixty-foot-long private rail coach, outfitted with sleeping berths and a galley, thereby facilitating procurement of lodging and meals during a time when public accommodations, even in the Midwest, were increasingly difficult for blacks to obtain. The Page Fence Giants had little difficulty, though, in booking games, playing in 112 towns in seven Midwest states. Pulling their splendid coach onto a sidetrack wherever the team was booked, they preceded their games with a boisterous parade through town astride the wares of another team sponsor, the Monarch Bicycle Company of Boston. The team won 118, lost 26, and tied 2, with the National League's Cincinnati Reds administering two of the defeats. [18]

White left the Page Fence Giants after just one season, returning east to join the Cuban X Giants through 1899. But in 1900, when the Page Fence Giants moved to Chicago, White rejoined them. Now called the Chicago Columbia Giants, they played at the former grounds of the Chicago Cricket Club and the future home of both Charles Comiskey's White Sox and Rube Foster's Chicago American Giants. Sol. White the historian judged them "the finest and best equipped colored team that was ever in the business."[19] They later merged into the confluent destinies of several local teams and became the Leland Giants (and eventually the Chicago American Giants).

The team was sponsored by a group of African American business and professional men known as the Columbia Social Club. Like the Page Fence Giants, who were a manufacturer's promotional campaign, the Columbia Giants were not a speculative entrepreneurial venture, relying on gate receipts to stay alive. Their function was not so much to make money as to embellish the prestige of Chicago's ambitious black bourgeoisie. In this respect, the Chicago Columbia Giants were redolent of the earliest era of black baseball in the East, when a game between aristocratic gentlemen's clubs was part of a festive social romp, topped off by a smashing buffet, presented by the host club. But by 1900, the gentlemen of Chicago's black middle class had replaced playing with paying, and simply bought a team.

Following the turn of the century, the racial oppression of the 1890s continued and even worsened. Yet African American baseball proliferated to the extent that no one team could dominate black baseball in the East as the Cuban Giants and Cuban X Giants had done in the 1880s and 1890s. By 1907 White could list nine black professional teams – all named Giants – within one hundred miles of the Queen Mother of African American baseball cities, Philadelphia.[20]

In 1902, after one last season with the Cuban X Giants, White became co-owner of the Philadelphia Giants. He managed the ballplayers, while H. Walter Schlichter managed the office. White continued to play until 1909, his last year with the team, when he was forty-one years old. Sol. White's Philadelphia Giants negotiated the turbulent and suddenly teeming waters of African American baseball in the East with impressive skill. Writing of White in 1927, the *Pittsburgh Courier* referred to "the heyday of his glory of 1905, 06, and 07."[21] Many of the greatest black players of the Deadball Era played for Sol. White, players of unsurpassed brilliance, such as John Henry Lloyd, Pete Hill, Danny McClellan, and the incomparable Rube Foster, to name but a few.

Lloyd was a key figure in both the alpha and the omega of the Philadelphia Giants' salad days. In 1905 White destroyed the Cuban X Giants by luring Lloyd to the Phils. In 1909 the Leland Giants, now run by Rube Foster, similarly destroyed White by spiriting "the black Honus Wagner" to Chicago. Thereafter, Sol. White's impact on the contemporary game declined sharply. He managed for a few years, then, in 1912, at the age of forty-four, he returned to his native Bellaire, Ohio, and remained there, in an unknown capacity, for eight long years. He reappeared sporadically in the Negro Leagues of the 1920s, serving as an executive, a manager, and a coach in 1920, 1924, and 1927. During the 1930s he worked on securing Yankee Stadium as home ground for an African American team.

Thankfully, he retained his vigorous enthusiasm for the game, providing articles and interviews of great historical value in prominent black newspapers, such as the *Age* and the *Amsterdam News* of New York City, as well as the *Pittsburgh Courier*. He spent the last third of his life in Harlem, where he told the *Pittsburgh Courier*, he "like[d] to go to the library and read good books."[22] It is believed that Sol. White died in New York City in 1955, at the age of 87. It remains unknown if he ever married or had children.

Sol. White on Black Baseball

Since the advent of the colored man in baseball, this is the first book ever published wherein the pages have been given exclusively to the doings of the players and base ball teams. – Sol. White, Sol. White's Official Base Ball Guide: History of Colored Base Ball

Nothing is known of Sol. White's education prior to his enrollment in Wilberforce University in Xenia, Ohio, where he spent four consecutive winters starting in 1896.[23] Records recently retrieved by Wilberforce librarian Jacqueline Brown reveal that at least two of those academic years were spent in the English Preparatory Department, where he received good grades. He also served in the Corps of Cadets, whose commandant was Lt. Charles Young, only the third black graduate of West Point, and one of the most distinguished black soldiers in the history of the United States Army. One can only imagine how the gregarious White must have bedazzled his fellow students with tales of his summers spent with the

Cuban X Giants. In any case, Wilberforce gave him his final preparation to write black baseball's first history.

The original edition of *Sol. White's Official Base Ball Guide* was physically small, measuring only 5¾ by 3½ inches. The text (including box scores, instructional essays, and poetry) occupies only about 50 of the book's 128 pages. Fifty-seven photographs of teams, owners, and players take up most of the balance. Fourteen pages of advertisements appear, many purchased by alcohol and tobacco products, who strenuously courted the trade of the sporting set.

White published his history when he was at the zenith of his career in African American baseball, but it was a time of severe hardship for most black Americans. In the South, where 90 percent of the nation's black population resided, civil rights and social justice were distant dreams. The Ku Klux Klan punished noncompliance to white supremacist rule with intimidation and terror, while politicians pandered to the most vile Negrophobia to succor votes. Georgia's James K. Vardaman denounced the black Americans as a "lazy, lying, lustful animal which no conceivable amount of training can transform into a tolerable citizen." Tom Watson, also of Georgia, howled, "What does Civilization owe to the Negro? Nothing! Nothing!! Nothing!!!"[24]

In 1908 Benjamin R. ("Pitchfork Ben") Tillman addressed the United States Senate after three days of racial bloodshed in Abe Lincoln's own Springfield, Illinois. The so-called one-eyed plowboy of South Carolina politics excoriated northerners (and probably made many squirm with guilt) for their hypocrisy: "The brotherhood of man exists no longer[,] because you shoot Negroes in Illinois, when them come in competition with your labor, as we shoot them in South Carolina when they come in competition with us in the matter of elections. You do not love them any better than we do. You used to pretend that you did, but you no longer pretend it, except to get their votes."[25]

In the halls of learning, racism gained a foothold through contortions of Darwin's writings on evolution. Popular culture certainly offered no shelter from the storm of racial animosity. Among the most acclaimed nonfiction books of the time were Charles Caroll's *The Negro a Beast*, of 1900, and Robert W. Shufeldt's *The Negro, A Menace to American Civilization*, published in 1907, the same year as Sol. White's book. While a book must not be judged by its cover, sometimes its title will do.

A year earlier, Thomas Ryan Dixon's novel *The Clansman* was a runaway bestseller. Set in South Carolina during Reconstruction, the book portrayed African Americans in the most bestial terms. In 1915, D. W. Griffith adapted the novel for the first feature-length American movie, "The Birth of a Nation," which set new standards of technical, artistic, and commercial accomplishment. Woodrow Wilson, a college chum of Dixon's, proclaimed that Griffith "wrote history with lightning."[26] But racial propaganda, not accuracy, was served by Griffith's images and Wilson's lofty acclaim heaped another shovel of despair on the smoldering embers of hope for African Americans.

In 1908, the year after Sol. White's *Guide* appeared, another nineteenth-century black ballplayer published a book that had nothing to do with baseball. The author was Moses Fleetwood Walker, and the book was *Our Home Colony: A Treatise on the Past, Present and Future of the Negro Race in America*. Twenty-four years after becoming the first African American in Major League baseball, Walker was now a radical separatist, an apostle of Bishop Henry McNeal Turner's advocacy of returning the race to Africa.

Examining the course of American race relations, Walker concluded that "[t]he Negro can never be raised to an equal point in Civilization while occupying his isolated position in the United States." Lynching statistics indicated to him that racism "has reached such a degree of virulence that under its influence reasoning men perform like wild animals." Walker, who was educated at Oberlin College and the University of Michigan, warned that "[t]he time is growing very near when the whites of the United States must either settle this problem by deportation, or else be willing to accept a reign of terror such as the world has never seen in a civilized country." Indeed, "the only practical and permanent solution of the present and future race troubles in the United States is entire separation by Emigration of the Negro from America. Even forced Emigration," he emphasized, "would be better for all than the continued present relations of the races."[27]

Few people heeded the former barehanded catcher's counsel, and Walker never removed himself from Ohio, much less the United States. Yet there was no question that black Americans continued to be systematically and relentlessly deprived of opportunity and hope across the entire spectrum of American life. In housing, education, and employment; in politics, government, and the law; in literature, science, and history: indeed, in virtually every aspect of the country's life and thought, in degrees ranging from trivial to grave, America proclaimed itself a "white man's country."

The African American's legal status had steadily deteriorated since the United States Supreme Court began diverting the benefits of Reconstruction legislation from the black population to the Gilded Age's corporate business interests. In the civil rights cases of 1883 they declared unconstitutional legislation enacted in 1875 to forbid racial discrimination in public accommodations and places of public amusement. As a result, railroad conductors, ticket vendors, and hotel desk clerks gradually came to establish and enforce community racial boundaries. The crippling effect of this development on the care and feeding of African American baseball teams was obvious.

In 1890 Frank Grant's Harrisburg team joined the Atlantic Association in midseason. Although White praised the team's owners for insisting that Grant be allowed into the League, he probably was unaware that they agreed that Grant would be the only black player on the team, an accommodation to antiblack sentiment in the League that cost Grant's one black teammate, Clarence Williams, his job.[28] The heightened complexity of owning a team with even merely one African American soon became apparent when the Clayton House Hotel, in Wilmington, Delaware, refused to accept Grant's patronage, in response to complaints from white borders. According to *Sporting Life*, "The white players determined to stick by their sable-hued companion and all marched out of the hotel in high dudgeon over the refusal to accommodate Grant. Another hotel was sought, where the players were given rooms with the understanding that Grant must eat with the colored help or get his meals elsewhere. He accepted the latter alternative."[29]

Throughout the 1890s and beyond, episodes of this nature accumulated until Jim Crow practices came to be the cornerstone of American race relations. In the national game, no less than anywhere else, racial discrimination became taken for granted as natural and inevitable. It was soon forgotten that race relations had not always been quite so intolerant.

The history of baseball in the nineteenth century, as well as the career of its first historian, illustrated the shifting sands of racial attitudes in the nation. Sol. White's was a tragic generation of African Americans, and not just for ballplayers. Born within a few years of the Civil War, these men entered manhood at a time in the 1880s when the future brutal protocols of discrimination seemed by no means inevitable. But careers were soon dashed when the wounds of white hostility were treated with the tincture of black repression. White Americans sought harmony in consigning the fate of black fellow-citizens to the mercies of their most implacable foes.

In *The Strange Career of Jim Crow*, C. Van Woodward wrote of "a twilight zone that lies between living memory and written history," when "old and new rubbed shoulders – and so did black and white – in a manner that differed significantly from Jim Crow of the future or slavery of the past.[30] It was a time of experiment, testing, and uncertainty – quite different from the time of repression and rigid uniformity that was to come toward the end of the century. Alternatives were still open and real choices had to be made.[31]

Sol. White's *Guide* describes this development in baseball. White's account of events of the black professional game's first two decades describes the creation of an entire black subculture of baseball, providing a case study of the broader theme of black America's struggle to respond to an increasingly hostile zeitgeist. Similar dynamics were at work across the spectrum of the African American experience: in religion, entertainment, journalism, the arts, fraternal societies, business associations, and countless other realms. All would react to exclusion by creating institutions that imitated the standards of the white community that had rejected them. Meanwhile, they retained vestiges of the black heritage that was the root cause of that exclusion.

In a section of his *Guide* entitled "The Color Line," White wrote that "[i]n no other profession has the color line been more rigidly drawn than in baseball." He recalled the more tolerant time of just two decades earlier, and noted the intervening deterioration. In public accommodations, for example, the black ballplayer "suffers great inconvenience, at times, while traveling. The situation is far different today in this respect than it was years ago. At one time the colored teams were accommodated in some of the best hotels in the country, as the entertainment [in 1887] of the Cuban Giants at the McClure House in Wheeling, W. Va., will show." Furthermore, he wrote, "such proceedings on the part of hotel-keepers . . . will be difficult to remedy."[32] Difficult, indeed.

Even worse than Jim Crow's mundane inconveniences was the imposition upon all African Americans, including those in baseball, of a dual personality. The black American was made constantly aware that he was simultaneously both black *and* American, and the two were not always in harmony. Indeed, to white supremacists they were mutually exclusive, as expressed by novelist Thomas Ryan Dixon when he sneered, "Who thinks of a Negro when he says 'American'?"[33] James Weldon Johnson wrote of this duality as "the dwarfing, warping, distorting influence which operates upon each and every coloured man in the United States. He is forced to take his outlook on all things, not from the view-point of a citizen, or a man, or even a human being, but from the view-point of a *coloured man*."[34]

W.E.B. DuBois put it more angrily in *The Souls of Black Folk*:

> It is a peculiar sensation, this double-consciousness, this sense of always looking at one's self through the eyes of others. One ever feels his twoness, – an American, a Negro, two souls, two thoughts, two unreconciled strivings; two warring ideals in one dark body, whose dogged strength alone keeps it from being torn asunder.
>
> The history of the American Negro is the history of this strife, – this longing to attain self-conscious manhood, to merge his double self into a better and truer self. In this merging he wishes neither of the older selves to be lost. . . . He simply wishes to make it possible for a man to be both a Negro and an American, without being cursed and spit upon by his fellows, without having the doors of Opportunity closed roughly in his face.[35]

In baseball, too, onerous demands were placed upon African American players solely due to race. Even during the most hopeful times of the 1880s, before unrestrained apartheid came to prevail, it was clear that even first-class players remained second-class citizens. For the black player, professional skill was necessary, but hardly sufficient, to play ball with whites. The growing anger and spite of cohorts on the diamond and spectators in the grandstand made it quite clear that, while all players were expected to master their skills in handling bats and balls, only African Americans had to handle brickbats and blackballs. And matters would get far worse before they got any better.

Sol. White the historian drew upon the career of Sol. White the ball-player to commiserate with the plight of black players. Although a man of optimistic mien, he was clear-eyed about baseball's color line and its debilitating effect on the black player. "As it is," he lamented, "the field for the colored professional is limited to a very narrow scope in the base ball world. When he looks into the future he sees no place for him. . . .

Consequently, he loses interest. He knows that, so far shall I go, and no further, and as it is with the profession, so it is with his ability."[36]

Nonetheless, White remained hopeful that the barriers eventually would tumble, perhaps quite suddenly, and African Americans would partake of the blessings of true athletic democracy.

"Base ball is a legitimate profession [he wrote]. As much so as any other vocation, and should be fostered by owners and players alike . . . it should be taken seriously by the colored player, as honest efforts with his great ability will open an avenue in the near future wherein he may walk hand-in-hand with the opposite race in the greatest of all American games – base ball."[37]

Even in the darkest of times, White continued to hope that "some day the bar will drop and some good man will be chosen from out of the colored profession that will be a credit to all, and pave the way for others to follow."[38] Black baseball's first historian would have to wait a biblical forty years for Jackie Robinson to become that "good man," to "pave the way." But as distressing as matters were for African Americans in 1907, at least black baseball had rebounded from more desperate times.

During the hard years of 1892 through 1894, the Cuban Giants were the only black professional team in the nation, and in 1893, the year economic historians associate with the word "panic," even the estimable "Cubes" could not make it to the field. Despite a few details, events from the 1880s related in *Sol. White's Official Base Ball Guide* have been sufficiently verified by modern research of contemporary newspaper accounts to lend credibility to Sol. White the historian. This is very good news to historians of the black game in the 1890s, for by then there was virtually no press coverage to substantiate or refute him. Come the turn of the century, though, black baseball in the East and Midwest became vibrant once again, despite the toxic atmosphere that enveloped black America.

Sol. White the historian may have remained optimistic in the face of daunting circumstances because Sol. White the ballplayer had known better times himself. He was aware not only that the Walker brothers had played the white game at its highest level in 1884, but that Major League teams in 1886 and 1887 offered to sign Fleet Walker, George Stovey, and the Cuban Giants' Arthur Thomas.[39] White may have reasoned that race relations in baseball (and elsewhere) were malleable, and a situation that had deteriorated in the past had the potential to improve in the future.

Sol. White may also have reckoned that it was only a matter of time before the persistently elusive realization came to the white American mainstream that by banishing black players, white baseball damaged itself. Aside from considerations of human justice, the game's patrons and proprietors rejected the nourishment the game needed to become its best. Make no mistake about it, lily-white baseball was an inferior product. Discrimination prevented entire generations of white fans from watching dozens of the greatest players of all time, while white owners ignored an ever-growing market of avid black fans. American baseball would attain fulfillment only when it cured itself of this racial anorexia, in which it merely starved itself into a diminished condition.

Meanwhile, African American baseball persevered. Back in 1888 the *New York Age* wrote that:

> For the last two seasons the residents of the old Dutch town owe much to the Cuban Giants for the amount of life they have given the place and the interest stimulated in this national sport. If any one doubts the popularity of this colored team, let him stand at 14th Street Ferry upon a Saturday afternoon and hear the comments and see the immense crowds flocking to their games. . . . This is another way of cultivating esteem and respect for the race, and it is a good way, judging from appearances.[40]

As African American baseball was driven underground, the esteem and respect *for* the race that it produced among white fans became internalized into a special esteem and respect *within* the race. Segregated black baseball reached its apex with the Negro Leagues and was especially resplendent in the East-West All-Star game, the annual centerpiece of black baseball from its inception in 1933. Played in Comiskey Park every year, the game drew crowds of more than 40,000, in many years far surpassing attendance at the Major League counterpart. Each year the Illinois Central Railroad added dozens of coaches to accommodate the fans flocking to Chicago to participate in the midsummer festival of black baseball excellence, a gratifying spectacle *of* blacks *for* blacks. The world Sol. White the ballplayer helped create and Sol. White the historian recorded, the earliest black baseball community, had survived many perils and come to this glorious feast. And, for the black ballplayer, the best was yet to come.

Sol. White wrote his history, as he put it, "to follow the mutations of colored base ball, as accurately as possible, from the organization of the first colored professional team in 1885, to the present time."[41] Despite occasional errors, he quite admirably achieved his objective. His literary style, while workmanlike, was hardly reminiscent of Francis Parkman . . . or even Fleet Walker. But he was entitled to the grit pride he later felt about his history. Twenty years after the book's publication, the *Pittsburgh Courier* reported that "Sol.'s personal copy of his own book is the only one he knows about and it would be a historical tragedy if this should be the last."[42] In 1936 H. Walter Schlichter, publisher of *Sol. White's Official Base Ball Guide* sent one of his last two remaining copies to White upon the latter's request. "The other one," he wrote, "I will not part with at any price."[43]

Considering the innumerable ways in which artifacts as valuable as Sol. White's history of the birth of black baseball are, almost routinely, lost, forgotten, or destroyed in the course of time, today's historians are grateful to have this account of black baseball's genesis. For Sol. White's greatest triumph, in a lifetime of devotion to the game he loved so dearly, was the historian's quintessential bounty: he rescued merit from oblivion.

NOTES

1. *Sporting Life*, June 29, 1895.

2. S. White, *Sol. White's Official Base Ball Guide: History of Colored Base Ball*, (Philadelphia: 1907), 30, 41.

3. *Pittsburgh Courier*, March 12, 1927.

4. White, *Guide*, 25.

5. White, *Guide*, 25.

6. The *New York Sun* is reprinted in *Sporting Life*, September 5, 1988.

7. *Sporting Life*, April 13, 1887.

8. *Sporting Life*, May 18, 1887

9. R. J. Nemec, "That National Colored Baseball League of 1887," unpublished datasheet.

10. *Sporting News*, May 31, 1887.

11. White, *Guide*, 17.

12. White, *Guide*, 81.

13. For a complete account of events in the season, see J. Malloy, "Out at Home: Baseball Draws the Color Line, 1887," *The National Pastime: A Review of Baseball History* 2, no. 1 (Fall 1982): 14–28.

14. R. Peterson, *Only the Ball Was White: A History of Legendary Black Players*

and *All-Black Professional Teams before Black Men Played in the Major Leagues*, (Englewood Cliffs NJ: Prentice Hall, 1970), 33.

15. White, *Guide*, 25.

16. *Minor League Stars, Volume 3*, (Society for American Baseball Research: 1992), 4.

17. *New York Amsterdam News*, December 18, 1930.

18. For information on the Page Fence Giants: R. Nemec, "A Team of Negro Players," unpublished datasheet; T. E. Powers, "The Page Fence Giants Play Ball," *The Chronicle: The Quarterly Magazine of the Historical Society of Michigan*, 19:1 (Spring 1983): 14–19; and R. Bak, "Swinging With the Page Fence Giants," *Detroit Monthly*, April 1993, 23.

19. White, *Guide*, 33.

20. White, *Guide*, 35.

21. *Pittsburgh Courier*, March 12, 1927.

22. *Pittsburgh Courier*, March 12, 1927.

23. White, *Guide*, 8.

24. T. F. Gossett, *Race: The History of an Idea in America* (Dallas: 1963), 271, 253, respectively.

25. Gossett, *Race*, 280.

26. S. Synnestvedi, *The White Response to Black Emancipation Second-Class Citizenship in the United States since Reconstruction*, (New York: 1972), 119.

27. M. F. Walker, *Our Home Colony: A Treatise on the Past, Present and Future of the Negro Race in America*, (Steubenville OH: 1908), 41, 26, 29, and 31, respectively.

28. White, *Guide*, 23; *Cleveland Gazette*, August 2, 1890.

29. *Sporting Life*, August 9, 1890.

30. C. V. Woodward, *The Strange Career of Jim Crow*, 2d rev. ed. (New York: 1966), xii, 26.

31. Woodward, *Strange Career*, 33.

32. White, *Guide*, 81, 83.

33. G. Osofsky, ed., *The Burden of Race: A Documentary History of Negro-White Relations in America*, (New York: 1967) p. 190.

34. J. W. Johnson, *The Autobiography of an Ex-Coloured Man*, (New York: 1960 [1912]), 21.

35. W.E.B. DuBois, *The Souls of Black Folk*, (New York: 1969 [1903]), 45–46.

36. White, *Guide*, 128.

37. White, *Guide*, 71.

38. White, *Guide*, 85.

39. *Trenton True American*, June 29, 1886; *Newark Daily Journal*, April 9, 1887.

40. *New York Age*, July 28, 1888.

41. White, *Guide*, 5.

42. *Pittsburgh Courier*, March 12, 1927.

43. H. Walter Schlichter to Sol. White, July 18, 1936, National Baseball Hall of Fame Library, Cooperstown, New York.

SCOTT ROPER

"Another Chink in Jim Crow?"

Race and Baseball on the Northern Plains, 1900–1935

O N   T H E   N O R T H E R N   P L A I N S, baseball developed and maintained an integrated status based on race and ethnicity before most other regions in the United States. Even there, most nonwhite players were strongly dissuaded from playing the game at the amateur and semi-professional levels. Newspaper articles from the early twentieth century demonstrate that most African Americans were subjected to shoddy treatment and harsh racism. White baseball players only welcomed the participation of whites and Native Americans, the latter a result of America's attempt to integrate and "civilize" Native Americans into white American culture. This essay demonstrates how these issues were present throughout the Northern Plains states between 1900 and 1935.

An Overview of Baseball in the American West

Miners, homesteaders, and soldiers were the three groups most responsible for baseball's diffusion to the trans-Mississippi frontier. Baseball existed in mining communities around Helena, Montana, at least as early as 1867.[1] The chief surgeon at Fort Buford, Dakota Territory, Dr. James P. Kimball, reported that a number of soldiers played baseball on the Northern Plains as early as 1869.[2] By 1873, with the arrival of the Seventh Cavalry's Benteen Base Ball Club in Dakota Territory, baseball already was well established along the Missouri River.[3] Groups of homesteaders followed, bringing the game with them from the eastern United States.[4] On the Northern Plains, most of these players were white; only after 1890 did nonwhites become prominent as baseball players in the region.[5]

The federal government encouraged Native American involvement in baseball and other sports as part of its program to assimilate Native Americans into American culture and society. Baseball was a mainstay at many government-established boarding schools, where Native Americans learned Anglo-American customs and were forced to relinquish their native culture.[6] Captain Richard H. Pratt created the first major boarding school at Carlisle, Pennsylvania, in 1879, hoping to "kill the Indian and save the man." By 1900, 113 such schools existed throughout the United States.[7]

After their education, most Native Americans either returned to reservations or entered so-called civilized society. Many Native Americans favored athletics, and those who played baseball in boarding schools continued to do so after their education days ended.[8] Some, such as Charles Albert Bender (16 years, 210–127 won-loss record), and Jim Thorpe (6 years, 289 games, .252 batting average), became successful Major League ballplayers. The abundance of teams originating on reservations in the Dakotas, however, suggests that many Native Americans returned home to play on amateur and semi-professional teams.[9]

Some whites who played baseball did not readily accept African Americans into American baseball. Although black athletes began to play baseball as early as whites, they were barred from some professional leagues as early as 1867.[10] By the late 1880s, all-black teams such as New York's Cuban Giants, named in the belief that white Americans would more readily accept Hispanics than African Americans, barnstormed throughout the United States.[11] Brothers Moses Fleetwood and Welday Walker broke the color barrier in 1884, playing for the American Association's Toledo club after competing in integrated college and semi-professional leagues.[12] In the late 1880s, however, "Cap" Anson of the Chicago White Stockings refused to play against African Americans, whom he referred to as "no-account niggers" and "chocolate-covered coon(s)." This attitude led to the unwritten rule barring African Americans from playing professional baseball.[13] In 1898, Bert Jones, the last black man in professional baseball before reintegration in 1946, left the Kansas State League for the all-black Chicago Unions.[14]

Black athletes nevertheless continued to play baseball, mainly on segregated clubs. All-black teams representing Nashville, Kansas City, Winnipeg, St. Paul, and the United States military played against teams from the Northern Plains throughout the early twentieth century.[15] In 1901, an African American team arose in Fargo, North Dakota, playing at least one game against an all-white team from the city.[16] Such developments as these were followed in the 1920s by the formation of the Negro National and American Leagues, organizations that protected players from financially exploitative booking agents.[17] Winter leagues, meanwhile, offered the chance for all-black All-Star teams to play against teams consisting of white (and sometimes Native American) Major Leaguers in California and Latin America.[18] Still, segregation remained at the professional level until 1946.

Attitudes toward minority baseball players in Montana and the Dakotas generally did not differ much from those elsewhere in America west of the Mississippi River. Native Americans were accepted and encouraged in their baseball endeavors, while most African Americans were ridiculed, often finding themselves the targets of racist insults when they played. Incidents of racism most often were directed at players on teams made up entirely of African Americans, particularly if the club originated outside the Northern Plains. Still, some teams consisting solely of white men did encounter nonwhite players and teams, giving the media ample time to air their attitudes and opinions on the matter.

Native Americans on the Northern Plains, 1900–First World War

For a newspaper writer to identify a baseball player according to race can be construed as racism, particularly if the identifying label is demeaning, unjustly sets a person apart from others of similar caliber because of skin color, or is used in conjunction with an insult. Although newspaper writers and editors on the Northern Plains occasionally referred to Native Americans by race, their acts of identification usually were more ethnocentric than racist.

Throughout the summer of 1900, for instance, the *Sioux Falls* (South Dakota) *Argus-Leader* carried reports of the Flandreau Indians, many of whose players were Native Americans. Unlike their treatment of white players, media sometimes singled out particular Native American players on white teams simply because of their ethnicity. On June 5, the day after exceptional performances by two players on the Scotland, South Dakota, baseball team, the newspaper noted that the two were "Indian."[19] In light of the federal government's attempts to integrate Native Americans into the culture and society of the United States, such incidents as this one demonstrate how sports columnists either encouraged Native Americans to "Westernize" or viewed Native American baseball players as proof that acculturation was possible. Editors of other city newspapers operated with the same basic attitudes. In 1905, the *Dakota Herald* reported that in a game between the Boston Bloomer Girls and the Yankton team, one of the key plays was made by the Indian catcher for the Bloomers: "[The ball was thrown home], where the Indian was waiting. . . . The Indian was knocked to his knees."[20]

The pro-Native American attitude continued into the next decade. In 1912, the author of an article appearing in the local newspaper in Bismarck, North Dakota, commended the Bismarck Indian School's baseball team for its "good work, especially when it is considered that the school has no coach."[21] In another North Dakota newspaper, neither race nor ethnicity was ever mentioned in the coverage of games in Great Bend or Hunter, in spite of the fact that players with Native American names, such as White Eagle and Big Chief Hoff, played for the two teams. [22] In neglecting the issue of race, the newspaper's editor demonstrated an acceptance of Native Americans as baseball players.

Such acceptance varied, however, from person to person and place to place. In fact, one article dating from 1905 claimed that "in the matter of errors Day, Armours Indian shortstop, was the chief offender."[23] The article also referred to Day by race as the "bronze-colored shortstop." The author's mention of ethnicity and skin color was unwarranted; used in conjunction with criticism (Day was the only player, white or Native American, singled out), the remarks would now be regarded as racist. In another incident, a newspaper referred to "6000 people besides 1000 Indians (who) witnessed the game" at the annual Chautauqua. [24] This report suggests a propensity to view Native Americans as subhuman. Still, negative remarks regarding Native American baseball players were quite rare. For all the articles appearing in seven major newspapers of North and South Dakota in 1900, 1905, 1912, and parts of other years, these two reports are the only known instances of specifically anti-Native American bias.

African Americans and Baseball

The attitudes of the media were far from positive in their treatment of black baseball players before the First World War. Few African Americans have *ever* lived on the Northern Plains, so newspapers were more likely to cover all-black, out-of-state touring teams than specific players from within the region.[25] As a result, most comments regarding African American baseball players were directed toward players from outside the Northern Plains.

One all-black team that traveled through Montana and North Dakaota in 1900 was the Nashville Students, a group of traveling musicians that boasted a baseball team. The group passed through Miles City, Montana, without incident. In fact, the *Bismarck Tribune* neglected to mention the fact that the baseball team, which the Bismarck team defeated easily, was all-black.[26] A day after the Students played the Jamestown High School baseball team, however, the local newspaper published a derogatory article about the "colored" players, ridiculing the team's coaches and its players' honesty, integrity, and abilities:

> Had the colored aggregation played a stronger game at the start there is no question that the Jamestown boys would have went after them hard and won by a much greater score. . . . The visitors evidently believed in coaching and had three coaches at work most of the time. Their work was quite amusing. . . . M. P. Morris was umpire for the first two innings but the colored team kicked on one of his decisions and he retired in favor of a member of the minstrel troupe who made a few unsatisfactory decisions.[27]

The Nashville Students forged on to Fargo, where the team met with further attacks. When the *Fargo Forum* reprinted comments made by the Students' catcher, it ridiculed his speech patterns: "'Dat's de best ball game I evern was in – even if we did get beat.'"[28] Its general account of the game also was derogatory: "At Bismarck and Jamestown the coons had not made a particularly good showing. . . . The "culled gemmen" had something up their sleeve, however, and saved their crack pitcher for the Fargo game."[29]

The liberal use of stereotypical phrases and racist slang continued. The following year, under the title "Chased Coon," the *Fargo Forum* printed an account of a ball game between a white club and "the sons of Ham."[30] The paper also ridiculed a pitcher for the team from Lakota, North Dakota, referring to him both as a "cullud gemmen" and as the Fargo team's "dusky rival."[31] By 1912, the paper's basic attitude had not changed. On June 26, the *Fargo Forum* announced that a team from neighboring Moorhead, Minnesota, would play a "colored aggregation," known as the Tennessee Rats.[32] Two days later, the newspaper ridiculed black players in general: "As coaches no race has anything on the coon race for making fun and as base runners they are funny as a bunch of monkeys and can sprint some."[33] When the Moorhead team finally defeated the Tennessee Rats on July 1, the *Fargo Forum* reprinted a common racist joke about the "Colored Gentlemen: "The rats produced four pitchers during the game, but the Moorhead boys had their batting eyes with them all afternoon and 'all coons looked alike' to them."[34]

The *Fargo Forum*, however, may be an extreme example of racism in the baseball world of the Northern Plains. The *Grand Forks* (North Dakota) *Herald* generally did not distinguish between black and white players. Likewise, newspapers in Yankton, South Dakota, and Sioux Falls, South Dakota, never referred to any players as being black. Still, the Fargo and Jamestown, North Dakota, newspapers demonstrate that racism existed to a strong degree in the Dakotas, just as it did elsewhere in the country.

Plains Baseball between the World Wars

Between the world wars, baseball on the Northern Plains opened its doors to African Americans. Newspapers also continued to report the status of the Native American baseball community. Although the plight of minorities in baseball improved, many in the media still were quick to differentiate between white and black baseball players.

Newspapers on the Northern Plains generally looked upon Native American baseball players as equal to white players. In fact, the press virtually ceased its practice of differentiating between Native Americans and whites. In 1924, the Cannonball Indians consisted of several Native American players, such as Bear Goose and Young Bear, but the *Bismarck Tribune* never referred to the players' ethnic background except with regard to the team's nickname. [35] In 1935, the *Minot* (North Dakota) *Daily News* referred to "Jerome, Indian hurler." [36] "Indian" referred to the Belcourt team's nickname, not to the player's ethnic background. As with the Cannonball Indians before them, the Belcourt Indians, based on the Turtle Mountain Reservation, included several Native Americans on its roster. Therefore, in the interwar years, Native Americans generally were accepted as a permanent part of the baseball world; only a few team names identified a team's ethnic background.

African American Baseball Players between the World Wars

The post–First World War years witnessed the partial acceptance of African Americans into Northern Plains baseball. In 1925, a team from Plentywood, Montana, "engaged a noted colored pitcher, John Donaldson."[37] Although he commanded the respect of opposing players, he was known as "'that cul'd gentleman, Mr. Donaldson'" to newspaper columnists. [38]

Still, such references as these were a vast improvement over the language favored by the *Fargo Forum* at the beginning of the century.

By the mid-1930s, many towns on the Northern Plains, particularly those in North Dakota, recruited the services of paid black athletes. People had begun to realize that African Americans could play as well as whites. In October, 1934, an all-black "All Star" team representing North Dakota's semi-professional leagues defeated a team of white American League All-Stars in games at Valley City, Bismarck, and Jamestown.[39]

Treatment of black semi-pro players varied by place and by situation. In 1931, Crookston, Minnesota recruited Negro League stars for an all-black team. Kansas City Monarchs pitcher Chet Brewer (incomplete record: 15 years, 89–69 win-loss record, principally with Kansas City [see editorial note]) was one of those recruited, and apparently was treated well in Crookston:

> The first Sunday I was up there in Crookston, I said, "I'm going to church. . . . I'going to see what these people are going to do." I walked in, dressed nice, walked right down the middle, looked at the minister, sat there. When the minister finished the sermon, he almost ran to the door to get there ahead of me, shook my hand, told me how happy he was that I came to his service, invited me to Bible class. I was just like one of the citizens.
>
> That was one of the most beautiful summers I lived. We were the only colored in town. . . . I told the hotel man that I was going to send for my family and wanted to rent a house. He said, "There's a big house over there a couple doors from the mayor. . . . I'll tell you what: you can get things out of my store room – beds and things." The hotel man and that restaurant owner, they furnished my house for me.[40]

Leroy "Satchel" Paige (30 years, 153–110 win-loss record) arrived in Bismarck under different circumstances. After Paige argued with the management of the Negro Leagues' Pittsburgh Crawfords over salary, Bismarck car salesman, mayor, and baseball manager Neil Churchill recruited him to pitch on an otherwise all-white team in 1933.[41] (The club added several other Negro League players to its roster over the course of the 1934 and 1935 seasons.) When Paige found out that he would be "playing with some white boys," he felt that he had "cracked another chink in Jim Crow."[42] Paige, however, unlike Brewer, did not play for an all-black team. As a result, despite the cultural similarities between Crookston and Bismarck, Paige was victimized by racism from the start of his year in North Dakota: "I got a pretty cold shoulder. Churchill wanted me, but those white ballplayers weren't too sure they did. . . . But when they saw me pitch, they wanted me more than anybody. But getting everybody else to want me was something else. Most of the folks were pretty nice, but there were some of those other kind, like you run into everywhere."[43]

The "other kind" of people, whom Paige refers to as "mean folk," refused to rent Paige and his wife a place to live. Finally, Churchill found the Paige family a place to live in a refurbished railroad freight car.[44]

In the process of integration, some racially motivated problems erupted in Northern Plains baseball. The Jamestown and Devils Lake, North Dakota, teams, for instance, released their African American players after the 1934 season, choosing to field all-white teams.[45] The following season, an on-field fight nearly erupted between the white Jamestown players and the black members of the Valley City team after Jamestown's catcher allegedly directed a racial slur toward Valley City's Art Hancock.[46] Only after the local police were called onto the field was order restored.

Racism also existed among players on the same team. In 1933, Satchel Paige chastised Bismarck's outfielders for making a few fielding errors. The outfielders walked away from Paige, one of them muttering what Paige thought sounded like "dirty nigger." The following inning, the outfielders refused to take the field, leaving Paige, the catcher, and the Bismarck infield to face the opposing hitters. The crowd thought the scenario was a stunt, and Paige saved his honor by striking out the three batters he faced. After the inning, Paige and the team's outfielders apologized to each other over their disagreement, and the outfielders returned to their positions for the remainder of the game.[47]

The newspaper columnists of the Northern Plains readily agreed that many of the African American players were stars. They generally ignored the fact, however, that, in terms of playing ability, African Americans were equal to their white counterparts. The *Bismarck Tribune* described Chet Brewer as "ace hurler of the Kansas City Monarchs and ranked next to Satchel Paige among the nation's leading colored hurlers."[48] Sportswriters readily compared Brewer to other black pitchers, but they hesitated to directly compare black pitchers to their white counterparts.

As if to accentuate differences in playing abilities, sportswriters continued to differentiate between black and white players. Local newspapers nearly always referred to African American players such as Paige,

Brewer, Quincy Troupe, Red Haley, Ted "Double Duty" Radcliffe (incomplete record: 12 years, 53–33 win-loss record), and Hilton Smith (13 years, 73–32 win-loss record) by such adjectives as "dusky," "Negro," "ebony," "colored," and the derogatory "Ethiopian." [49] Newspaper articles never contained commensurate references to white players.

When quoting blacks, authors and editors continued to exaggerate African American speech patterns. The *Bismarck Tribune* printed a picture of Paige, entitled "Yo'all Can't Win," with the following caption: " 'I'm shoa gonna have that new c-a-a,' " asserted the lean, ebony Satchel Paige. . . . Reports from Kansas City say that the stalwart Negro right-hander has been promised a new automobile if he and the Capital City crew cops the championship." [50]

After Bismarck won the championship, neither the media nor the "baseball establishment" would accept African Americans on the same level as whites. The *Bismarck Tribune* referred to the Major League scouts at the Wichita tournament as "Ivory hunters," meaning that scouts attended the games to seek out white athletes and not black players. [51] According to the *Minneapolis Tribune*'s George Barton, in an article reprinted in the Bismarck newspaper: "Bismarck has in Satchel Paige, Negro, a pitcher who, if he were white and eligible to play in organized baseball, would bring around $100,000 in the open market. . . . Many a Major League scout . . . wished he were white. . . . Were he Caucasian instead of Ethiopian, Paige would take his place alongside of the Dean brothers, Carl Hubbell, Lingle van Mungo and other pitching greats of the Major Leagues." [52]

The Bismarck newspaper also reprinted a racist cartoon of Satchel Paige. The athletes pictured along the right side of the cartoon, to whom Paige is compared, were drawn with monkey-like characteristics. Although the term "Ethiopian" was degrading to African Americans, the artist likened Paige's pitching style to an "Ethiopian war dance." The caricature of Paige himself looks nothing like him; the nose and the lips on the drawing are severely exaggerated and disproportionately large. [53]

In spite of the racial problems on the Northern Plains in the 1930s, the very presence of African American players constituted a major advancement toward interracial respect over previous decades. In the 1920s, Scobey, Montana, responded to Plentywood's signing of John Donaldson by signing white players, including former members of the Chicago White Sox, who were banned from professional baseball for allegedly "throwing" the 1919 World Series.[54] The 1930s, particularly after Bismarck's success, witnessed the rapid integration of most teams on the Northern Plains. According to Donn Rogosin, most Dakota cities had added blacks to their teams by the end of 1935.[55]

*

African Americans suffered intense prejudice in baseball on the Northern Plains from 1900 through the Great Depression. Native American players were more readily accepted because of the movement to incorporate Native Americans into the culture and society of the United States. Attitudes toward black athletes often reflected racism; writers of newspapers in the region made no attempt to hide racist feelings.

Still, the participation of minority groups in Montana and the Dakotas indicated important trends in baseball at the national level. Several Native Americans have been inducted into the National Baseball Hall of Fame, and the American League's Cleveland Indians were named in honor of Louis Francis Sockalexis, a Native American who played on the team in the 1890s.[56] The status of Native American baseball players has remained nearly equal to that of their white counterparts, though recently their numbers have dwindled in professional baseball. Although research remains to be conducted on the subject, the reasons for the small numbers may be rooted in the extreme poverty on most American reservations, which limits the opportunities for Native Americans to attend colleges and receive exposure as baseball players.

For African Americans, the implications of integrated baseball were even more important. After 1898, black athletes rarely had the chance to play competitive baseball on integrated teams. With some exceptions, most integrated games occurred between all-black and all-white (or mixed white and Native American) teams. Between the wars, the integration of African Americans into white semi-pro leagues on the Northern Plains accelerated, preceding the integration of professional baseball. Professional baseball remained segregated until 1946, when Jackie Robinson played his first Minor League game for Montreal.

Soon after, the Nashua (New Hampshire) Dodgers of the New England League became the first professional team based in the United States to integrate its roster. The national success of the 1935 Bismarck club and similar teams may have hastened the change in attitude toward black baseball players among the whites who controlled the professional baseball leagues.

NOTES

Editor's Note: All records cited in brackets are deemed by the editor to be of Major League status and are mentioned without qualification.

1. D. A. Smith, "A Strike Did Not Always Mean Gold," *Montana, The Magazine of Western History* 20:3 (July 1970): 76.

2. "Medical History of Fort Buford, Dakota Territory, 1868–95," Washington: National Archives, 1960. Dr. James P. Kimball was the medical officer who wrote about baseball at the fort in 1869.

3. H. H. Anderson, "The Benteen Base Ball Club: Sports Enthusiasts of the Seventh Cavalry," *Montana, The Magazine of Western History* 20:3 (July 1970): 84.

4. S. Roper, "The Origins and Diffusion of Baseball in Bismarck, North Dakota, 1865–1901," Unpublished paper (University of North Dakota Department of Geography, Grand Forks, North Dakota, 1991).

5. Data compiled by comparing names of Bismarck residents who played baseball in Bismarck, North Dakota, between 1873 and 1901 with data obtained from the original enumeration sheets of "The Tenth Census of the United States, 1880"; "The Twelfth Census of the United States, 1900"; and "The Dakota Territorial Census, 1885." Players' names originally appear in Roper, "Orgins."

6. H. Seymour, *Baseball: The People's Game* (New York: Oxford University Press, 1990), 397–80.

7. Seymour, *People's Game*, 380–81.

8. Seymour, *People's Game*, 391.

9. Newspaper columnists in the Dakotas frequently reported the results of games between local teams and reservation clubs. Major newspapers in Bismarck, Fargo, Grand Forks, and Minot contained references to all–Native American teams in settlements such as in Solen, Flandreau, Standing Rock, Hunter, Great Bend, Belcourt, Cannonball, White Earth, Fort Totten, and the Fort Lincoln Indian School, among others.

10. Seymour, *People's Game*, 532; idem, *Baseball: The Early Years* (New York: Oxford University Press, 1960), 42.

11. N. J. Sullivan, *The Minors: The Struggles and the Triumph of Baseball's Poor Relation from 1876 to the Present* (New York: St. Martin's Press, 1990), 189.

12. Sullivan, *Minors*, 187–88; Seymour, *People's Game*, 547.

13. Seymour, *People's Game*, 552-53; Sullivan, *Minors*, 187–88.

14. Sullivan, *Minors*, 188.

15. *Grand Forks Herald*, April 1–September 30, 1900, 1910, and 1920; *Fargo Forum and Daily Republican*, April 1–September 30, 1900, 1910, 1920, and 1935; *Jamestown Daily Alert*, July 30, 1900; *Bismarck Tribune*, April 1–September 30,

1900, 1910, 1920, and 1934, and March 23–August 31, 1935; Seymour, *People's Game*, 566.

16. *Fargo Forum*, July 31, 1900, 5.

17. D. Rogosin, *Invisible Men: Life in Baseball's Negro Leagues* (New York: Atheneum, 1987), 9–10.

18. L. (Satchel) Paige, *Maybe I'll Pitch Forever* (New York: Grove Press, 1963), 77–83.

19. *Souix Falls Argus-Leader*, June 5, 1900, 6.

20. *Dakota Herald*, July 21, 1905, 2.

21. *Bismarck Tribune*, June 25, 1912, 5.

22. *Fargo Forum*, June 18, 1912, 9.

23. *Dakota Herald*, July 25, 1905, 2.

24. *Fargo Forum*, July 22, 1901, 3.

25. S. A. Roper, "African Americans in North Dakota, 1800–1940," Master's Thesis, Department of History, University of North Dakota, Grand Forks, North Dakota, 1993.

26. *Bismarck Tribune*, July 19–July 31, 1900.

27. *Jamestown Daily Alert*, July 30, 1900, 3.

28. *Fargo Forum*, July 31, 1900, 5.

29. *Fargo Forum*, July 31, 1900, 5.

30. *Fargo Forum*, May 6, 1901, 4.

31. *Fargo Forum*, June 17, 1901, 4.

32. *Fargo Forum*, June 26, 1912, 8.

33. *Fargo Forum*, June 28, 1912, 3.

34. *Fargo Forum*, July 1, 1912, 3.

35. *Bismarck Tribune*, June 2, 1924, 6; July 7, 1924, 6; July 14, 1924, 6.

36. *Minot Daily News*, August 23, 1935, 6.

37. G. Lucht, "Scobey's Touring Pros: Wheat, Baseball, and Illicit Booze," *Montana, The Magazine of Western History* 20:3 (July 1970): 88.

38. Lucht, "Scobey's Touring Pros," 93.

39. *Bismarck Tribune*, October 6, 1934, 8; October 8, 1934, 6; J. B. Holway, *Black Diamonds: Life in the Negro Leagues from the Men Who Lived It* (New York: Stadium Books, 1991), 19.

40. Holway, *Black Diamonds*, 28–29.

41. Paige, *Maybe*, 75; *Bismarck Tribune*, April 13, 1935, 6.

42. Paige, *Maybe*, 75.

43. Paige, *Maybe*, 75

44. Paige, *Maybe*, 75–76.

45. *Bismarck Tribune*, May 9, 1935, 10; May 12, 1935, 12.

46. *Bismarck Tribune*, May 31, 1935, 7.

47. Paige, *Maybe*, 77.

48. *Bismarck Tribune*, August 24, 1935, 6.

49. *Bismarck Tribune*, March 25–September 1, 1935; *Fargo Forum*, April 1–August 31, 1935; *Minot Daily News*, April 1–August 31, 1935.

50. *Bismarck Tribune*, August 17, 1935, 6.

51. *Bismarck Tribune*, August 8, 1935, 8.

52. *Bismarck Tribune*, August 31, 1935, 6.

53. *Bismarck Tribune*, August 28, 1935, 6.

54. Lucht, "Scobey's Touring Pros," 89.

55. Rogosin, *Invisible Men*, 140.

56. L. Reidenbaugh, *Take Me Out To the Ball Park* (St. Louis: Sporting News Publishing, 1987), 94.

JERRY JAYE WRIGHT

From Giants to Monarchs

The 1890 Season of the Colored Monarchs of York, Pennsylvania

I N 1888, A COLUMN in the *Sporting News* stated: "There are players among these colored men that are equal to any white players on the ball field. If you don't think so, go out and see the Cuban Giants play. This club, with its strongest players on the field, would play a favorable game against such clubs as the New Yorks or Chicagos."[1]

By the latter part of the nineteenth century, white baseball had long abandoned its origins as a simple boy's game and gentleman's social pastime, and evolved into a muscular professionalism. Popularized during the Civil War, and now a product of postwar prosperity, baseball rose to new heights of national prestige and commercial reward. Now, in the late 1880s, African American baseball embarked on a similar course as its white counterpart, and established itself as a viable economic entity with the birth of the Cuban Giants in 1885. This successful black enterprise led to the creation of a black subculture of baseball; black reporters for black newspapers writing for black fans about black players and managers on teams owned by black investors. For more than six decades, this was the future of Jim Crow baseball.[2]

Neither ethnically Cuban nor physiologically Giants, the Cuban Giants Base Ball Club played a key role in professional baseball's halting and uncertain drift toward the color line. A line that extended from racial tolerance of black players on white teams, to all black teams in otherwise all white leagues, to black teams in black leagues. The Cuban Giants experienced each of these stops along the color line and ultimately became the model for the final stop, which endured more than sixty years before the line ended with the signing of Jackie Robinson in 1947.[3]

From their formation in the late summer of 1885 to 1891, the Cuban Giants were the most successful and boasted, from time to time, some of the best black players of all the Negro Leagues, both nineteenth and twentieth century.[4] According to former Giant and later black baseball historian Sol. White, the Club was organized from a group of Long Island waiters who entertained guests of the Argyle Hotel in Babylon, New York, by playing baseball.[5] To conceal their ethnic heritage, the players spoke inarticulate gibberish while on the field in order to pass for Spanish, thus masking racial exclusion from the game and making it socially acceptable to compete against all-white clubs.[6] Considering the hostile attitude of white Americans toward blacks, however, it is doubtful the incorporation of "Cuban" into a team's moniker would deceive the knowledgeable baseball fan.

While there is speculation as to how many tables these players ever actually waited, or with respect to their gibberish verbalization, in the fall of 1885 Walter Cook, a wealthy Trenton, New Jersey, businessman, purchased the Giants and began replacing the alleged waiters with quality salaried black players. Cook hired Virgin Islands native S. K. Govern (colored) as manager, and sent the team to Cuba to hone their baseball skills during the winter months. A more probable basis for "Cuban" as the Giants' surname was derived from playing in Cuba, rather than nonsense chatter on the field in America.

In February 1886 the Giants returned to Florida and began playing their way northward with exhibition games. The Club enjoyed considerable success, even challenging white Major League clubs.[7] But despite the club's rise to prominence, social bias and discriminatory practices of the period continued to relegate their schedule to independent and Minor League teams, most frequently of the same complexion, black. From 1889 to 1891, however, this exclusion from organized league play would change.

On November 19, 1888, at the Washington Hotel in Philadelphia, delegates and proxies representing eight cities in three states – Delaware, New Jersey, and Pennsylvania – met to organize the Middle States League. The new league marked an important step for colored baseball. The New Jersey delegate was none other than S. K. Govern, manager of the Trenton-based Cuban Giants, and representative of the club's new owner, John Bright.[8] Because League organizers viewed the Giants as a drawing card, they were admitted, seemingly without incident, and thus became the first all-black team to compete in a racially mixed, yet predominantly white, league.[9] Racial controversy did arise, however, midway through the season, and was perhaps ultimately responsible for the outcome of the League's 1889 pennant race.

On June 10, 1889, the *Harrisburg Daily Patriot* reported that when the League was formed "there was much complaint about admitting the Cuban Giants, principally on account of their color, and now that they are proving their superior strength against all the other clubs in the league the complaints have become more general and bitter." [10] These complaints continued to build through the remainder of the season, and were not limited exclusively to the Cuban Giants. On July 19 the *Harrisburg Daily Patriot*, writing of a League game between Harrisburg and the New York Gorhams (a black team), stated that "the Gorhams, like the Cuban Giants, are dirty foul-mouthed ball players and the umpire should compel some of them to quit the grounds. During the game one player proclaimed the umpire 'was a liar,' and another exclaimed, 'Oh, Jesus' after the umpire made his decision. Some other of their dirty tricks will not be mentioned." The article concluded, "Why cannot a Negro baseball player be just as respectable as a White one?" [11] Whether the derogatory language, the color of their skin, or that the Giants won ten of fourteen games against Harrisburg had a bearing on the journalist's commentary, it did kindle a competitive spirit between the two clubs and the Harrisburg faithful. [12]

With their superior performance on the field, the League's inaugural season came to a close with the Cuban Giants in first place, a few percentage points ahead of the Harrisburg club. Harrisburg protested on grounds that the Giants had played fewer games, and the awarding of the pennant was turned over to a League committee. [13] Through a series of decisions on appealed games, the League adjusted the totals to give Harrisburg a record of 64–19 (.771), barely ahead of the Cuban Giants' 55–17 (.764), and thus the championship. [14]

While the decision to allow a committee to determine the championship was unusual, the committee's rationale for its decision was scandalous and, in light of media commentary during the season, potentially racist. Or was it? With the loose control of League policies and frequent failure to uphold its constitution, such a procedure was not surprising. During the season, franchises in larger cities defied League policy and refused to play contests with clubs in smaller markets, or moved the games to locations, usually their own facility, that would ensure a larger gate. Additionally, scheduled League home games were postponed, regardless of the competition, if another could be scheduled with a more lucrative club. Both Harrisburg and the Cuban Giants were guilty of such violations. But John Bright appears to have been the most frequent violator. He seized every opportunity to move League games to Trenton, and took his Giants at a moment's notice to New York or Washington DC where he was assured larger profits. Bright also attempted to count his non-League conquests as League games.[15]

The degree to which such violations contributed to the League committee's decision is unclear and at best, confusing. But, considering the apparently greater violations of the Cuban Giants, perhaps it was justified. The Harrisburg club was awarded two victories by forfeit against Wilmington when that club disbanded. But the decisive blow for the Cubans came when four of their victories were disallowed on the grounds that the ball used in these games, although furnished by the Giants' opponents, violated League regulations.[16]

The Cuban Giants immediately filed a protest with the League, and for months Mr. Bright heatedly argued that he was robbed of the pennant. The protest dragged on, and with the eventual reorganization of the League, was never acted upon. To the baseball purist of Harrisburg, a championship had been won. But the real significance of the 1889 baseball season was that an "intense rivalry" between Harrisburg and the Cuban Giants had been unleashed, and this would continue with the Colored Monarchs of York, Pennsylvania.

The Colored Monarchs of York, Pennsylvania, 1890
Robert Peterson, in his book, *Only The Ball Was White*, wrote that "tracing the course of the organized Negro Leagues is rather like trying to follow a single black strand through a ton of spaghetti. The footing is infirm, and the strand has a tendency to break off in one's hand and slither back into the amorphous mass."[17] The Cuban Giants were at the forefront of Peterson's "spaghetti" theory. Not only were they neither Cubans nor Giants, sometimes, as in 1890, they weren't even the "Cuban Giants."

On November 2–3, 1890, the Middle States League was reorganized and renamed the Eastern Interstate League at a meeting in Harrisburg. Despite having "interstate" in its name, it was commonly referred to as the "Pennsylvania League," as the six clubs that comprised it were located in Pennsylvania: Allentown, Altoona, Easton, Harrisburg, Lebanon, and York.[18] The Cuban Giants were not represented. The usual League business transpired – election of officers, constitution adoption, scheduling, and so forth – and a second meeting was scheduled for February 24, 1890.

In the months prior to the February meeting two events occurred that would have significant bearing on the League's franchises. The first involved Samuel Crook, head of the syndicate that owned Harrisburg's Middle States League franchise of 1889. While the syndicate was no doubt pleased about last season's championship, they did not share the grousing about the Cuban Giants. Despite John Bright's claim that the Cuban Giants would be based in Trenton for the 1890 season, rumor suggested that Crook's group planned to obtain a second franchise in Harrisburg and sign every player from Trenton's Cuban Giants to staff it.[19] The second event was York's application for League membership filed February 12, 1890, by William E. Whorl. At this time, however, York's application appears to have had no connection with eventual League decisions or its organization.[20]

When the League's February meeting was called to order, the second-franchise-in-Harrisburg rumor became reality. It did not, however, include the Cuban Giants. Challenging Crook's syndicate for the Harrisburg franchise was local businessman Henry Fleming with his newly formed Island Base Ball Club and its pirated manager from last season's championship team, James Farrington. The League quickly determined that there would be only one franchise per city and immediately began voting procedures to determine which faction's club would represent Harrisburg. Following fifteen cast ballots, the result was a tie. A compromise was suggested in which Fleming would pay the syndicate $500 for the franchise. Crook refused, demanding $1,500. Neither club could agree. But when a sixteenth ballot was taken, Mr. Fleming's new club was suddenly unanimously admitted as Harrisburg's entry into the League and granted permission to adopt the nickname "Ponies" from last year's club.[21]

What actually happened to swing a unanimous vote is unclear. While York's application was also accepted at the meeting, there was no evidence of possible collusion until late April when the York Base Ball Club made application to the court of York County, Pennsylvania, for a charter of incorporation. According to the document, "Harrisburg Group, Inc." put up $1,500 in capital, which allowed York representative William Whorl to sell $500 worth of stock at $15 per share.[22] Was "Harrisburg Group, Inc." actually Crook's Harrisburg Syndicate? The $1,500 in capital was the exact amount Crook had demanded from Mr. Fleming for the Ponies. And with the stock arrangement, Harrisburg Group, Inc. had controlling interest in the York Base Ball Club, and to some degree, Harrisburg had a second franchise in the Eastern Interstate League.

Further evidence of the Harrisburg-York connection appeared in the *York Gazette* to the effect that "Harrisburg People have obtained the grounds here and plan to place a team of colored players in a new league."[23] Sol. White went a step further stating, "A party of Gentlemen who backed the Harrisburg Club of '89, secured the grounds in York, and signing the Cuban Giants placed them in York as representatives of the Eastern Interstate League."[24] But as late as March 13, 1890, owner John Bright was still saying his "Giants will be located in Trenton and not Harrisburg or any other Pennnsylvania city."[25] By mid-April, however, Crook and his syndicate had quietly signed the majority of Bright's Giants and began scheduling exhibition games in York.

Why was it seemingly so easy to attract the Giants to tiny York, Pennsylvania? Several factors may have fostered the move. Evidence suggests that Harrisburg ran the Eastern Interstate League, and it was clear at the reorganization meeting that they discouraged out-of-state clubs, specifically the Cuban Giants.[26] While John Bright's business acumen had been valuable for getting his Giants placed into a league in 1889, his penurious dealing with his players fostered unhappiness and occasional turnover in personnel.[27] When the new league instituted a virtual player salary cap of $75 per month – a $25 increase over the Middle State League – to assure that all players were paid equally, it enticed renegade players,[28] and perhaps the Cuban Giants. The League and Harrisburg club may well have viewed the Monarchs of York in the former light.

To what degree, if any, each of these events were responsible for the Giants' migration to York is unknown. They did, however, mark the total breakup of the original Cuban Giants.[29] Under new manager, J. Monroe Kreiter Jr., the new aggregation of old Cuban Giants now fancied itself the "Colored Monarchs of the Diamond," but commonly were known as the "Monarchs of York."[30] In the breakup process, Bright lost eight of his top players in the exodus to York, and two, believe it or not, to the new Harrisburg club.[31]

Angered by Crook's acquisition of the Cuban Giants for York, Harrisburg manager Farrington defied any racial criticism and immediately signed Giants catcher and Harrisburg resident Clarence Williams. On

April 17, Farrington, in a telegram from New York, informed the team's directors that he had also signed Giants third baseman, Frank Grant. [32] York, too, claimed to have signed Grant, and took issue with Farrington through an appeal to League President, W. H. Voltz, and a suit brought before Judge Joseph Simonton of the Harrisburg Municipal Court. Voltz made his ruling on May 19, Judge Simonton on June 6; Grant would play for Harrisburg's Ponies. [33] To offset the loss of Grant, Crook and his Monarchs invaded the New York Gorhams' camp and signed Sol. White, Andy and Oscar Jackson, and catcher William Jackson of Detroit.

The League and court decisions, as well as the entire scenario, served to intensify the Harrisburg-Giants rivalry of the previous season. When League play began March 1, the new Ponies picked up with the Monarchs of York where their predecessor left off with the Cuban Giants in 1889, slugging it out for the League lead.

Both teams opened on the road, and when they met in Harrisburg for two games on March 12 and 13, York had a 6–2 record while Harrisburg was 7–1. York defeated the Ponies twice, and returned home to York to a rousing reception. Some two thousand fans followed the Spring Garden Band as the team paraded through town to Center Square along Market Street. Following speeches by players, manager Krieter, and club directors Charles Young and William Hill, the team was treated to a lavish dinner at Welsh's Restaurant. [34]

Located less than twenty-five miles to the south of Harrisburg, York's proximity allowed Crook and his investors to closely monitor the club from League headquarters. Further, the town's mostly German-immigrant population supported baseball and displayed, seemingly, no racial prejudice. While York's 1889 team representative had been successful (45–28), the community soon became disillusioned with transient players and their drunken disorderliness. [35] York's baseball complexion, as it were, changed for the 1890 campaign. With a unified team, the city immediately accepted the Monarchs as their own, right down to their uniforms. While manager Kreiter lobbied to have "Monarchs" lettered across the chest of each uniform's shirt, club directors decided the name "York" in black letters "would be the only name on the team uniforms." [36]

Team members were quartered at the home of Mrs. L. Pollard and Mr. G. Robinson, but took meals in local restaurants and generally had the run of the town. [37] Only two incidents were reported during the season that might be construed as racial, and each occurred while the team was playing on the road. When the Monarchs arrived in Allentown, their accommodations were scattered all over town. Manager Kreiter refused to take the field until the entire team was housed at one hotel. They were so accommodated and showed their appreciation for a good night's rest by defeating their host, 14–7, the following day.[38]

By the end of June 1890, the Eastern Interstate League was a three-team race, with York, 27–10, leading Harrisburg, 27–15, and Altoona, 27–16. Other League teams became frustrated with the Monarchs' superior play, voicing their contempt on the field and in the press. Following an 8–5 win over Easton, Pennsylvania, Easton fans taunted the victors with, "Why don't the Black-and-Tan's get into a bigger league?"[39]

The Monarchs continued their League domination, and by late July, only Harrisburg still challenged them for the pennant. But, for a second time, these "X" Cuban Giants were denied the championship by a Harrisburg Club. On July 21, with York (40–16, .714) barely ahead of Harrisburg (39–25, .609) in the standings, Harrisburg's directors drove their team of Ponies into another league, the Atlantic Association.[40]

The loss of Harrisburg was so critical that within two days the Eastern Interstate League was dissolved.[41] There was feeling among York fans that Harrisburg had jumped to the Atlantic Association (AA) to save embarrassment should they lose the pennant. In truth, Harrisburg had been courting the Atlantic Association since late June. But because of the club's black players, Williams and Grant, the AA was not eager to accept the Ponies.[42]

Having suddenly been deprived of the chance for a League pennant, York fans became even more frustrated when Crook and his syndicate elected to move the Monarchs of York to Harrisburg. From the capital city they retained their York affiliation and continued to play teams in the defunct Eastern Interstate League and wherever they could find a game. By season's end, the Monarchs had traveled some six thousand miles in Pennsylvania and New Jersey, visited more than fifty different towns and cities, and compiled an overall record of 88 wins and 27 losses.[43]

During the winter of 1890–1891, the Cuban Giants players were reunited with their "Cuban Giants" uniforms. Owner John Bright was able to regain, without litigation, the services of Frank Grant, Clarence Williams, and others who had left the fold. Together once more, the team prepared for its third consecutive season of play in 1891. But for the second straight year, the Cubans were fleeced of their players, this time by Ambrose Davis and his New York Big Gorhams. It was the same scenario, only this time in a "NEW" York.

Regardless of the Cuban Giants' origin, their creation and gradual evolution marked the birth of organized black baseball. As the black game developed simultaneously with, yet separately from, its white counterpart, it created a subculture that enabled black baseball to retain its own distinct identity. Without a game of their own, playing (supposedly "American") baseball and engaging in it as a business enterprise was an attempt by African Americans to achieve full socialization, to be accepted. Despite more than sixty years of oppression, the survival of African American baseball demonstrated resourcefulness, persistence, and an energetic ability, both on and off the field, to make the most of any dispiriting situation.

During their first three seasons, in three different cities and under two assumed names, the Giants experienced and overcame various forms of oppression. In so doing, they ultimately became the model that propelled black professional baseball into the twentieth century and led to the organization of the Negro Leagues. York, Pennsylvania, with its Monarchs was the first of many small, predominantly white towns to foster black baseball; the first of so many, many stops along baseball's indecorous color line.

NOTES

1. *Sporting News*, September 5, 1888.

2. J. Malloy, "The Birth of the Cuban Giants: The Origins of Black Professional Baseball, 1885–1886," paper presented at the Cooperstown Symposium for Baseball and the American Culture, National Baseball Hall of Fame, Cooperstown NY, 1992 (reprinted elsewhere in the present volume).

3. On April 10, 1947, Jackie Robinson became the first African American in the modern Major Leagues when Branch Rickey and the Dodgers purchased his contract from the Montreal Royals of the International League.

4. For an overview of the formation of the Cuban Giants, see R. Peterson, *Only The Ball was White: A History of Legendary Black Players and All-White Professional Teams Before Black Men Played in the Major Leagues* (Englewood Cliffs NJ: Prentice Hall, 1970), 34–39; and S. White, *Sol. White's Official Base Ball Guide: History of Colored Base Ball* (Philadelphia: H. Walter Schlichter, 1907), 11–13; for a history of the Argyle Hotel, see, S. M. Aldrich, "The Argyle Hotel, Babylon, New York, 1881–1904," Transcript, Babylon Public Library.

5. A similar account of the birth of the Cuban Giants appears in the *New York Age*, October 15, 1887.

6. A. F. Harlow, "Unrecognized Stars," *Esquire Magazine* (September 1938): 75; Prior to Harlow's article there is no reference to the Giants' on-field verbalizations. But since the article such reference is rarely omitted.

7. The Giants played two Major League clubs, losing to both: the New York Metropolitans, 11–3, and the Philadelphia Athletics, 13–7. Observers gave testimony that the victors needed help from the umpires. *Trenton Times*, May 10, 1886.

8. *Reach's Base Ball Guide* (Philadelphia: A. J. Reach, 1889), 33; The League franchise cities were Frankfort and Wilmington DE, Trenton NJ, and Harrisburg, Lancaster, Norristown, Philadelphia, and Reading PA.

9. During this period various leagues had clubs with one or two black players on their rosters. The New York Gorhams was an all-black club, but they joined the Middle States League in midseason.

10. *Harrisburg Daily Patriot*, June 10, 1889.

11. *Harrisburg Daily Patriot*, July 19, 1889.

12. While media commentary was racist, it was most likely intended to fuel the rivalry that had emerged between the two clubs.

13. League president William H. Voltz appointed a confidential committee. Harrisburg club manager James Farrington attended the committee meeting, however, but left the room before votes were cast and the decision made.

14. *Spalding's Official Base Ball Guide* (Chicago: A. G. Spalding and Bros., 1890), 89.

15. Such tactics were not exclusive to the Middle States League. Newspapers from other League cities, as well as national sporting papers of the period, are filled with accounts of postponement, rescheduling, awarding of wins on technicalities, moving of venues, and other incidents of the kind.

16. In midseason, the League adopted the Keefe and Bucannon ball following complaints by players that the Mason ball was too soft. The new-ball rule went into effect July 31, 1889 (*Harrisburg Daily Patriot*, July 29, 1889), but when the Giants played at Norwalk on July 31, the outlawed Mason ball was nonetheless used. The Giants reported the violation to League president Voltz, and the Giants won by forfeit (*Harrisburg Daily Patriot*, August 2, 1889). No further reference is made to ball violations prior to the committee's determination of the championship.

17. Peterson, *Only the Ball was White*, 80.

18. At the League's initial organizational meeting, clubs from Delaware, New Jersey, and New York expressed interest in joining, but did not follow through.

19. *Harrisburg Daily Patriot*, January 20, 1890; *Cleveland Gazette*, April 5, 1890.

20. *York Gazette*, February 15, 1890.

21. *Sporting Life*, December 11, 1889; *Reach's Base Ball Guide*, 24; *Harrisburg Daily Patriot*, February 26, 1890.

22. Document of Incorporation, York Base Ball Club, York County Courthouse; *York Gazette*, April 21, 1890.

23. *York Gazette*, April 18, 1890.

24. White, *Guide*, 21.

25. *Harrisburg Daily Patriot*, March 13, 1890.

26. *Sporting Life*, December 11, 1889. During the Middle States League's 1889 season, member clubs, including the Giants, accused Harrisburg of running the League. Ironically, Harrisburg accused League president Voltz and Giants' owner John Bright of collusion in League matters.

27. Malloy, "Birth of the Cuban Giants."

28. *Reach's Base Ball Guide*, 33.

29. The *Harrisburg Daily Patriot*, April 18, 1890, reported the significance of the breakup. While not denoting the same team, however, the name Cuban Giants continued to identify black baseball teams in many forms for decades: X Cuban Giants, Cuban X Giants, and so forth.

30. White, *Guide*, 23; *York Gazette*, April 23, 1890.

31. *New York Clipper*, December 29, 1888; *Cleveland Gazette*, April 5, 1890. The eight Giants lost to York were pitchers William Malone and William Seldon, and position players Ben Boyd, Jack Frye, Abe Harrison, Arthur Thomas, Billy Whyte, and George Williamson.

32. *Harrisburg Daily Patriot*, April 19, 1890. Frank Grant was the Giants' second baseman, and, except for the 1890 season, predominantly played that position his entire career.

33. *Harrisburg Daily Patriot*, May 20 and June 9, 1890.

34. *York Gazette*, May 15, 1890.

35. *Harrisburg Daily Patriot*, February 5, 1890; *York Gazette*, February 7, 1890. Before the Cuban Giants took up residence in York, Joseph DeVine, manager of York's 1889 club, applied to manage the city's 1890 team, stating that "I will be able to place a better team in the field than the hayseeds of last (year), and also a sober club."

36. *York Gazette*, April 23, 1890.

37. *York Gazette*, April 21, 1890.

38. *York Gazette*, April 26, 1890.

39. *York Gazette*, June 27, 1890.

40. *Spalding's Base Ball Guide*, 168; *Harrisburg Daily Patriot*, July 21, 1890; *York Gazette*, July 21, 1890.

41. Several of the League's smaller franchises had been in serious trouble

financially, placing the League's existence in jeopardy. Harrisburg's withdrawal was the final straw.

42. Harrisburg was approached in June 1890 to purchase the AA's Washington DC franchise. They declined. But when the Jersey City NJ franchise folded, Harrisburg agreed to join the League as a replacement (*Harrisburg Daily Patriot*, July 21, 1890). The AA constitution barred black players, and Harrisburg negotiated to keep both Williams and Grant. There was a compromise; Grant was allowed to play, but Williams was given his release.

43. *Cleveland Gazette*, October 11, 1890.

GUY WATERMAN

Racial Pioneering on the Mound

Don Newcombe's Social and Psychological Ordeal

JACKIE ROBINSON'S magnificent achievement as the first black man to cross organized baseball's color line in the twentieth century has been justly praised and documented in countless newspaper and magazine pieces, plus books, including the well-researched and broadly conceived treatment by historian Jules Tygiel, *Baseball's Great Experiment: Jackie Robinson and His Legacy.*[1]

Less celebrated are other black players who stepped across the line right behind Robinson, facing almost as much hostility and tension as the first man: outfielder Larry Doby, who broke the barrier in the American League later in 1947; pitcher Dan Bankhead, the first black to pitch from a Major League mound, also in 1947; and finally, Roy Campanella and Don Newcombe, who joined Robinson as leading stars of the strong Brooklyn teams of 1949 and the 1950s.

In honoring Robinson, we honor the first black batter, baserunner, and fielder to confront white opponents on a Major League diamond in this century. An examination of contemporary press accounts, however, suggests a hypothesis that the first black *pitchers* of these years confronted special social and psychological barriers of their own. This article will review some of this evidence. If the hypothesis is worth further study, social and recreational history should provide data for a clearer understanding of the special obstacles, in the form of racial insecurities and resentments rampant during the 1940s, that were met and overcome by these pioneering black pitchers. Notable among these pioneers and their tribulations was the experience of Don Newcombe.

Unique Role of Early Black Pitchers

Consider for a moment what it meant to be among the first black pitchers in the 1940s. A pitcher's role is notably different from other players'. This difference resulted in significantly different social and psychological pressures on the pioneer black pitchers.

In baseball's metaphor of life, there is a big distinction between the roles of batters/fielders and the pitcher. A batter is one man facing nine opponents. It has been said often enough that baseball differs from its principal rivals in mass media sports in that in football eleven men line up against eleven men on every play; and in basketball five against five; but in baseball the classic confrontation is batter against pitcher, one against one, with no support, no way to get help.[2] This is true only to a point: as soon as the batter makes any headway – that is, hits the ball – suddenly he has not just one opponent but nine, all ready to work together to put him out. He still has almost no support whatever from his teammates, but the lucky pitcher has now acquired a lot of allies. The same is true of the baserunner, although the involvement of a batter wearing the same uniform and possibly another baserunner or two slightly improves the odds. Still, the defense has the advantage of nine against two, or three, or four.

Consider what this meant when Jackie Robinson first stepped into a Major League batter's box in 1947. What his white opponents saw was one lone black facing a team of nine entrenched white men. Looked at from one perspective, this added to the pressures on Robinson. But it also reduced, in the minds of his opponents, the sense of being threatened by a black man. At least he was just one; they had nine on their side, and one of theirs held the ball.

Now consider the position of the first black pitchers. For the first time in modern Major League baseball, white batters found themselves going up to the plate to confront a big black man, standing tall on a mound just sixty feet away, and holding that hard white ball in his hand. The roles were now reversed. The white batter was, for the first time in this century, in the role of one man facing a black opponent, with the black man having a lot of team support and the white man none.

Of no little consequence was the fact that the black man had the ball and would be throwing it hard and dangerously close to a white man's head. Roger Angell has pointed out, with characteristic grace and clarity: "A great number of surprising and unpleasant things can be done to the ball as it is delivered from the grasp of a two-hundred-pound optimist, and the first of these is simply to transform it into a projectile. Most pitchers seem hesitant to say so, but if you press them a little they will admit that the prime ingredient in their intense personal struggle with the batter is probably fear."[3]

Also relevant was the size of the first black pitchers: Dan Bankhead, Satchel Paige, and Don Newcombe were all well over six feet tall.[4] All these factors combined to magnify an unprecedented insecurity and consequent sense of threat in the minds of white batters. Of course, on one level, this worked to the advantage of the black pitcher. Don Newcombe recalled his acceptance as one of the first two blacks to play Minor League ball at Brooklyn's farm team in Nashua, New Hampshire. Newcombe explained the lack of difficulties he was subjected to thus: "I had the ball in my hand. Nobody was going to bother me."[5]

But on another level, resistance of whites to their unwonted role as oppressed instead of oppressors created underlying tensions that even Jackie Robinson had not faced. For this reason, the first black pitchers deserve a large measure of respect for having confronted pressures of their own, pressures from which Robinson, Doby, and Campanella were excused.

Recall that these events took place in a Jim Crow America. Throughout many states of the union, blacks were not allowed to go to the same schools as whites; *Brown v. Board of Education of Topeka* was not decided by the Supreme Court until May 17, 1954. Not until the following year did Rosa Parks refuse to give her seat to a white man on a bus in Montgomery, Alabama, upsetting segregation in transportation. Throughout much of the country, a black person could not enter a restaurant of his or her choice, could not check into the better hotels, could not even wait for a train in the same waiting room. Lynchings were not uncommon in the Deep South, the Ku Klux Klan a respected force. White athletes were not accustomed to sharing locker rooms and showers with the "other" race. It is – fortunately – difficult for those of the last couple of generations to conceive of the separation of the races during the late 1940s, the indignities routinely applied to every black, and the rigid patterns and habits of thinking imposed on both races. This is the background against which we must try to view white perceptions of the first black pitchers.

Newcombe's Niche in Baseball History

Don Newcombe was one of several men who first stepped into the role as the big black man up there on the mound holding the ball. He was not the first black pitcher in the Majors. That honor went to Dan Bankhead in 1947. Bankhead, however, appeared in only four games, pitching ten relatively ineffective relief innings, with an ERA of 7.20 and no decisions in each. He was then gone for two years before coming back briefly in 1950 and 1951. In the American League, the inimitable Satchel Paige made a far more successful debut for Bill Veeck's pennant-bound Cleveland Indians in 1948, starting seven games and relieving in fourteen, posting a 6–1 record with a 2.48 ERA. Paige, however, was in a better position than younger pitchers to withstand pressures. Over forty years old (how much over was uncertain at the time), a veteran of many barnstorming appearances against white opponents, and a self-assured, philosophical old wizard, Paige was immune to the tensions and self-doubts that plague most rookies.

Don Newcombe came up to the Dodgers in 1949. Immediately he pitched well and became a mound mainstay of the Dodgers in their race to the National League pennant. He started 31 games that year, despite missing the first month of the season, posted a 17–8 record, and was named National League Rookie of the Year. He showed he could hit as well: throughout the big man's career, he was effective at bat as well as on the mound, compiling a .271 lifetime average, along with a .367 slugging percentage, and saw frequent (87 appearances) service as a pinch hitter.

Newcombe was the first pitcher of his race to become a big-time winner. He did so as a young man: just twenty-three years old when he was called up. That fall he went on to become the first black pitcher to start a World Series contest, being handed the ball for the 1949 opener against the New York Yankees and Allie Reynolds. (Paige had put in an uneventful two-thirds of an inning in relief in the 1948 Series.)

Newcombe became an unprecedented focal point as the first young black pitcher to win big in the hitherto-segregated Majors. The great black players of the past four decades have almost universally credited Jackie Robinson as the man who made their careers possible. Willie Mays has been quoted as remarking: "Every time I look at my pocketbook I see Jackie Robinson."[6] This debt is properly assigned. But all black *pitchers* of the Majors owe another, if lesser, debt to Don Newcombe as the man who blazed the way for *them*. Bob Gibson, Ferguson Jenkins, Dave Stewart, and so many other men of talent and achievement have been treading in the footsteps of a trail first broken by big Don Newcombe in 1949.

Newcombe was the first of his race against whom white batters had to step in all season long. Furthermore, Robinson, the star of 1947, was an articulate, well-educated, wholly admirable figure. Campanella, the new star in 1948, was a good natured, roly-poly bear of a man, whom no one could dislike. But Newcombe had neither of these winning qualities. To white ballplayers who had never had to face a black pitcher before, he was perceived as just a big (6'4", 220 pounds) black man who was up to no good out there on the mound. In fact, for a while, Newcombe's promotion to the Major League level was delayed due to fears that he would not prove as tractable as Robinson and Campanella. Burt Shotton, when sending Newcombe back down to Montreal in April 1949, commented, "I think he can pitch in the Majors, but he might undo everything those other fellows have accomplished."[7] Black reporters charged that "his habit of popping off" was why Newcombe was being held back.[8] The *Afro-American* called him the "problem child of the Dodger organization," in contrast to the exemplary Robinson and Campanella.[9] In short, Newcombe was the first black star who ideally fitted the negative stereotype that, at some level, white ballplayers dreaded.

Press Coverage of Newcombe in 1949

When he first broke into organized baseball, Newcombe experienced the same indignities as Robinson, Campanella, and other pioneering blacks. At spring training in 1947, the four blacks in the Dodger camp were assigned a third-rate hotel and soon developed dysentery. "I go so weak," recalled Newcombe for historian Tygiel, " I could hardly swell up your lip with a fast ball."[10] In St. Louis, during Newcombe's first regular season, the Dodgers stayed at the fashionable Chase Hotel, except for the blacks, whose Jim Crow hotel was not air-conditioned during St. Louis's hot spells. "In retrospect," commented Newcombe, "I wonder just what we were thought of. What kind of animals were we that nobody wanted us?"[11]

But by 1949, Robinson and Campanella were accepted as stars without regard to color, as integral parts of the fine Dodger team. Newspaper coverage routinely referred to Robinson as Brooklyn's star second baseman, without mentioning race. Newcombe, however, was characteristically identified by color: "Don Newcombe, big Negro righthander" (*New*

York Times, May 21, 1949);[12] "Newcombe, huge Negro righthander" (AP, May 22, 1949);[13] "Don Newcombe, Negro righthander" (*Chicago Tribune*, May 23, 1949);[14] "Don Newcombe, the huge Negro rookie" (*Washington Post*, August 1, 1949);[15] "big Don Newcombe, husky Negro pitcher" (AP, August 22, 1949);[16] "the giant Negro righthander" (*New York Times*, August 29, 1949);[17] and so forth.

Recalling such references is not intended to impute bigotry to the reporters or their newspapers. Indeed in some cases references to race may have been meant as commendation of the performance of a pioneering black ("Negro" in 1949 terminology). Rather, the point is that race seemed to loom with larger significance for a big fastball pitcher than for the nonpitching stars of the same era.

Consider this sequence of stories. An Associated Press wire story datelined May 17, 1949, opens: "With Jack Robinson scoring from second on a bunt and Roy Campanella hitting a two-run homer, the Brooklyn Dodgers scored six runs in the eleventh inning today in whipping the Chicago Cubs, 8–5."[18] There is no mention of race for the two stars of the day. The next day Campanella was featured in the AP story, again with no mention of race.[19] On May 22 Robinson appeared prominently in the story, and still with no mention of his race.[20] On May 22 the AP story began: "The Dodgers won the opener 3–0 behind Don Newcombe. Newcombe, huge Negro righthander, made his first Major League pitching [appearance] for Brooklyn in the opener and turned in a sparkling 5-hitter."[21] Alone of the three, the pitcher was linked to his race. Two days later Robinson belted two home runs in one game, and his name was put in the wire service's lead sentence, though again with no identification of his color.[22] In the *Chicago Tribune*, stories of May 18 and 19 reported the heroics of Robinson and Campanella, with again no mention of race, but on May 23 referred to "Don Newcombe, Negro righthander."[23] Press stories at this time also covered Larry Doby of the Cleveland Indians, who was off to a fast start in 1949, but virtually never troubled to mention the color of his skin.[24]

The May stories might at first appear explainable on the grounds that Newcombe was making his debut in the Majors, and therefore newspaper readers would not know he was black unless told, whereas Robinson, Campanella, and Doby were already known. The differential treatment continued all season, however, not in every story, but often enough to show that the blackness of a pitcher seemed to carry more significance than the blackness of any other player. Here are examples:

1. A wire story of August 1: "A masterful pitching job by Don Newcombe, the huge Negro rookie."[25]

2. Wire story on August 22: "For big Don Newcombe, husky Negro pitcher, it was his sixth loss."[26]

3. The *New York Times* on August 29: "Neither the number thirteen nor slugging Ralph Kiner held any terrors for big Don Newcombe at Ebbets Field yesterday. The giant Negro righthander made his thirteenth triumph of the season a 4-hit shut-out as" (a question may be raised here whether these references to superstition had racial stereotypes as their origin; possibly not.)[27]

4. *New York Times* on September 3: "Brooklyn's strong-armed Negro righthander put on a gaudy show."[28]

5. *New York Times* on September 25: "It was a wonderful evening for the giant 24-year-old Negro righthander."[29]

Throughout these months, press write-ups of Robinson, Campanella, and Doby do not appear to have mentioned race. One exception may be noted, and the context may be relevant. The fiery Robinson was just beginning to emerge from the constraints imposed on him by Branch Rickey to ensure his acceptance. On September 21 he exploded in an argument with an umpire and was thrown out of the game. In this story, the *New York Times* uncharacteristically referred to him as the "star Negro second baseman of the Brooks."[30] In fact the write-up of this game, played in St. Louis, southernmost city in the National League as then constituted, hints at racial divisions in the crowd reaction: "A large number of the fans were rooting violently for the Dodgers, and were even more vociferous after the unfortunate incident that caused Robinson's eviction."[31]

But in the absence of such special circumstances, it appears that press coverage of black stars in 1949 omitted reference to race for nonpitchers, while often identifying Newcombe's blackness. Again, let it be emphasized, this observation is not intended as a charge of racism against the reporters or their papers, but as evidence that race loomed larger in everyone's mind when a big pitcher held the ball and stood on that raised mound than when a white pitcher looked down from the mound on a black batter.

When the Dodgers won a close-fought pennant by one game over the

Cardinals, and went on to the Series and played against the Yankees, Newcombe's race was once again a focus of write-ups. On September 24, with Brooklyn trailing St. Louis by a half game, Newcombe won a key victory and was identified as "the giant 24-year-old Negro righthander."[32] The *New York Times* described the World Series opener as matching New York's Allie Reynolds "and Donald Newcombe, giant Negro right-hander."[33] The *Chicago Tribune* that day referred to "the big Negro."[34] None of these stories identified which nonpitchers on the team were blacks.

The *San Francisco Chronicle*, calling Newcombe the "rookie Negro righthander," went on to give a long rhapsodic account of the pitch-ers' duel between Reynolds and Newcombe, closing with a tribute to the excellence of the latter's losing effort, including this obvious racial pleasantry: "His was the labor magnificent, even though the rewards were memories that will haunt him until he gets as old as Satchell [*sic*] Paige, and, brethren, that's old."[35]

Such repeated press references underscore the impression, otherwise difficult to document, that everyone involved was more conscious of race when a dominating black pitcher took the mound, controlling the ball on every pitch, than when one or two blacks entered the lineup at other positions. If this hypothesis has value, it tends to support the idea that Newcombe's performance under pressure was subject to unprece-dented stresses, encountered by no one else as intensely or as consistently. Newcombe was the first regular starting pitcher of his race. That special tension was always present when he took the mound. He was black and he *was* big. White batters in the Major Leagues had never faced this particular scenario as part of the regular rotation. Newcombe was surely aware of the psychology of the situation. ("What kind of animals were we . . .")

Don Newcombe in his prime was an impressive, complex, and pow-erful figure. In later years, his career came to an early end amid the disgrace of alcoholism. Yet the big man overcame that enemy, too, and returned to become a counselor to big league athletes coping with the fatal temptations of alcohol and drug abuse. In 1979, he received the Ernie Meld Award as the "figure who has contributed greatly to the overall image of professional baseball both on and off the field." Prior winners had included such other admirable role models as Ernie Banks, Roberto Clemente, and Phil Niekro.

Younger players had good reason to heed his message. No one knew better than Don Newcombe the meaning of pressure. Taking his life as a whole in perspective, very few responded with greater courage.

NOTES

1. J. Tygiel, *Baseball's Great Experiment: Jackie Robinson and His Legacy* (New York: Vintage Books, 1984).

2. The point is almost a cliché in baseball writing. One excellent example may be found in J. B. Holway, *The Pitcher* (New York: Prentice Hall, 1987), 1–2.

3. R. Angell, *Five Seasons: A Baseball Companion* (New York: Popular Library, 1978), 11.

4. On all factual and statistical matters, my source is the indispensable "Big Mac": *The Baseball Encyclopedia*, 8th ed. (New York: Macmillan, 1990).

5. Newcombe, quoted in Tygiel, *Baseball's Great Experiment*, 151.

6. Willie Mays, quoted in D. Q. Voigt, *American Baseball, Volume III: From Postwar Expansion to the Electronic Age* (University Park and London: Pennsylvania State University Press, 1983), 51.

7. Burt Shotton, quoted in Tygiel, *Baseball's Great Experiment*, 287.

8. "Don Newcombe Becomes Dodger Pitcher," *Afro-American*, May 21, 1949, 6.

9. "Newcombe Victor in Initial Start," *Afro-American*, May 28, 1949, 5.

10. Newcombe, quoted in Tygiel, *Baseball's Great Experiment*, 175.

11. Newcombe, quoted in Tygiel, *Baseball's Great Experiment*, 146.

12. "Slaughter's 3-Run Double Helps Munger Subdue Brooklyn, 6 to 2," *New York Times*, May 21, 1949, 17.

13. "Raffensberger Hurls Reds to 1-Hit, 2–0 Victory over Dodgers," *Washington Post*, May 23, 1949, 12. The wire story is datelined May 22.

14. "Dodgers Beat Reds, 3 to 0; Lose 2d, 2 to 0," *Chicago Tribune*, May 23, 1949, 4.

15. "Bums Whip Cards, 4–2, Behind Newcombe; Still 1 1/2 Back," *Washington Post*, August 1, 1949, 10.

16. "Braves Do It to Dodgers Again, 5 to 0," *Washington Post*, August 22, 1949, 8.

17. "Dodgers' Newcombe Takes No. 13, Tripping Pirates on 4-Hitter, 9–0," *New York Times*, August 29, 1949, 20.

18. "Bums' 6 Runs in 11th, Win over Cubs, 8–5," *Washington Post*, May 18, 1949, 17.

19. "Dodgers Overwhelm Cubs, 14–5; Campanella, Snider Homer," *Washington Post*, May 19, 1949, 23.

20. "Brooklyn Erupts for 8 in 9th to Club Cards, 15 to 6," *Washington Post*, May 22, 1949, 20.

21. "Raffensberger Hurls Reds to 1-Hit, 2–0 Victory over Dodgers," *Washington Post*, May 23, 1949, 12.

22. Robinson Hits Two Homers, Bums Win, 6–1," *Washington Post*, May 25, 1949, 14.

23. "Cubs Lose, 8–5 in 11th," *Chicago Tribune*, May 18, 1949, 1; "Dodgers Rout Cubs, 14–5," *Chicago Tribune*, May 19, 1949, 1; "Dodgers Beat Reds, 3–0; Lose 2d, 2 to 0," *Chicago Tribune*, May 23, 1949, 4.

24. See, for examples, "Dobson vs. Al Benton in Sox-Indians Clash," and "Larry Doby Only Clouter – Now – on Staggering Indians," both in *Boston Globe*, May 21, 1949, 4; "Senators Beat Indians, 6–2, Behind Hudson," *Chicago Tribune*, May 26, 1949, 4; "28,573 See Nats Beat Tribe, 6–2, Behind Hudson," *Washington Post*, May 26, 1949, 4B; and "Doby Hits 500-Foot Homer," *Boston Globe*, May 26, 1949, 30.

25. "Bums Whip Cards, 4–2, Behind Newcombe; Still 1 1/2 Back," *Washington Post*, August 1, 1949, 10.

26. "Braves Do It to Dodgers Again, 5 to 0," *Washington Post*, August 22, 1949, 8.

27. "Dodgers' Newcombe Takes No. 13, Tripping Pirates on 4-Hitter, 9–0," *New York Times*, August 29, 1949, 20.

28. Dodgers Blank Giants and Cut Idle Cards' Lead to 1 ½ Games," *New York Times*, September 3, 1949, 8.

29. "Dodgers, Cards Win," *New York Times*, September 25, 1949, 1.

30. "Dodgers Break Even with Cardinals, Stay Game and Half Out of First Place," *New York Times*, September 22, 1949, 42.

31. "Dodgers Break Even," *New York Times*, September 22, 1949, 42.

32. "Dodgers, Cards Win," *New York Times*, September 25, 1949, 1.

33. "Yankees Triumph over Dodgers, 1–0, on Henrich Homer," *New York Times*, October 6, 1949, 1.

34. "Yanks, 1 Up, Pick Raschi Today," *Chicago Tribune*, October 6, 1949, 1.

35. "Yankees Take Series Opener, 1–0," *San Francisco Chronicle*, October 5, 1949, 1H.

JEAN HASTINGS ARDELL

Mamie "Peanut" Johnson

The Last Female Voice of
the Negro Leagues

You want to know what it's like
Being colored?
Well,
It's like going to bat
With two strikes
Already called on you.
    – Waring Cuney, quoted in Harold Seymour, *Baseball: The People's Game*

J ACKIE ROBINSON LIVED THOSE LINES ten years later, coming to
bat with two metaphorical strikes – call them racial prejudice and
the weight of tradition – against him. History has testified to his
character and endurance in securing a place in Major League baseball. Yet
as Robinson and the black players who followed him into white baseball
succeeded, black fans were abandoning the Negro Leagues, which had
been a source of pride and a cultural rallying place in black communities. During their struggle to survive in the early 1950s, the Leagues
resorted to many types of marketing strategies. Which is how, six years
after Robinson's history-making appearance, a skinny second baseman
broke the gender line in the Negro Leagues. In 1953, the Indianapolis
Clowns signed second baseman Toni – that's Toni with an *I* – Stone
for $12,000. (In 1947, Jackie Robinson's first contract in Brooklyn was
$5,000, the minimum Major League salary).[1] And when the Kansas City
Monarchs signed Stone away for the 1954 season, the Clowns signed two
more women: Connie Morgan, who replaced Stone at second base, and a
utility fielder/right-handed pitcher of Bobby Shantzian stature (5'4", 120
pounds) named Mamie "Peanut" Johnson. Of this sorority of three, only
Johnson survives.

*

I met Johnson during Labor Day weekend 1999 at a women's amateur baseball tournament in Bethesda, Maryland, where she had been invited to coach first base, and I followed up with a lengthier interview at the Negro Leagues Gift Shop in Mitchellville, Maryland, where she then worked. The *Biographical Encyclopedia of the Negro Leagues* reports that Johnson played one year with the Clowns, compiling a 10–1 record. Other sources, however, give her a three-year career, with a record of 11–3 in 1953 and 12–4 in 1955. Eric Enders, of the National Baseball Hall of Fame and Museum, points out that Negro Leagues records for these years are incomplete and that it's quite possible she did play three years. Johnson herself claims three years. At any rate, some fans view Mamie "Peanut" Johnson's career as an interesting footnote to the waning years of the Negro Leagues. Yet the stories of such players who fought for a place on the game's margins add richness and texture to baseball history and insights into the culture of the times. To place Johnson's career in context, some background on black women's baseball is helpful.

Black Women Played, Too

Nearly a hundred years ago, to aspire as a black female – if you could even find such a woman – to play the National Pastime was akin to trying to enter the game with three strikes against you. "There are very few women, especially colored women, who even understand a game of baseball when they see it played, to say nothing of taking part in a game," reported a dispatch in 1908 from Louisville to the black newspaper the *Freeman*.[2] Thus women such as Mrs. Henry Newboy, who worked as the secretary for her husband's ball club, were a novelty: "Mrs. Newboy is an expert at the game and practices with the club," reported the *Freeman* with some wonder "[She] understands and can play baseball and enjoys the diamond dust."

Some forward thinkers in the black community wanted more Mrs. Newboys. As the *Freeman* editorialized in the same issue: "Our neighbors' wives and daughters (white) take interest in athletics, and why not those of our race? Athletics are not copyrighted; they are at the disposal of each and every one. . . . Push it along. Take up athletics, girls; take physical exercises; get interested in the games of the field, diamonds, and in other pastimes of the like. Enjoy life as it is; don't make it what it isn't or what it should not be."

The year 1908 also saw a black girls' team organized in Springfield,

Ohio, with plans under way to play teams from other cities in Ohio and Indiana. There was talk of forming a league, to be known as the Colored American League for Girls. The president of the Springfield club, C. L. Mayberry, said: "You are aware there is but little that the girls of our race can find to do. . . . If this project can be made a success . . . it will be opening fields for our girls that have hitherto been closed. . . . Why wait until the white girls have worn all of the 'new' off? . . . I believe that if this is encouraged by men of influence and men of means, it will mean worlds for our girls."[3]

Occasionally black women played on black men's teams: as early as 1917, Pearl Barrett played first base for the Havana (Cuba) Red Sox. But as James A. Riley has noted, "the Sox's caliber of performance was not regarded as on par with the big leagues."[4] And in 1933, the Cleveland Giants fielded a second baseman named Isabelle Baxter. (In a game against the Canton Clowns, Baxter had one error in five fielding opportunities (a wide throw to first after stopping a "spectacular" ball behind first), and went one for three at the plate. These events were reported in much the same way as those of early white female ballplayers: as anomalies that quickly faded from the diamond, for in those years, women of any color were allowed forays into the game simply for the purposes of publicity and increased attendance. Black women who played consistently did so with their own kind, for black women's teams continued to crop up. For example, in *The People's Game*, Harold Seymour cites a 1933 edition of the *Defender* announcing the formation of a women's team in Steelton, Pennsylvania.

Of the three women who played in the Negro Leagues, only Connie Morgan benefited directly from these early attempts to include black girls in the National Pastime: as a teenager, she played for five years on an all-girl ball club, the North Philadelphia Honey Drippers, where she compiled a .368 batting average. The other two women played primarily with black men: Toni Stone played with the House of David, the San Francisco Sea Lions, and the New Orleans Creoles, while Mamie Johnson grew up playing on black men's sandlot, amateur, and semi-pro teams. So, four decades after it was suggested that black women might benefit from taking up athletics, these three were discovering that baseball could come to mean, in the words of the *Freeman*, "worlds to them."[5]

Knocking Birds Out with Rocks

Several sources have reported that Mamie "Peanut" Johnson was born on September 27, 1932, in Long Branch, New Jersey. Johnson told me she was born in 1935 in Ridgeway, South Carolina, to Miss Belton and Mr. Harrison (she declined to give their first names). Growing up during the Depression in the rural South, Mamie was unaware that women could be paid to play baseball. In the hamlet where she first lived, Johnson grew up "knocking birds out of the trees with rocks."[6] She recalls an uncle who was an accomplished ballplayer and instructed her in the game. "I was very, very young when I started playing ball down South. That was all we really had to do at that particular time. We made our own baseballs out of stone, twine, and masking tape. I learned to play with the fellows and it was enjoyable to me."[7]

By then her father had moved to Hartford, Connecticut, where he began another family. Her mother would later tell her that she came by her baseball talents honestly: "She said my father was a real good ballplayer, that every time she looked at me, she saw him." When her mother moved to Washington DC in search of better economic opportunities, and with the goal of owning her own home, Mamie was left in the care of her grandmother. She says both women and her uncle encouraged her to go after whatever she wanted to do. For Mamie, that meant playing ball.

When Mamie was eight years old, her grandmother died, and the girl moved north to Long Branch, New Jersey, where she lived with a maternal aunt and uncle for three years. She joined the Police Athletic League (PAL), which she credits as a great help to her as an athlete. At age nine, she was the sole girl on the baseball team and says the experience challenged her to concentrate on improving her game. When she moved to Washington DC at age eleven, she continued to play sandlot baseball with the boys, as well as some girls' softball. She returned to New Jersey each summer and stayed on when she was fourteen. It has been reported that she played football for Long Branch High School. When I asked her about this, she replied, "I was not really on the football team. I used to mess around with the kids, but playing varsity [for a girl] was not allowed. People," she added, "want to think that we are so fragile, but we are not."[8] Even so, her stature presented a challenge – at age fourteen, she weighed between ninety-five and one hundred pounds.

After graduation from Long Branch High School in 1949, Mamie studied at New York University before returning to Washington DC, where she played semi-professional baseball with various clubs. When she conceived a child, she continued playing ball until she was seven months pregnant. In 1952 she approached a white Alexandria (Virginia)-based women's team for a tryout. "They looked at me like I was crazy," she recalled, "as if to say, *what do you want?*" It was Johnson's first bruising encounter with racism. Johnson, who had experienced different cultures in the South and in the North, puts it this way: her life in "South Carolina was black and New Jersey was white. . . . I went to an all-white high school in New Jersey and was never treated differently. Washington DC," she says, "taught me segregation." The experience disappointed her but did not undermine her confidence. "I felt like I was just as good, and looked just as good, and could play just as good."

"I'm glad they turned me down," she adds. "Otherwise, I would have been just another woman who played woman's baseball."[9] Indeed, about a year later, she realized how lucky she was when a former Negro Leagues ballplayer named Bish Tyson spotted her pitching for a men's semi-pro team. He introduced her to Bunny Downs, the business manager of the Indianapolis Clowns. Downs gave her a tryout and afterwards told her to go meet the bus. Mamie Johnson was on the team.

Johnson says she was treated very well by her male teammates – in her words, "beautiful, honey, beautiful. . . . There was a different breed of young men back then than we have now. We were raised different and that made our character different. . . . Young men came from families where they were taught character and respect."[10] The term "respect" frequents Mamie's conversation. When another reporter inquired as to hanky-panky on the club, Johnson shook her head. "If you're out there doing what you're supposed to be doing, your teammates . . . give you the respect you're due. . . . Respect is the greatest thing in the world; it will take you farther than money."[11] She gave a similar, no-nonsense answer when I mentioned that Ila Borders had found some of the wives of her teammates in the Northern League to be less than congenial toward her traveling with the team: "That's stupid," Johnson retorted. "She's out there to play." She herself says she encountered no suspicious wives. "Why would they be jealous of me? I had my own [man]. I rode on the bus day and night, met everybody's wife, and had a good time. Really, I don't understand that. . . . I loved being a female on the team. I had twenty-six wonderful brothers."

This being baseball, there was, of course, hazing. When speaking with the media, Johnson takes the same attitude toward sexism as Toni Stone and Ila Borders: to have complained or reported such incidents would have reflected poorly upon their professionalism, their ability to "take it," and would have gained them the reputation of a whiner. They are probably correct. So they tend to downplay such experiences, especially the more appalling ones. Even so, Johnson sometimes threw at the batters "because sometimes, honey, you just get mad."[12]

Johnson did share this anecdote: A player named Barnes, whose first name she doesn't recall – it might be Tom Barnes, pitcher and outfielder for the Memphis Red Sox in 1950–55 – liked to razz her repeatedly. One day, with Johnson pitching and Barnes waiting to step into the batter's box, she remembers him saying, "How do you expect to strike anybody out and you're not as big as a peanut?"[13] Johnson told him to step up to the plate, and she silenced his banter in the most effective way by striking him out. She considers that strikeout to be one of her most satisfying. And that, she says, is how she got her nickname, "Peanut."

A couple of incidents at the 1999 Bethesda amateur tournament illustrate Johnson's style on the diamond: On a close play at first, the black umpire and Mamie saw the play differently. Mamie questioned his eyesight; the umpire stood his ground, eventually lecturing her, "On a bang-bang play you hear it, you don't see it."

"Look, I been playing ball fifty years and more, so don't go trying to teach me this game," retorted Mamie, and on it went. Jim Glennie, the president of the American Women's Baseball League and the coach of the Michigan All-Stars for that tournament, watched the exchange from the bench with some envy. "Black teams just seem to develop a fun atmosphere," he said. "The ump and Mamie – I call that an ice-breaking exchange; now they know one another." Mamie Johnson and the ump continued their verbal jousting for the rest of the weekend.

Another example: During the championship game in the Bethesda tournament, Mamie and Jerry Dawson, the white coach for the New England team, saw a play differently. She again expressed her opinion until Dawson told her to quit talking. Johnson turned the air blue with an impressive exposition of the epithet "motherfucker." When the inning was over, she returned to the bench, still fuming, still spewing epithets, and Dawson's apology did little to calm her. "Nobody tells me to be quiet," she said to nobody in particular.

When we met the following afternoon at the Negro Leagues Gift Shop in Mitchellville, the encounter with Dawson was still on her mind. Johnson nodded at the old signs on the wall, from segregation days, which read: "We serve colored carryout only. . . . No dogs, Negroes, Mexicans . . . colored seated in rear." She said, "This is the way the dummy acted yesterday – I don't know what made me react so quickly, unless it was him talking to me like I was somebody's child."

Bus Travel

With that, Johnson returned to the subject of her years in black baseball. Bunny Downs handled the logistics of women traveling with a busload of ballplayers. With most of the games played at night, the team often slept on the bus, and the Clowns had one fine bus, according to Johnson. When accommodations were available, a woman enjoyed an advantage. "The fellows would stay mostly in the dingy hotels or whatever, but we stayed in people's home[s], where it was very nice."

Through baseball, Johnson traveled to virtually every state in the union and into Canada. Unlike Toni Stone, who used her travels to visit libraries and learn about African-American history, Johnson demonstrated little interest. Perhaps this was a difference of temperament, for Johnson had told me, "If it don't interest me, I don't have time for it." Or perhaps it was a result of environment: Stone grew up in the urban North (St. Paul, Minnesota) in a family that stressed education and disdained her tomboy baseball-playing ways, while Johnson was a child of the rural South, whose family encouraged her athletic talents. Stone wanted to come to terms with her heritage, to stretch toward the possibilities, while Johnson seemed more inclined to accept the hand blacks were dealt. An interviewer, unfamiliar with the chronology, once asked Mamie how the civil rights movement affected her team. Johnson simply replied that the black teams got along well because they accepted the situation as it was: "It kept down a lot of difficulties. . . . We knew segregation was there and we didn't put ourselves in a position for it to affect us. Because if I know that you don't want me at your house then I am not going to come there. And it is the same thing with the restaurants. If I know . . . they are not going to serve, then why am I going? I mean, that's stupid."[14]

Johnson finds it more difficult to navigate the uncertainties of today's integrated times, unsure of which whites are friendly. Scars are evident from a life lived during the twentieth century's sea change in race relations. Her recent celebrity as a former Negro Leagues player has tried her patience and her trust. "The media writes what it sees and some that they don't see," she says. "Sometimes they blow it out of proportion. Better if they got *all* the facts before they started writing."

Nevertheless, when I telephoned early in 2000 to confirm some of the details of our interview, Johnson stated that she thought she should be paid for talking to me. She said she was tired of being ripped off by people making "a pile of money" off her story, and no amount of explanation – that the preparation of this essay for a baseball conference involved no payment, or that my contract with a university press to write a book about women and baseball would not even cover my research expenses – budged her in the slightest: "I've been advised that I should be paid."

Johnson referred me to her agent, a woman named Hazel Woods, of the Negro Leagues Yesteryear Foundation. Woods explained that the foundation represents "all of the living Negro Leagues players" and operates in their best interests. Just because I was not financially profiting from telling Johnson's story didn't mean that others wouldn't pick up my research and make money from it. The conversation was cordial, but I got no further with Hazel Woods than I had with Mamie Johnson. Not one fact would be confirmed.

Good Enough to Be There?

James A. Riley has called the Indianapolis Clowns the forerunner of the Harlem Globetrotters, who "always provided the crowds with a blend of baseball and showbiz."[15] If you had the talent of, say, Satchel Paige, you could afford to fool around and still look good, but the women players took the game seriously. The issue of why they were on the team touches a nerve in Johnson. One of Mamie's claims to fame is that Satchel Paige taught her how to throw a curve ball properly. "He just showed me how to grip the ball to keep from throwing my arm away, 'cause I was so little." Once she learned it, she said, "I was damn good."[16] Johnson has also been quoted thus: "I am an old Negro League baseball player," she says, not a bit immodestly. "I was good enough to play."[17] And in the *Baltimore Sun*: "People say Toni and Connie and I were gimmicks. Well, we weren't gimmicks; we were good enough to be there."[18] One of her former teammates supported that view in the *Sun*: "Gordon 'Happy' Hopkins of Hyattsville [Maryland] says he was pleased to play second base on days when Johnson took the hill. 'We didn't clown around. It wasn't a show. Mamie could pitch. I ain't lying.'"[19]

In his 1996 memoir, *I Was Right on Time*, Buck O'Neil also speaks to the issue. O'Neil had once tried to sign Bob Gibson with the Kansas City Monarchs and tells of his response: "Thanks for the offer . . . but I'm hoping to play ball for the St. Louis Cardinals."[20] O'Neil continues, albeit reluctantly:

> A few years before, Bob Gibson might have jumped at the chance to play for the Kansas City Monarchs. But Negro baseball was no longer the glorious enterprise it had once been. In 1954 our highest-paid player was actually a woman. Forgive me, Ora [O'Neil's wife], I don't intend to demean women, but we had signed Toni Stone away from the Indianapolis Clowns not because she was the best second baseman around but because she could give us a boost at the gate. Tony was a pretty fair player. . . . She ran well, and she knew what she was doing around the bag. But she wasn't of the same caliber as our other players, and the pitchers did take it easy on her when the game wasn't on the line.[21]

Window

Nevertheless, the Negro Leagues' declining years opened a window of opportunity for the three women, one they would not have had but for the integration of the Major Leagues. Mamie Johnson may have come to the Negro Leagues as their glory was fading, but not all the shine had quite gone. As she told one reporter, she remembers thinking, "Wow, look at me! I'm out here pitching in front of 80,000 people. And I'm a *girl*. . . . We would fill up Comiskey Park and Yankee Stadium when the white players couldn't."[22]

Baseball was Mamie's life at this time – she told me it was the best time of her life – and she did not hold other employment. When she played in Baltimore, in Virginia, and in Griffith Stadium, her relatives and her husband came to the games. Johnson was once asked how her husband felt about her baseball career. Ever the independent thinker, she replied, "Well, it didn't make any difference because I was going to play anyway. So whether he liked it or not it was immaterial to me because that was something that I wanted to do."[23]

A reporter once asked if she recalled hearing any stories about Negro Leagues baseball during the Depression. Johnson's reply illustrates much of her philosophy toward the game and toward life:

> No, people want to say that it was hard but when you are doing something

that you want to do and that you enjoy doing it is not that hard because the hard part of it you don't even think about. . . . A whole lot of fellows wanted to say that it was hard but I don't see where it was hard. Even with the older fellows that were there way before me – they don't emphasize the hardness of it because this was something that they wanted to do. They were ballplayers and there wasn't much pay or whatever but they enjoyed it. It was something they wanted.[24]

Johnson had given birth to a son in 1952, and when she was on the road with the Clowns, she left him in the care of her mother. She says her career in the Negro Leagues ended when she acknowledged it was time to go home and be a mother, not without regrets. "I wish I hadn't had him so young," she told me. "He cut off a whole lot of my life, things I would have done." She returned to Washington DC and went to nursing school. She underwent a divorce, married again, and adopted another son. She worked for thirty years as a licensed practical nurse at Sibley Hospital in Washington DC and at local nursing homes. But she wasn't through with baseball. She continued playing sandlot ball and coaching youth baseball for years, and she has a message for the girls of today: "I want all girls to know that if you're athletic, do it. Even if you don't succeed, try. Do what you want to do, because if you don't you're never going to succeed."

As it does for many aging fans and former players, the game still gets her up in the morning and keeps her going. At age sixty-seven (or seventy), she works five days a week as the manager of the Negro Leagues Gift Shop. During the summer of 1999, she coached the Mitchellville Tigers of the Babe Ruth League. Periodically Johnson appears at various baseball functions. In February 2000, she traveled to Kansas City to appear in a forum on black women in sports, where, the curator of the Negro Leagues Baseball Museum noted, "she was just as feisty as ever." In October 1999, Jim Glennie invited her to Arizona for a women's amateur tournament. She has appeared in a Canadian film about women in baseball. In March 1999, she was a guest of the Clintons at the White House. Just don't call her a museum piece – she is apt to say, "I'm not going anyplace. I'm still here."

She currently lives with her mother on the northeast side of Washington DC, in a home the latter purchased more than fifty years ago. So mother achieved her dream of home ownership, and daughter achieved her dream of playing professional baseball. Considering Johnson's life in baseball, the *Freeman*'s advice of 1908 returns to mind: "Enjoy life as it is;

don't make it what it isn't or what it should not be." This is impossible advice for a 5'4" black woman who came of age in the mid-twentieth century. Mamie Johnson had undeniable baseball talent or she would not have gotten as far as she did, but to "enjoy life as it is" would have meant not scrapping for her place in baseball. For a woman, to dream of playing professional baseball is to strive to make life – and baseball – "what it isn't" (a gender-blind game) and, some would say, "should not be."

Mamie Johnson still has a couple more baseball dreams and during our interviews was passionate about the possibilities. She hopes to found a local junior Negro League, from T-ball to eighteen-and-over. So far, she has rounded up enough boys for three teams, and should any girls want to play, she says, "Hey, come on in. . . . All they need is an opportunity when they're young."

Next door to the Negro Leagues Gift Shop is the site of her other dream, a rough baseball diamond. "It's an old field where the Mitchel-lville Tigers played in the 1940s," Johnson explains. "It has so much historic value – and that's the field I want to use." Walking the field, you notice the silhouette of the pin oaks that shape the outfield boundaries and the wooden stands that sag beneath a barren tree. A flattened white tube sock and an empty Budweiser can are evidence that not so long ago a game was played – a sandlot team, the Black Sox, plays here. But the property is for sale, and because the land fronts on Highway 301, a renovated ballpark is not an economic probability. Johnson's dream is a long shot, but that's nothing new.

NOTES

1. Eric Enders, of the National Baseball Hall of Fame, adds, "What we don't know is what Robinson made in his first year with Montreal." Telephone interview, March 12, 2000.

2. "Baseball among the Fairer Sex Coming into Prominence," *Freeman*, December 26, 1908.

3. "Baseball among the Fairer Sex," *Freeman*.

4. J. A. Riley, "Lady at the Bat," *Diamond* (March/April 1994): 22.

5. "Baseball among the Fairer Sex," *Freeman*.

6. Mamie "Peanut" Johnson, personal interview, Mitchellville, Maryland, September 7, 1999.

7. R. Cottingham, "Oral History Project on Mamie "Peanut" Johnson Good-

man," University of Baltimore, December 10, 1998. Courtesy of the Babe Ruth Museum, Baltimore, Maryland.

8. Johnson, personal interview.

9. D. Britt, "Following Her Heart to Pitcher's Mound," *Washington Post*, September 10, 1999, 1, 8.

10. Cottingham, "Oral History Project," 6.

11. Britt, "Following Her Heart," 8.

12. C. Thomson, "Making Pitch for Women," *Baltimore Sun*, June 22, 1999, 4.

13. Britt, "Following Her Heart," 8.

14. Cottingham, "Oral History Project," 9.

15. Riley, "Lady at the Bat," 22.

16. Britt, "Following Her Heart," 1.

17. *Base Runner*, newsletter of American Women's Baseball League (September 1999).

18. Thomson, "Making Pitch for Women."

19. Thomson, "Making Pitch for Women."

20. B. O'Neil, *I Was Right on Time* (New York: Fireside Books, 1996), 194.

21. O'Neil, *I Was Right on Time*, 194–95.

22. Britt, "Following Her Heart," 8.

23. Cottingham, "Oral History Project," 10.

24. Cottingham, "Oral History Project," 9.

Effa Manley

A Major Force in Negro Baseball in the 1930s and 1940s

Effa Manley, co-owner of the Newark Eagles, a Negro baseball team, was one of the most colorful and influential people in Negro baseball during the 1930s and 1940s. As one writer noted, "[n]o figure cast a larger shadow in Negro baseball in its late period than the amazing Effa Manley."[1] In the 1930s and 1940s women were second-class citizens and blacks had few, if any, rights. She managed to become a respected force, not only in the Negro Leagues, but also in the black civil rights movement.

Effa Manley's birth, as her life, was filled with controversy. Although people assumed she was a light-skinned black, she claimed that she was white. According to her, her mother was white, of German and (Asian) Indian descent. Effa claimed that her mother, who did sewing for wealthy white families, became pregnant by her white employer, John Marcus Bishop, a well-off Philadelphian. Her black stepfather, Mr. Brooks, sued Mr. Bishop for alienation of his wife's affections, and in an out-of-court settlement Mr. Bishop paid $10,000. Effa grew up in a black community and culturally always identified with blacks.[2] Within the black community, she rarely discussed her heritage. Most friends and acquaintances assumed she was black. One of her players described her "as a light-skinned black woman."[3] Effa's life became almost totally involved with baseball and civic affairs after she married Abe Manley, a successful numbers racketeer. Both were avid baseball fans, and both were to become an instrumental force in Negro baseball. Appropriately, they met at the 1932 World Series and were married the next June.[4]

Marriage to Abe changed Effa's life. His wealth enabled her to be part of Negro high society. As Effa bluntly put it, "I was a bastard and 75 years ago that was a terrible thing. . . . I was not accepted into the better circles of Negro society until I met Abe."[5] After marrying Abe she became a queen of Negro society and was very active in civic affairs and a crusader for Negro rights. In 1935, disturbed that stores in Harlem refused to hire black salesladies, Effa, with the Rev. Johnson, formed the Citizen's League for Fair Play. The group picketed stores along 125th Street with the slogan, "Don't shop where you can't work."[6] It took six weeks, but in the end, the owners relented, and a year later approximately three hundred Negroes were employed on 125th Street.[7]

"Stop Lynching"

As an activist for Negro rights, she often used Newark Eagles baseball games to promote special causes. According to writer Donn Rogosin, "probably the most remarkable special day in Negro baseball history" was when Effa Manley staged a "Stop Lynching" benefit in Ruppert Stadium. She was treasurer of the NAACP in New Jersey at the time and wanted to raise funds for what she considered one of the most important Negro issues. Her usherettes wore sashes that read "Stop Lynching" and went through the stadium collecting funds.[8]

During the Second World War, she did her part to support the war effort. A news photo shows her pinning an NAACP Crusade for Liberty button on the Deputy Mayor of Newark.[9] Another time, she invited the entire 372nd Regiment, a select black military unit, to a game as her guest.[10] She also paid for a bus to bring performers to Fort Dix to entertain the soldiers. As a member of a government gas-rationing committee, she heard hardship cases to decide whether or not a person should receive extra gas rations. She was also very proud of the fact that fifty-four Negro baseball players volunteered to serve during the Second World War.[11]

It was an interesting turn of historical events that provided her husband, Abe Manley, with the opportunity to become a Negro baseball magnate. In 1931, the Negro National League (NNL), which had been founded in 1920 by Rube Foster, dissolved. The Depression had taken its toll on gate receipts and by 1931 many teams had failed. A few teams continued to barnstorm, but organized black baseball was at an end. Negro baseball was in need of a large infusion of dollars and gambling money soon came to its aid. With most legitimate black businesses either destroyed or weakened by the Depression, the only people in the black community with large amounts of capital were the numbers-racket kings. To gain respectability and leadership in the black community, many became involved in legitimate businesses, charities, or civil rights activism.[12]

Gus Greenlee, policy (numbers) king of Pittsburgh's Hill district, saw baseball as his opportunity for gaining legitimacy. He spent $100,000 to build the first completely black-owned stadium in baseball and persuaded his friends in the numbers racket to help him establish the new, or second, Negro National Baseball League in 1933. Numbers bankers Abe Manley of Newark, Tom Wilson of Nashville, Ed "Soldier Boy" Semler of New York City, and Sonny "Man" Jackson of Homestead, New Jersey, joined him.[13]

Effa Manley's account of how the new league got started is a little different. She said that Greenlee helped to reorganize the NNL in 1933, but that this endeavor was unsuccessful. "Everything was run in a permissive, self-defeating, and entirely unorthodox manner."[14] She claimed that it was her husband, Abe, who completely reorganized the League and made it into a professional organization in 1935. "There were twelve Negro baseball teams, operating all over the country dependent entirely on booking agents. . . . (Abe) was interested enough to want to see them organized into a league. And he got five of the teams in the East to go along with him and set up the Negro National League on condition that he would operate a team out of Brooklyn."[15] Gus Greenlee was renamed president of the new organization and Abe Manley became treasurer.[16]

In an interview in 1977, Effa said that Abe's motive was that he had "retired from his real estate business. . . . So he was no doubt looking for something to do and this was something that just caught his fancy."[17] Effa laughed during the interview when she said that her husband was "retired from the real estate business," bud did not elaborate. In an earlier interview in 1975 with Henry Hecht of the *New York Post*, she was much more direct. Effa said, "Abe was a numbers banker in Camden and he came to New York when the Camden gangsters wanted to take over. They threw a bomb into a club he owned and the D. A., a personal friend of his, told him, 'Abe, you better get out of town.' "[18] Abe took his advice. In another interview in 1977 with Allen Richardson, a graduate student, she reflected back and then, as if thinking to herself, said, "I've often wondered if he (D. A.) was on Abe's payroll, because he bothered so."[19]

Abe was a wealthy, powerful man with an avid interest in Negro baseball, so owning a baseball team appealed to him. He had the money to invest in developing players and could afford the luxury of not always making a profit. As Effa said, "He went into it (baseball) head first with his mind made up to spend any amount of money he had to." Over the years he invested over $100,000 in the team. When he finally sold the team in 1947, according to Effa he got about 5 percent of his investment back.[20]

Olive Brown, sports editor of the *New Jersey Herald* in 1950, credited the Newark Eagles with having developed more Major League Negro stars than any other team.[21] And as Effa said, "Abe died feeling he had made a great contribution to Major League baseball."[22] Effa always gave credit to Abe for founding the Newark Eagles and for developing so many players. For whatever reason, she also felt it important to stress how honest he was. Maybe it was because Abe's bankroll came primarily from illegal numbers gambling. In her Chandler Oral History interview in 1977, she made a point of saying how everyone liked Abe and how Dan Burley, a black sports editor, nicknamed him "honest" Abe.[23]

Honesty may have been a relative term for Effa, however. Perhaps she considered her husband more honest than many other owners. At any rate, there is evidence that Abe bent the rules in order to have a winning team. In 1942 he signed a talented Paterson, New Jersey, Eastside High School senior, Larry Doby, to the Eagles' roster and paid him $300 a week to play until college started in the fall. Abe was right about Doby's talent; Doby later became the second black in modern Major League baseball when he signed with the Cleveland Indians. The only problem with his signing of Doby was that he listed him on the roster as Larry Walker from Los Angeles. The pseudonym was used to protect Doby's status as an amateur, so he could play in college. Of course, this was illegal.[24]

"Honest" Abe

Effa, as noted above, was always quick to point out Abe's honesty. Once she proclaimed that Abe "always paid his taxes." Donn Rogosin believes that she may have boasted too much about her husband's tax return. He says, "It seems probable, given the massive ignorance of white authorities about Negro baseball, that the numbers income was shielded as baseball profits. And of course, both baseball admissions and gambling receipts were almost always cash."[25]

But baseball was more than an investment for Abe. He enjoyed traveling on the road with his players and being a part of their lives. There was also status in owning a team. Baseball was an integral part of the black community and one of the few arenas for legitimate black achievement. When Abe got the franchise, Effa immediately assumed an active role as co-owner of the Eagles. She took over the day-to-day business operations of the club, so that Abe could concentrate on recruitment of players. As business manager, Effa made all the hotel and other arrangements for road trips, managed the company payroll, bought the team's equipment, and handled promotions and publicity. As Effa said, "(I) succeeded in setting up a system of public relations that eventually made the Newark Eagles one of the most talked-about teams in the country." [26] As co-owners, the two complemented each other and never had any substantive disagreements.

Abe apparently never did any actual scouting. Friends and acquaintances would tell him about a hot prospect. Abe would then take a look and decide whether or not to offer the player a contract. Supposedly, these tips came from people just doing him a favor. But when Abe died in 1952, Effa had second thoughts about the arrangement. She said, "I found an awful lot of notes where this one owed him so much. . . . So I tore them all up, because I knew I would never be able to collect them. . . . Whether that was the way he (Abe) paid them off, I don't know." [27] No doubt, Effa would have handled things in a more professional manner. As Jerry Izenberg, sports columnist for the *New York Post* has noted, "She ran an operation far more professional than some of her counterparts in the Major Leagues." [28] What is amazing is that Effa, prior to marrying Abe, had had no financial experience. After graduating from William Penn High School in Philadelphia, she had done millinery work. [29] But she was a born businesswoman.

She also knew how to get publicity. When Abe acquired the team, she immediately mailed out special invitations for the inaugural game to important officials and other dignitaries. She got Mayor La Guardia to throw out the first ball. Some of the other people who accepted her invitation were Charles C. Lockwood, justice of the court of appeals for the state of New York, Lowell Thomas, famous radio commentator, Jimmy Powers, sportswriter for the *New York Daily News*, and George W. Harris, editor-in-chief of the *Daily News*. [30] All in all there were 185 distinguished guests in the stands. [31] Unfortunately, only about 2,000 of the projected 10,000–15,000 fans showed up for the game and the Eagles lost to the Homestead Grays, 21–7. [32] Effa recalled, "I never saw so many home runs in my life. . . . I went home in the third inning and had my first drink of whiskey."[33] George Giles, the Eagles first baseman, remembers that opening day at Ebbets Field and how mad Effa Manley got when the team lost. "The Homestead Grays near killed us! . . . Mrs. Manley left. When she was displeased, the world came to an end. . . . Mrs. Manley didn't like a loser."[34] When the Eagles had a losing season that first year, she was instrumental in firing the old manager and having Abe appoint this same George Giles, the new first baseman, as manager. Giles said he was surprised when Abe came up to him and said, "My wife wants you to manage the ball club."[35]

One group she found she had little control over was the white press. She was disappointed when she realized that the white newspapers had a "freeze-out" policy in regard to writing about Negro baseball. Fortunately, the black newspapers gave full coverage and baseball for them was always a major event.[36]

Disappointment

The Eagles' first year of operation, in Brooklyn, was a disappointment. They were unable to compete with the Brooklyn Dodgers for fans. The Manleys decided that if they were to survive financially, they had to move the franchise. Abe negotiated with the owner of the Newark Dodgers, a black semi-pro team, and bought the franchise as well as the contract for Raymond Dandridge, a promising third baseman. In 1936, the team officially became the Newark Eagles.[37]

As was true of all Negro baseball teams, the Eagles played their games in leased stadiums that Major or Minor League clubs owned. In Brooklyn, the Eagles leased from the Dodger organization and, in Newark, they leased Ruppert Stadium from New York Yankees management. White professional baseball may have banned blacks from playing in their league, but they were not adverse to making a profit off them. The usual arrangement was that the Negro club paid a percentage of the gate – often 20 percent.[38]

In 1936, each team in the NNL was scheduled to play approximately fifty League games, in addition to as many exhibition games as they liked so long as the latter didn't conflict with regular League play. As Effa says, this sounded all right until one realized that teams could often make more money playing exhibition games against semi-pro teams.[39] Booking agents took full advantage of this fact. Not only did they book most exhibition games, but certain agents had exclusive rights with Major League organizations to schedule games in their stadiums. White booking agents such as Abe Saperstein (owner and organizer of the Harlem Globetrotters) and Eddie Gottlieb had a virtual monopoly on scheduling. They often charged Negro teams as much as 40 percent of gross gate receipts for their services. Because of these types of arrangements, Branch Rickey referred to the Negro Leagues as "rackets."[40]

Abe Manley was opposed to allowing these booking agents to control scheduling and tried to convince the NNL owners to do their own scheduling. It was a losing battle. Effa said, "[I]t was one time I disagreed with him, but not to any great extent. . . . I could see that it was going to cost us money."[41] And it did. The booking agents retaliated and failed to schedule the Eagles for the highly profitable Sunday and holiday games in the big cities.[42] Effa blamed the booking agents for the fact that the Eagles franchise was financially unsuccessful.[43]

Although Effa claimed in later years that she disagreed with her husband's protest against the booking agents, newspaper articles written at the time give a different perspective. An article in the *Afro-American* stated that in a "fiery speech," Effa sought the dismissal of Tom Wilson, the president of the NNL because of his approval of an agreement that gave Gottlieb, the booking agent, 10 percent on promotion of League games in Yankee Stadium.[44]

Effa was noted for taking an active part in all League meetings. Believing in her own convictions, there were times when she gave unsolicited, and often unappreciated, advice to other owners. Dan Burley, sports editor for the *Amersterdam News*, wrote, "Effa Manley has long been a sore spot in the NNL setup . . . the rough and tumble gentlemen comprising its inner sanctum have complained often and loudly that 'baseball ain't no place for no woman.' "[45] Although the other owners may have complained, they respected her financial judgment. Effa handled all the finances of the NNL even though Abe was the official treasurer.[46]

In matters of League policy, business affairs, or issues of civil rights, she was respected. When, however, it came to day-to-day operation of the team, she often was considered a nuisance by the team's managers. Two Newark managers, Willie Wells and Biz Mackey, said they had difficulty working with her.[47] One favorite story about her meddling ways is the time she supposedly sent a message down to the Eagles' manager to pitch Terris McDuffie, her favorite pitcher. She wanted her girlfriends to see how handsome he was.[48] Another story, which may be exaggerated, is that of how Willie Wells, who played in addition to managing, came to be knocked unconscious. Bill Byrd, the Baltimore Elite Giants pitcher, beaned him when the latter was looking up at Effa Manley to get her signal as to where to hit; he failed to see the pitch and got hit in the head.[49]

Effa Manley believed that she was instrumental in developing players' careers. Most players would have agreed. For example, George Giles, who joined the Eagles in 1935, remembered how she told everyone that he was a great first baseman. He said, "I got some pretty good write-ups there – Dan Parker in the *American*, Ed Sullivan . . . in the *News*. Just through her."[50]

The very first season of play in 1935, worried about what her players would do in the off-season for employment, Effa arranged for a man in Puerto Rico to sponsor a winter team. With Vic Harris, who managed the Homestead Grays, she assembled a team composed of both Eagles and Grays to play under the Brooklyn Eagles' name. As she said, "Puerto Rico accepted them with open arms, put them right in their league."[51] The team did their part and won the pennant. As Effa recalled after sending the first team down to Puerto Rico, "from then on a boy that we'd been giving five hundred dollars a month [to] could go down there and get a thousand."[52] In later years, this became a mixed blessing. Latin American countries ended up raiding some of the best players from the Negro League during the regular season. Although there is no doubt that Effa was mad about Mexico, the Dominican Republic, and other countries stealing her best players, she never blamed the players for leaving.

The Family

The Manleys treated their boys as family. As Effa said, "We did favors and tried to help when any of the boys needs us. . . . The thing that Abe was proudest of is the fact that most of our boys made good."[53] Larry Doby, for example, felt so close to the Manleys that he asked them to be the godparents of his first child.[54] Monte Irvin, short of cash for a down payment on a house, borrowed two or three thousand dollars.[55] Lenny Pearson, who became a Newark tavern owner after leaving the Eagles, recalled, "After I quit playing, she started me out in business. She interceded for me and spoke to people and helped me. She financed the first tavern I ever had. A beautiful, beautiful person in all ways."[56]

She was, however, also noted for having favorites. Players who weren't on her favored list often feared her. Johnny Davis, an outfielder and pitcher for the Eagles in the 1940s, recalled that he wasn't one of her favorites. "I stayed as far away from that woman as I could. When she had a meeting, I stayed in the back of the room."[57] He also recalled how she would reprimand a player if he did something she didn't like. "[S]he had an apartment house in Crawford Street, and she'd get you down there and, boy, she'd blast you. Maybe you didn't have clean white socks on your uniform, or you looked sloppy on the field, or your shirt was torn."[58] As Max Manning, an Eagles pitcher recalled, "Abe . . . mostly stayed in the background. . . . Effa . . . ruled the roost."[59] There was no doubt that Mrs. Manley was the boss, and a mixture of fear and team pride probably kept many players in line. As Johnny Davis said, "When I first started playing baseball, you needed drugs to stay awake! But we never thought about drugs or anything. We were Mrs. Manley's boys."[60] Indeed, her assertive manner may have been instrumental in averting a threatened player's strike at the annual East-West Game. She proclaimed to the strike committee that "no Newark Eagle was gonna strike, period."[61]

Effa may have kept the players in line, but it was Abe who decided which players to purchase. In 1938, he bought Satchel Paige from Gus Greenlee, owner of the Crawfords. According to Effa, Abe paid $5,000 for Satchel and, to the best of her knowledge, this was the only time in the history of the Negro League that money was paid for a player.[62] According to Donn Rogosin, the sale price was closer to two or three thousand dollars, which Rogosin considered a bargain-basement price for the most famous personality in Negro baseball.[63] Regardless of what the price was, it was too much because Paige left to play in Mexico and Abe never got his money back. Effa claims that Satchel wrote and said he'd play for the Eagles if she'd be his girlfriend. She never responded.[64]

The 1930s and early 1940s were difficult times for Negro baseball. Most teams were underfinanced, overextended, and operated in the red.[65] The Second World War, however, changed all this. During the war years attendance reached all-time highs. In 1944, attendance at Negro baseball's East-West Game was 46,247, while the Major Leagues' All-Star Game was only 29,589.[66] By the end of the war, Negro baseball was a $2,000,000 enterprise and represented one of the largest black dominated businesses in the United States.[67] Edsall Walker, former pitcher for the Homestead Grays and the Philadelphia Stars, believed that the Major Leagues became integrated after the war because black baseball outdrew white baseball. "If it weren't for the Negro leagues the Major Leagues would have folded. We were outdrawing them."[68]

There is a sad irony to this period. The combination of Negro base-ball's success and the patriotic spirit of black military units led to the integration of the Major Leagues. But it also sounded the death knell for Negro baseball. The issue of integration of the Major Leagues had been raised before the war, but it was a divisive issue. It took the war to change people's minds. In 1939, Shirley Povich of the *Washington Post* had said, "There's a couple of million dollars worth of baseball talent on the loose, ready for the big leagues, yet unsigned by any Major League clubs. . . . Only one thing is keeping them out of the big leagues – the pigmentation of their skin. . . . That's their crime in the eyes of big league club owners."[69]

Others, such as Ted Shane in a *Saturday Evening Post* article of July 27, 1940, derided Negro baseball. "[T]heir (Negro League) baseball is to white baseball as the Harlem Stomp is to the sedate ballroom waltz. . . . [T]hey play faster . . . clown a lot, go into dance steps, argue noisily and funnily."[70]

In 1942, a CIO union delegation called upon Commissioner Kenesaw Mountain Landis to integrate Major League baseball and the New York state legislature passed the Quinn-Ives Act, which banned discrimina-tion in hiring.[71] An editorial in the *Sporting News* of August 6, 1942, claimed that both blacks and whites preferred separate leagues.[72] Amer-ican League President Larry McPhail predicted the failure of the Negro Leagues if Major League baseball was integrated.[73]

Citizens Committee to Get Negroes into the Big Leagues

Motivated by McPhail's statement a Citizens Committee to Get Negroes into the Big Leagues was formed with the aid of the black press. Effa Manley, as a member of that committee, responded to McPhail in the *New York Daily Worker* by saying that "the Majors draft dozens of players from the Minors every season, but do those leagues fold up? Certainly not. In fact it improves them, because many hundreds of new stars take up the game, and interest generally is heightened by the addition of new talent."[74] Effa contended that, rather than Negro baseball owners blocking integration, they were on the contrary all supporting "the fight to end Jim Crow in the Majors." The allegation that owners wouldn't sell players to the Majors was, she said, "without a doubt the most stupid thing I have ever heard."[75]

After the war, integration of baseball became a major issue. The rallying cry became, "If he's good enough for the navy, he's good enough for the Majors."[76] And in 1946 the color line was broken when Branch Rickey signed Jackie Robinson to play for Montreal, a Triple A International League team.[77] Ironically, it was not until July 1948 that President Truman, by Executive Order 9981, provided for the integration of the armed services.[78] Baseball had taken the prior step toward integration.

Although integration of the Major Leagues would soon lead to the demise of the Negro Leagues, 1946 was the best year for the Newark Eagles. They beat the Kansas City Monarchs in the seven-game Negro League World Series. The team was superb and two players stood out – Larry Doby and Monte Irvin. In the final game, they scored the tying and winning runs for a 3–2 victory.[79] Both would later join the Major Leagues.

The Beginning of the End

The turning point for Negro baseball was near. In 1947 Jackie Robinson became a Brooklyn Dodger. There were sixteen black ballplayers now in organized baseball. Half of them were on Minor League Dodger teams.[80] Black fans in massive numbers began to abandon Negro baseball to see Jackie Robinson and other newly acquired blacks play. Attendance at Newark Eagle games plummeted from 120,000 fans in 1946 to 57,000 in 1947 to 35,000 in 1948, the last year of operation.[81] Yet when Effa Manley spoke out against black fans deserting black baseball, the press crucified her. They said, "The day of loyalty to Jim Crow anything is fast passing away. Sister, haven't you heard the news? Democracy is a-coming fast."[82]

Effa claims that prior to Rickey signing Jackie Robinson, she had gone to Washington DC to attend a meeting of the Minor Leagues and met with their president, George M. "Red" Trautman, to see if Negro baseball couldn't become a farm system. She got "exactly nowhere with Trautman."[83] If this had worked, she felt the Negro Leagues could have subsisted as a farm system for a long time.

When Rickey signed Jackie Robinson in 1946, the black press was ecstatic. At long last a black was going to play white professional baseball. The NAACP announced that the signing was "the most visible sign of change" in race relations.[84] After signing Robinson, Branch Rickey continued with his plan to integrate the Dodgers organization by recruiting

Don Newcombe and Roy Campanella. Rickey, who had been criticized for not compensating Bill Baird, co-owner of the Kansas City Monarchs, had his aides ask both Newcombe and Campanella whether they were currently under contract to any Negro team to avoid further conflict with the Negro Leagues. Don Newcombe wrote, "I am not under contract for my baseball services for any future time" and Roy Campanella denied that he was under contract with the Baltimore Elite Giants for 1946.[85] The owners of the Baltimore Elite Giants and the Newark Eagles felt differently, however. The Baltimore Elite Giants decided to let the issue pass, but Effa Manley acted. She wrote a number of letters to Rickey asking him to meet with her about his taking Don Newcombe from the Eagles. Rickey didn't reply.[86]

Although Effa was livid, she was smart enough to realize that there wasn't much that she could do. As she later recounted, "(Rickey) didn't give us five cents or say thank you. . . . And we couldn't protest. The fans would never have forgiven us. Plus it would have been wrong to have prevented them (Newcombe and Campanella) from going to the Majors."[87]

The Larry Doby Purchase

In 1947, Bill Veeck of the Cleveland Indians called Effa Manley. He said that he was interested in buying Larry Doby (12 years; .283 BA, 253 HR, 969 RBIS) from the Eagles and wanted to know what price they wanted for him. Effa replied, "Well, Mr. Veeck, if Larry has a chance to play for your club, I certainly won't stand in his way." Veeck said he'd pay $10,000. Effa, always a negotiator, immediately responded, "Mr. Veeck, you know if Larry Doby were white and a free agent, you'd give him $100,000 to sign with you merely as a bonus." Veeck then made a deal. He said that if Doby stayed with the organization over thirty days that he would give the Manleys another $5,000.[88] Larry Doby became the first black player in the American League.[89]

According to Effa this was the first time that anyone in the Major Leagues had compensated a team in the NNL or NAL for a player.[90] Effa had established a precedent and after that Major League owners paid on average about $5,000 for a player taken from the Negro Leagues.[91]

With the best players being drafted by the Majors and black fans deserting the Negro teams, the latter could no longer show a profit. In 1947, the Eagles had a loss of $20,000 and the Manleys sold the team to Dr. Young, a black doctor in Memphis, Tennessee. The stipulation was that he owned the contracts of the players.[92] Shortly after the sale, Effa read in the *Newark Evening News* that Branch Rickey had signed Monte Irvin to his St. Paul Minor League team. Irvin was one of the players whose contract she had sold to Young. She immediately wrote Irvin in Cuba where he was playing winter ball to verify the story.[93] Monte Irvin wrote back that he had signed with the Brooklyn Dodgers to play in St. Paul. He wrote: "I read in the paper that you had sold the team so there was not any hesitancy on my part, since I don't have too many years left to play. I sincerely hope that I did the right thing."[94]

Effa then hired Jerry Kessler, a lawyer, to contact Branch Rickey and say that Irvin was under contract to the Eagles. Rickey immediately called the Irvin deal off. The Negro press jumped all over her for destroying Irvin's chances.[95] Effa went to work to try to find another team for Irvin. She contacted the Yankees with no luck and then hit pay dirt with the Giants. They gave here $5,000 for Irvin. But Effa still wasn't happy. She said, "They paid me $5,000 lousy dollars for Monte Irvin. If he'd been white they'd have given me $100,000. . . . But I was glad to get it."[96] Of the $5,000, half went for Kessler's fee and the other half was equally divided between the Manleys and Dr. Young. Effa purchased a mink cape with their share. In her book (1976), she wrote: "I still have this cape in my possession, and occasionally I get it out and look at it. . . . It serves to remind me of yet another bit of baseball history in which I have been privileged to play a small role!"[97]

Twenty-five years later, when Monte saw her wearing it, he quipped, "You got a good deal on it." She responded, "Not as good as Horace." She was referring to Horace Stoneham, the Giants owner who paid her the $5,000.[98] Effa Manley, businesswoman to the end, believed that she had a right to collect on her player investments.

Effa Manley versus Jackie Robinson

Effa Manley defended Negro baseball against what she believed were slights or injustices. When Jackie Robinson authored an article in *Ebony* in 1948, "What's Wrong with Negro Baseball?" she was incensed. She immediately sent a letter to Jackie and countered with an article in *Our World*. To challenge the opinions of a black national hero took courage. None of the other owners of Negro baseball teams spoke out, but they appreciated Effa's outspokenness and wrote thanking her for setting Robinson straight.[99]

In her article, she blasted both Robinson and Major League Baseball. She said, "Major League tactics are ruining Negro baseball" and "some people are knifing it in the back. The most outrageous attack came from Jackie Robinson's widely publicized article in a national magazine. No greater ingratitude was ever displayed." After all, according to Effa, Jackie owed his opportunity to play for the Dodgers to Negro baseball.[100]

Jackie, for his part, had attacked every aspect of Negro baseball. He said, "the bad points range all the way from the low salaries paid players and sloppy umpiring to the questionable business connections of many of the team owners."[101] Among the problems he noted were owners' indifference to the welfare of their players' poor road accommodations, which ranged from uncomfortable buses to cheap hotels.[102] In her reply Effa suggested that perhaps Jackie Robinson had been used by the Major Leagues. She said, "I wonder if he's speaking his own mind or if his statement was for a purpose even he does not understand."[103] She further explained how most of the problems that Jackie cited were due to segregation and discrimination in American society and not the fault of Negro baseball. She blamed Jim Crow laws for the poor hotel accommodations available to blacks. She said, "Until Congress makes statutory changes about race prejudice in hotels, I'm afraid there's very little that we can do to better such accommodation."[104]

She also challenged the idea that Negro ballplayers were underpaid when the average player made a $100 a week. The average American worker in 1945 only made $44.39 a week.[105] Further, since most of the teams operated in the red, she felt the owners were particularly generous.[106] She then attacked the Major League owners for taking players from the Negro Leagues without compensation. She also attacked the press, both white and black, for treating Negro baseball as "the step-child of American sport."[107] She appealed to Negro fans to support their black teams and not to abandon them for white integrated teams. She said, "Gullible Negro fans who think white owners take on colored players through any altruistic pangs of democracy had better quit kidding themselves. There's a potential of two million Negro fans to draw from."[108]

Effa's attack on the fans and the press brought about an immediate reaction from the black press. John Johnson, sports editor of the *Kansas City Call*, a black newspaper, described her as "more or less widely known for her rather violent distaste toward Branch Rickey, for her fault-finding with the Negro press, and for her condemnation of Negro fans under the impolite term 'desertion of the colored game for mixed baseball.'" He disagreed with her that the fans were disloyal. After all, there would have been no Negro Leagues without fan support. What Effa saw as disloyalty, Johnson saw as progress. He said, "[The Negro fan] is going to see Robinson and Campanella and Doby and Paige play [in] the Majors. . . . He sees the best there is in the National Pastime. . . . This is democracy in sports; . . . it is something only the reactionaries would condemn." He then strongly urged Negro owners to "see sports not as Negro sports or white sports, but American sports."[109]

Ultimately Effa's appeal to the fans, the press, and Major League Baseball to keep Negro baseball alive fell on deaf ears. The Eagles folded in 1948 and so did two other teams in the NNL. The other three teams migrated to the Western League.[110]

The era of black baseball was coming to an end. The NNL had disbanded in 1948 and the NAL had only four teams by 1953, down from ten teams in 1949.[111] A few teams, however, were able to hang on financially by becoming unofficial farm clubs for the Major Leagues. The American Giants had a close relationship with the St. Louis Browns and the Monarchs with the New York Yankees.[112]

A combination of integration of the Major Leagues and changing American leisure patterns had taken their toll. Competing forms of entertainment, such as movies, travel, and other professional sports, predominantly basketball and football, had cut into spectatorship. With the invention of television, fans no longer had to travel to games. Major League games were brought into their living rooms. But it wasn't just Negro baseball that suffered. The All-American Girls Professional Baseball League folded in 1954, and many white Minor League professional baseball teams also went out of business. After the war, attendance at Minor League games declined from 42 million to 15.5 million. They were all causalities of changing times.[113]

Although it was sad to see Negro baseball disappear from the American scene, it was a victory for American society. It meant that black baseball players were no longer going to be second-class athletes, but rather were going to take their rightful place among white players. Integration of Major League Baseball paved the way for integration in other sports.

Effa Manley, until her death in 1981 at age eighty-one, devoted herself to keeping the history of Negro baseball alive and to gaining recognition for many of its ballplayers. Her *Negro Baseball . . . Before Integration,* written with Leon Hartwick, a professional writer, was published in 1976. She wrote numerous letters to both the National Baseball Hall of Fame and to the *Sporting News*, trying to get recognition for the Negro Baseball Leagues and the players. When the Hall of Fame finally recognized eleven players of the Negro Leagues, she was delighted, but she thought that many more players should have been chosen. She begged the Hall of Fame to admit others. She said that if it wasn't possible to enshrine others, a plaque listing the names of the great Negro players should be installed and a Negro section be established.[114] Her requests were denied.

In 1985, four years after Effa's death, the Hall of Fame added an exhibit on black ball. Effa's picture is prominently displayed in that exhibit, though she would doubtless be disappointedto learn that her name is not included among the women owners in the "Women of Baseball" exhibit that was added in 1988. According to the curator, William Spencer Jr., the reason for her omission from the exhibit is that it would be redundant to list her name in both exhibits.

NOTES

1. D. Rogosin, *Invisible Men: Life in Baseball's Negro Leagues* (New York: Atheneum, 1983), 108.

2. Effa Manley, interview by Bill Marshall, October 19, 1977, A. B. Chandler Oral History Project, University of Kentucky Library, Lexington, Kentucky.

3. Rogosin, *Invisible Men*, 109.

4. J. B. Holway, *Voices from the Great Black Baseball Leagues* (New York: Dodd Mead, 1975), 319.

5. H. Hecht, "Woman with a Mission," *New York Post*, September 15, 1975.

6. D. Rogosin, "Queen of the Negro Leagues," *Sportscape* (Summer 1981): 18.

7. "Prominent Women," newspaper article, June 20, 1936 (NBHFL).

8. Rogosin, *Invisible Men*, 94.

9. News photo, NBHFL.

10. Rogosin, *Invisible Men*, 94.

11. Effa Manley, interview by Bill Marshall.

12. J. Bruce, *The Kansas City Monarchs: Champions of Black Baseball* (Lawrence: University Press of Kansas, 1985), 83.

13. A. Ashe Jr. *A Hard Road to Glory: The History of the African American Athlete 1919–1945*, Vol. 2 (New York: Warner Books, 1988), 33.

14. Effa Manley and Leon Hardwick, *Negro Baseball . . . Before Integration* (Chicago: Adam Press, 1976), 41.

15. Effa Manley, interview by Bill Marshall.

16. Manley and Hardwick, *Negro Baseball . . . Before Integration*, 42.

17. Effa Manley, interview by Bill Marshall.

18. Hecht, "Woman with a Mission."

19. A. Richardson, "A Retrospective Look at the Negro Leagues and the Professional Negro Baseball Players" (MA Thesis, San Jose State University, 1980), 158.

20. Effa Manley, interview by Bill Marshall.

21. Manley and Hardwick, *Negro Baseball . . . Before Integration*, 97.

22. Holway, *Voices*, 325.

23. Effa Manley, interview by Bill Marshall.

24. J. Moore, *Pride Against Prejudice: The Biography of Larry Doby* (New York: Praeger, 1988), 10–20.

25. Rogosin, *Invisible Men*, 107.

26. Manley and Hardwick, *Negro Baseball . . . Before Integration*, 51.

27. Richardson, "A Retrospective Look," 177.

28. J. Izenberg, "Black Baseball Had Its Pride and Pros," *New York Post*, February 21, 1989.

29. Effa Manley, interview by Bill Marshall.

30. Manley and Hardwick, *Negro Baseball . . . Before Integration*, 43–44.

31. Holway, *Voices*, 319.

32. Manley and Hardwick, *Negro Baseball . . . Before Integration*, 44.

33. Holway, *Voices*, 320.

34. J. B. Holway, *Black Diamonds: Life in the Negro Leagues from the Men Who Lived It* (Westport CT: Meckler Books, 1989), 65–66.

35. Quoted in Holway, *Black Diamonds*, 66.

36. Manley and Hardwick, *Negro Baseball . . . Before Integration*, 44, 46.

37. Manley and Hardwick, *Negro Baseball . . . Before Integration*, 47.

38. Holway, *Voices*, 320.

39. Manley and Hardwick, *Negro Baseball . . . Before Integration*, 44–46.

40. J. Tygiel, *Baseball's Great Experiment: Jackie Robinson and His Legacy* (New York: Vintage Books, 1984), 23.

41. Effa Manley, interview by Bill Marshall.

42. Manley and Hardwick, *Negro Baseball . . . Before Integration*, 50.

43. Effa Manley, interview by Bill Marshall.

44. A. Carter, "Split Looms in BasBorica, Metro Clubs Try to Oust Tom Wilson," *Afro-American*, February 10, 1940.

45. D. Burley, "Dan Burley's Confidentially Yours," *Amsterdam News*, February 21, 1942.

46. Manley and Hardwick, *Negro Baseball . . . Before Integration*, 54.

47. Rogosin, *Invisible Men*, 109.

48. Rogosin, *Invisible Men*, 109; R. Peterson, *Only the Ball Was White: A History of Legendary Black Players and All-Black Professional Teams before Black Men Played in the Major Leagues* (Englewood Cliffs NJ: Prentice Hall, 1970), 137.

49. Rogosin, *Invisible Men*, 74.

50. Holway, *Black Diamonds*, 66.

51. Effa Manley, interview by Bill Marshall.

52. Effa Manley, interview by Bill Marshall.

53. Holway, *Voices*, 326.

54. S. Hoskins, "Abe Manley, Baseball Founder Buried," *Afro-American*, December 20, 1952.

55. Holway, *Voices*, 326.

56. Holway, *Voices*, 326.

57. Holway, *Black Diamonds*, 162.

58. Holway, *Black Diamonds*, 162.

59. Holway, *Black Diamonds*, 124.

60. Holway, *Black Diamonds*, 124.

61. Rogosin, *Invisible Men*, 110.

62. Effa Manley, interview by Bill Marshall.

63. Rogosin, *Invisible Men*, 137.

64. E. Manley, "Negro Baseball Isn't Dead! But It Is Pretty Sick," *Our World*, August 1948, 27–29.

65. Tygiel, *Baseball's Great Experiment*, 23.

66. Ashe, *A Hard Road to Glory*, 2:39.

67. Tygiel, *Baseball's Great Experiment*, 24.

68. Quoted in C. Smith, "Rejoicing, Urgently, For Times Long Gone," *New York Times*, August 12, 1991.

69. S. Povich, "This Morning," *Washington Post*, August 7, 1939.

70. Quoted in Ashe, *A Hard Road to Glory*, 2:37.

71. Tygiel, *Baseball's Great Experiment*, 38.

72. Tygiel, *Baseball's Great Experiment*, 38–39.

73. Ashe, *A Hard Road to Glory*, 2:38.

74. N. Low, "Would Negroes in the Majors Hurt Negro Baseball? Certainly Not, It Would Help, Says Negro Club Owner," *Daily Worker*, August 13, 1942.

75. Low, "Would Negroes . . . ?"

76. Quoted in Bruce, *Kansas City Monarchs*, 98.

77. A. Rust Jr. *"Get That Nigger Off the Field!"* (New York: Delacorte Press, 1976), 67.

78. N. Wynn, *The Afro-American and the Second World War* (London: Paul Elek, 1976), 119.

79. Rogosin, *Invisible Men*, 19.

80. Rust, *"Get That Nigger Off The Field!"*, 63.

81. Bruce, *Kansas City Monarchs*, 116.

82. Bruce, *Kansas City Monarchs*, 116.

83. Richardson, "A Retrospective Look," 167.

84. Bruce, *Kansas City Monarchs*, 114.

85. M. Polner, *Branch Rickey: A Biography* (New York: Atheneum, 1982), 175.

86. Tygiel, *Baseball's Great Experiment*, 87.

87. Effa Manley, interview by Bill Marshall.

88. Manley and Hardwick, *Negro Baseball . . . Before Integration*, 74–76.

89. E. Rust and A. Rust Jr., *Art Rust's Illustrated History of the Black Athlete* (Garden City NY: Doubleday and Co., 1985), 64.

90. Manley and Hardwick, *Negro Baseball . . . Before Integration*, 79.

91. Holway, *Voices*, 325.

92. Effa Manley, interview by Bill Marshall.

93. Manley and Hardwick, *Negro Baseball . . . Before Integration*, 89–90.

94. Manley and Hardwick, *Negro Baseball . . . Before Integration*, 89–90.

95. S. Williford, "Black Woman Owner of Newark Eagles, Negro Baseball Team, Mrs. Effa Manley: She Owned the Greats," *Los Angeles Sentinel*, April 19, 1973.

96. Quoted in Rogosin, *Invisible Men*, 216–17.

97. Manley and Hardwick, *Negro Baseball . . . Before Integration*, 92.

98. J. Izenberg, "Black Baseball Had Its Pride and Pros," *New York Post*, February 21, 1989.

99. Holway, *Voices*, 322.

100. Manley, "Negro Baseball Isn't Dead!", 27.

101. J. Robinson, "What's Wrong with Negro Baseball?" *Ebony*, June 1948, 16.

102. Robinson, "What's Wrong . . . ?", 17–18.

103. Manley, "Negro Baseball Isn't Dead!", 27.

104. Manley, "Negro Baseball Isn't Dead!", 27.

105. Wynn, *Afro-American and the Second World War*, 27.

106. Wynn, *Afro-American and the Second World War*, 27.

107. Manley, "Negro Baseball Isn't Dead!", 28.

108. Manley, "Negro Baseball Isn't Dead!", 28.

109. J. Johnson, "Sport Light: Crying for a Lost Cause," *Kansas City Call*, June 24, 1949.

110. Effa Manley, interview by Bill Marshall.

111. Bruce, *Kansas City Monarchs*, 120.

112. Bruce, *Kansas City Monarchs*, 119.

113. Bruce, *Kansas City Monarchs*, 118.

114. Richardson, "A Retrospective Look," 178.

WILLIAM C. KASHATUS

Dick Allen, the Phillies, and Racism

FROM THE DAYS of the Negro Leagues up to the present battles over merit-based excuses for the absence of blacks in management positions, baseball has long served as a barometer of the nation's racial climate. Nowhere is this more true than in Philadelphia, where the Phillies have suffered for their reputation as a racially segregated team in a racially segregated city. The case of Dick Allen is most often cited as the prime example of this inglorious history of race relations.

Allen, the first African-American superstar to don the red pinstripes, was at the center of controversy in the 1960s and mid-1970s when he played in Philadelphia. He exploded onto the scene in 1964, winning the NL Rookie of the Year Award for his .318 average, 29 homers, and 94 RBIS. It was a performance that kept the Phillies in the pennant race for most of the summer until their infamous collapse in the final two weeks of the season. Over the next seven years Allen established himself among the ranks of the game's superstars, becoming a consistent .300 hitter and averaging 30 homers and 90 RBIS a season. Those statistics, along with a 1972 MVP performance with the Chicago White Sox, earned him a hero's welcome when Allen returned to Philadelphia in 1975. Phillies management and the fans were convinced that his time away from the city had given him the maturity and experience needed to win the pennant for a budding contender. They were wrong.

While Allen's tape-measure home runs and exceptional speed gained for him the tremendous admiration of fellow players, his unexcused absences, candid opinions, and pregame beer drinking earned him some of the harshest press in the city's sports history. Through it all the specter of racial prejudice hung over Allen's relationship with the owners, the team, the press, and the city's fans. For some he was the quintessential rebel who did as he pleased when he pleased, with little regard for team rules or his teammates. For others he exemplified the emerging independence of Major League players as well as growing black consciousness in the game.

The controversy has made Dick Allen the greatest player not enshrined in the National Baseball Hall of Fame. Although he became eligible in 1982, his candidacy has been tainted by the scathing opinions of baseball writers like Bill James, who claims that Allen "used racism as an explosive to blow his own teams apart." James specifically cites Allen's 1965 fight with Frank Thomas, a popular white veteran who was subsequently traded, and the slugger's threat not to play in the 1976 postseason if the Phillies didn't make room on the roster for Tony Taylor, an aging Hispanic player, as examples of Allen's manipulative nature. James dismisses Allen's eligibility for the Hall on the grounds that he "did more to keep his teams from winning than anybody else who ever played Major League Baseball."[1]

This essay argues that Dick Allen was both a victim and a manipulator of racism on a team that had a poor history of race relations, but a team that was making an earnest effort to distance itself from that inglorious reputation during the 1960s. The tragedy of Dick Allen's relationship with the Philadelphia Phillies is that there always existed a fundamental level of distrust between the two that inevitably expressed itself – sometimes willingly, at other times quite unwittingly – in racial terms. That distrust has cost Allen a place in the Hall of Fame and the Phillies the opportunity to acquit themselves of an infamous reputation as a racist organization.

Defining Racism

At the root of the Allen controversy is a basic misunderstanding of racism. Too often society confuses racism with prejudice. Racial prejudice refers to individual beliefs and attitudes that frequently manifest themselves in psychologically or physically abusive actions toward people of color. Racism, on the other hand, cannot be fully explained as an expression of prejudice alone. It is a much broader cultural phenomenon, encompassing institutions as well as individuals and specific groups of people. David Wellman offers the most useful definition of racism as a "system of advantage based on race."[2] This definition suggests that racism is a form of oppression that involves cultural messages and institutional policies and practices, as well as the beliefs and actions of individuals.

To be sure, whites are uncomfortable with such a systematic definition because it contradicts traditional notions of American meritocracy, individual enterprise, and the mainstream belief that "success comes to those who earn it." It is easier to think of racism as a particular form of prejudice because notions of power or privilege can then quickly be dismissed. Too often this has been the case in Major League Baseball, where "color blindness" has become the convenient excuse for not promoting blacks, whether it be in the ranks of the players or in management.[3] Perhaps more unsettling for whites is that this definition exonerates people of color from the charge of racism, simply because they do not systematically benefit from it. In other words, people of color can and do have racial prejudices. Because of their minority status, however, they cannot benefit from institutional or cultural practices that favor whites, who intentionally or unintentionally benefit from racism.[4]

African-Americans struggle to establish an identity in a white mainstream society because of the racism inherent in it. The process of resolving the dilemma is especially difficult during late adolescence and early adulthood, when the individual is starting out on a career path and is forced to confront institutional policies that are racist. According to William Cross there are various stages of racial-identity development that unfold at this time, which include: encountering racism for the first time; immersion in a racist environment, where the individual begins to grapple with what it means to be a member of a group adversely affected by racism; internalizing those cues as well as stereotypes from a white world that reflect one's blackness back upon one; and internalization-commitment, in which the individual comes to terms with his or her own identity as a member of the African-American race.[5]

Each individual's experience with and resolution of this process is unique to his or her own circumstances. In Dick Allen's case the process resulted in the adoption of an oppositional identity. Initially he was the victim of racial prejudice, but as his career unfolded in Philadelphia he began to internalize the negative treatment he received from the fans and the media. By 1968 he had come to terms with an oppositional identity as a "rebel," and manipulated racism in order to get traded. In the process he only served to reinforce the negative stereotype that the fans and media had imposed on him in the first place.

Consciously at times, and unwittingly at others, the Phillies management indulged Allen and his personal irresponsibility because of his tremendous talent as well as their desire to distance themselves from a poor history of race relations. In fact, their handling of Allen reflected a double standard in which racism worked to his advantage. The fact that this exceptionally talented player was African American at a time when the Phillies were making a purposeful attempt to integrate seemed to re-inforce the front office's feeling that he was entitled to special treatment. Allen came to discover and exploit that feeling, first in the 1960s and later when he returned to Philadelphia in the mid-1970s.

Ultimately, both Dick Allen and the Phillies suffered from the consequences of their mutual distrust and actions.

Philadelphia in the 1960s

The Philadelphia Phillies' reputation as a racially segregated team in a racially segregated city is not without merit. During Jackie Robinson's quest to break the color barrier in 1947, the Phillies front office actually phoned Brooklyn Dodgers' president Branch Rickey before the two teams met and told him "not to bring that nigger here." Predictably, the Phillies treated Robinson the worst of any player in the NL whenever he appeared in Philadelphia. Pitchers threw at his head, infielders purposely spiked him on the base paths, and – in one of the lowest moments in baseball history – the team humiliated Robinson by standing on the steps of their dugout, pointing their bats at him and making gunshot sounds.[6] The Phillies were also the last team in the NL to integrate. They did not field a black player until 1957, when John Kennedy appeared in five games for the Phils at third base – a full decade after Robinson broke the color barrier. Even then the Phillies maintained segregated spring training facilities, a practice that was finally abandoned in 1962.[7] Like their baseball team, the city was also struggling with the issue of racism.

During the 1960s Philadelphia was experiencing middle-class "white flight" to the suburbs. Whites were escaping the crime, drugs, and gang warfare of north and west Philadelphia where the black population had relocated from the old-time ghettos. While whites made their new homes in the outlying suburbs of Merion, Abington, Haverford, Malvern, Swarthmore, and Bucks County, poor blacks who migrated from the rural South and other low-salaried city dwellers came to dominate the city's diminishing tax base. As expenses increased the city was forced to make decisions on questions of education, employment, and public welfare for which it was ill prepared. The "race factor" often became a rhetorical device for greater state and federal funding to meet those needs. In fact, the hope of the future for the city lay with upwardly mobile black families whose wage earners were employed in banks, insurance companies, law offices, and government agencies and who lived in sections of the city like Germantown, Mount Airy, Queen Village, and Fairmount.[8] But it was still a struggle for them.

Democrat James Tate, who favored the white working class and distanced himself from the downtown business and liberal communities, was mayor. His tenure was riddled by a succession of scandals and political quarrels. Charges of zoning concessions, extortion, and conflict of interest brought a series of resignations in high places. Pressing social concerns were largely ignored while a rising protest movement that was focused on civil rights for blacks erupted on the city's streets. Together with Philadelphia's rising crime rate, black protest accelerated white flight to the suburbs. To his credit Tate realized that the widespread unrest was fueled by both idealism as well as resentment, and he responded with a two-pronged approach.

To stem the tide of protest he appointed Charles Bowser, a young black lawyer, to head the Anti-Poverty Action Committee, an organization inspired by the federal government's War on Poverty. The appointment curried favor with the black community as Bowser worked hard to insure local community participation on public welfare issues. To address the pressing need for crime control, Tate appointed Frank Rizzo as police commissioner. Unfortunately, Rizzo's streetwise, shoot-from-the-hip, tough-cop style became synonymous with the public's image of Philadelphia – and it wasn't a good one. He antagonized the black community with his outspoken comments on race, voicing sentiments previously unspeakable among responsible public officials, couched in rhetoric of physical intimidation. The size of Rizzo's charisma and personality inspired unreasoned loyalty among whites, and fear as well as violent opposition among blacks. During his tenure as police commissioner "crime control" became a euphemism for "anti-black movements."[9]

The Phillies Integrate

Ironically, the Phillies might have been one of the few rays of hope for a city struggling with the issue of race relations in the 1960s. By that time it had become clear that the 1950 pennant-winning Whiz Kids' best days were behind them. Robin Roberts, the ace of that team, and Richie Ashburn, the sparkplug, were nearing the end of their brilliant careers. Age had also caught up with infielders Granny Hamner and Willie Jones, who were hampered by injuries. Other players had become lackadaisical and it showed in their performance. The team hadn't finished higher than fourth since 1953. It was time to rebuild. There were also clear indications that the Phillies were making an earnest effort to distance themselves from a segregationist past.

Owner Robert R. M. Carpenter Jr., who purchased the club in 1943, poured his energy and his family's fortune into giving dignity to what had traditionally been a losing franchise. Although he never expected to realize huge profits from the Phillies, he was a tough-minded businessman who used his family connections with the mammoth Du Pont Company to build a winner. Throughout the late 1940s and 1950s, when other NL clubs were scouting and signing black as well as Latin American ballplayers, the Phillies remained reluctant to do so, which only served to further the Phillies' reputation as a racist organization. Carpenter insisted that he wasn't "opposed to Negro players" but that he wasn't "going to hire a player of any color or nationality just to have him on the team." Admittedly, his reluctance to sign minority talent may have been due to his weakness for tall, strong pitching prospects and his devotion to the pennant-winning Whiz Kids, many of whom he kept around for too long. Perhaps the success of Roy Campanella and Hank Aaron, both of whom the Phils had had an opportunity to sign, convinced him otherwise. [10] Whatever the reason, Carpenter realized it was time for a change.

In 1960 he hired Gene Mauch, a little-known thirty-four-year-old manager and journeyman infielder of the American Association's (AA) Minneapolis Millers to replace Eddie Sawyer as the Phillies manager. Mauch was an ideal manager for the rebuilding process. He was a young disciplinarian who had come up through the Brooklyn Dodgers' organization in the late 40s. Having played for Branch Rickey, he experienced firsthand the process of integration and learned to respect the abilities of his black teammates. At the same time, his career batting average of .239 underscored the fact that the game had not come easy to him. He was a better tactician than player, and one who studied the game with exceptional attention to detail, a trait that would later earn him the moniker "Little General." On good days he was able to steal a victory by manipulating his roster one step ahead of the opposing manager. On bad days he'd overmanage, costing his team a victory that had been within reach. No one could deny, however, that Mauch had the temperament to manage. He was surly and sharp-witted, and he refused to back down from anyone, regardless of size or authority. The sportswriters loved him for the ease with which he conducted a postgame interview, serving up some of the most colorful – if not unprintable – quotes imaginable.[11]

When he assumed the Phillies post in the spring of 1960, Mauch immediately set a new tone. In a closed-door clubhouse meeting he criticized the players' off-the-field behavior and set a strict curfew. "I want my players to realize that baseball is their livelihood – not a way to have fun," he stated. "My ultimate goal is to get this ball club to a point where it won't need rules. But now they take privileges that good players on other clubs have to ask for. I think if a player doesn't have respect for himself, he'll have a hard time getting respect from someone else."[12]

Mauch, who was known to use racially inflammatory language, may not have been color-blind, but he, like new general manager John Quinn, certainly seemed to be "color-neutral" when it came to judging a player's abilities. Scouting reports indicate that the number of black players in the Phillies farm system, which consisted of approximately two hundred players on ten teams, jumped from three in 1958 to thirty-four in 1961 and steadily increased through the mid-1960s.[13] Among the more talented black players were outfielders Johnny Briggs, Richard and Robert Haines, Alex Johnson, Larry Hisle, and Ted Savage, pitchers Grant Jackson and Ferguson Jenkins, and, of course, the Phillies' first black superstar, Richie Allen. Nor did the Phillies seem to spare much expense in signing that talent. With the exception of Jackson, who signed for a $1,500 bonus, the others each received a bonus of $8,000 or more. Briggs and Jenkins received $8,000 each; Savage signed for $17,500; Johnson for $18,000; the Haines brothers for $40,000 each; Hisle, $50,000; and Allen for the unprecedented sum of $70,000.[14] Similar white talent signed during the 1960s received lower bonuses. Outfielder Joe Lis, for example, signed for $15,000 in 1964. Rick Wise, who would become the most consistent Phillies pitcher in the late 1960s, signed for $12,000 in 1963. Shortstop Larry Bowa, who would serve as the sparkplug for the pennant-contending Phillies of the late 1970s, received only $2,000 for signing in 1965.[15] If there was a racial bias in the Phillies' signing of prospects, it certainly seemed to favor the black players. Indeed, integration was a conscious process.

Player records from the late 1950s and the early 1960s always indicate the race of the black players. The scouting report on outfielders Richard and Robert Haines, for example, refer to them as "broad-shouldered Negroes." Ted Savage is listed as a "Negro athlete with good outfield potential because of his speed." Similarly, a separate roster of "Negro Players in Philadelphia National League Organization" was kept during the 1960s, listing both black and Hispanic players.[16] Though the Phillies were not the only team to confuse the identities of these two groups of players, the misconception that Hispanics are Negroes indicates a racial stereotyping by the team. The term Hispanic is an ethnic label, not a racial one. Hispanics are a racially mixed group, one that includes combinations of European white, African black, and indigenous American Indian. Just as in the black community, there can be wide color variations within the same Hispanic family. While it may have only been a matter of naiveté, to make "Hispanic" synonymous with "African American," as the Phillies had done, only served to reinforce the racism that already existed in the organization.[17]

John Quinn, who was hired by the Phils as general manager in 1959, also enhanced the racial composition of the team through trades. Some of his earliest deals involved two white players who would go on to become among the greatest names in Phillies history: Johnny Callison, who along with Allen would carry the offensive load for the pennant-contending Phillies in 1964, came from the Chicago White Sox for Gene Freese; and future Hall-of-Fame pitcher Jim Bunning, from the Detroit Tigers for Don Demeter. Other black players were added: Wes Covington from the Kansas City Athletics and Bill White from the St. Louis Cardinals. An increasing number of Hispanic players rounded out the roster, including Tony Gonzalez and Cookie Rojas from the Cincinnati Reds, Ruben Amaro Sr. from the Cardinals, and fan-favorite Tony Taylor from the Chicago Cubs.[18]

At the center of the rebuilding process, however, was Richard Anthony Allen. Born on March 8, 1942, in the small town of Wampum, Pennsylvania, thirty miles northwest of Pittsburgh, Allen was the youngest of three boys raised by a single mother. Era Allen was a dedicated parent with an unshakeable resolve to raise her sons with a deep and abiding respect for religion and for themselves, despite the poverty that surrounded them. Her God-fearing ways underscored both the compassion as well as the hard-line discipline she employed to nurture a close-knit family in this predominantly white but integrated community.[19] With a population of only one thousand residents, Wampum itself was an insular community beset by high unemployment and declining steel and cement industries that had once formed the backbone of its economy. Poverty was the most defining feature of this small hamlet tucked away among the scenic mountains and green countryside of western Pennsylvania.[20]

When he was a child, Allen would tag along with his older brothers, Ron and Hank, playing whatever sport happened to be in season. Being the youngest of the crowd, he constantly had to prove himself to his brothers and their friends. Eventually they came to accept him as a tough-hearted competitor and "one of their own." When an injury to Allen's right eye left the eyelid slightly contorted, they gave him the nickname "Sleepy" as a term of endearment.[21] By the time he was a senior at Wampum High School, Allen had established himself as an all-around athlete. One of only 5 blacks in a class of 146 students, he excelled at sports and this provided an identity that allowed him to be accepted by his white classmates. Following in his older brothers' footsteps, Allen became the star of the basketball team. As captain and starting guard he led Wampum to the Class B state championship.[22] But it was his talent as a power-hitting shortstop on the school's baseball team that captured the attention of John Ogden, a gruff, no-nonsense six-year veteran scout for the Phillies in 1960. Ogden was so impressed with the broad-shouldered all-around athlete that he courted the entire Allen family. He earned the trust of Era Allen by agreeing to sign all three of her sons to Phillies contracts. Of course, Richie's was the most lucrative at $70,000 – the highest bonus ever paid to a black ballplayer at the time. A personal visit to the young, impressionable ballplayer by former Negro League great William "Judy" Johnson, who had recently joined the Phillies scouting ranks, sealed the deal.[23]

To be sure, the Phillies were pinning their hopes on a player of Allen's caliber. Their dismal performances had become perennial and had begun to wear on their fans. The team hit rock bottom in 1961 when it suffered a twenty-three game losing streak, a Major League record that still stands today. In '62 they managed to climb out of the NL cellar, largely because two new expansion teams (the New York Mets and the Houston Colt 45s) provided the Phils with beatable opponents. Nevertheless, a nucleus of good, young talent existed within the organization.

In 1962, for example, Johnny Callison and Tony Gonzalez established themselves as solid outfielders with potent bats, hitting 23 and 20 home runs, respectively. Pitcher Art Mahaffey, a hard fastballer who struck out seventeen Cubs in one game the previous season, turned in an All-Star performance with nineteen wins. Chris Short, a twenty-four-year-old, strong-armed southpaw, added another eleven victories. Second base-man Tony Taylor established himself as captain of the infield and a reliable lead-off hitter. The team continued to improve in 1963, finishing in fourth place.[24] Allen would make them a pennant contender.

Encountering Racism

During his early years in the Minor Leagues, Dick Allen was an adolescent, encountering a new and heightened awareness of race that he had never experienced in his hometown of Wampum. As he moved through the farm system he was respected for his extraordinary athletic abilities, but kept at a distance – or worse, discriminated against – because of his race. The young shortstop had an impressive debut at Elmira of the New York-Pennsylvania League in 1960, hitting .281 in eighty-eight games. The following season he played at Magic Valley, Utah, in the Pioneer League, hitting .317 with 21 homers and 94 RBIS. When he was promoted to Double A at Williamsport in '62, Allen continued his prodigious power hitting, despite being moved to a new position. He hit Eastern League pitching at a .332 clip with 20 home runs and 109 RBIS while learning to play center field. It appeared as if the Majors were on his horizon. Allen realized that the Phillies already had a strong outfield with Covington, Gonzalez, and Callison, but he still believed they could use his bat and intended to win a spot on their roster for '63.

Invited to spring training that year, Allen hit nine home runs, the most on the club. But at the end of camp he was told that he needed more seasoning in the Minors, this time at their Triple A club in Little Rock, Arkansas. Allen pleaded with Quinn and Mauch to give him a shot at the Majors. They refused to listen. Allen had asked for a $50.00 raise as a symbolic reward for his season at Triple A.[25] Quinn probably interpreted the request as a demand by an ungrateful – if not cocky – young black who had been given the opportunity of a professional career. If so, the general manager's liberalism had its limits and the young slugger had exceeded them. Predictably, Allen became the first black ballplayer in Arkansas history and the season proved to be a nightmare.

At Little Rock, Allen was immersed in a racist environment where he had to grapple with a devalued status. That environment operated on the stereotype of blacks as troublemakers, criminals, or ignorant laborers. His emotional response was anger, confusion, and alienation.

On opening night a capacity crowd of seven thousand fans packed

Little Rock's Ray Winder Stadium to see history in the making. Outside, signs that read "DON'T NEGRO-IZE BASEBALL" and "NIGGER GO HOME" greeted Allen at the park. Inside sat Governor Orval Faubus, who had tried to bar black teenagers from attending Little Rock's Central High School just six years earlier, waiting to throw out the first ball. Allen was scared. Starting in left field for the Travelers that night, he botched the very first ball hit out to him. "It was a lazy fly," he remembered. "I just froze, then I took a few steps in and the ball flew over my head. I missed that ball because I was scared and I don't mind saying it."[26] Later in the game he made up for his miscue by hitting two doubles, the second one of which set up the Travelers' game-winning rally.

After the game Allen purposely waited until the clubhouse cleared before walking out to the parking lot. "When I got to my car," he said, I found a note on the windshield. It said. "DON'T COME BACK AGAIN, NIGGER." I felt scared and alone, and, what's worse, my car was the last one in the parking lot. There might be something more terrifying than being black and holding a note that says "Nigger" in an empty parking lot in Little Rock, Arkansas, in 1963, but if there is, it certainly hasn't crossed my path yet.[27]

Things only seemed to get worse as the season unfolded. Allen had to live with a family on the black side of town and could not be served in a restaurant unless accompanied by a white player. He was stopped routinely by local police for no apparent reason, received threatening phone calls, and was forced to endure the epithets of racist fans. Through it all there was very little support from the Phillies organization. With the exception of teammate Lee Elia, who encouraged the young, twenty-one-year-old prospect, Allen was a loner. While Manager Frank Lucchesi treated him just like any other ballplayer and respected his abilities, Lucchesi couldn't relate to the young player's circumstances, nor did he try.[28] In fact, no one could really understand Allen's situation. He was the only African-American on the team and he believed that the Phillies were using him to break the color barrier in Arkansas. What's more, the Phillies were still considered one of the most racist organizations in Major League Baseball. Integration was only the first step toward dismantling that reputation. Whether intentional or not, they neglected Allen, forcing him to fend for himself in an overtly racist environment.

"Sixty-three was the first season for Triple A ball down there," Allen recalled years later.

It was the first season with the Phillies as parent club – and no blacks. They had no choice but to bust it. I didn't know anything about the race issue in Arkansas and didn't really care. Maybe if the Phillies had called me in, man to man, like the Dodgers had done with Jackie Robinson and said, "Dick, this is what we have in mind. It's going to be very difficult but we're with you" – at least I would have been prepared. I'm not saying I would have liked it. But I would have known what to expect. Instead I was on my own.

I liked Frank Lucchesi's style as a manager. But he didn't understand me as a person. What did he know about abuse? While I was in bed listening to gunshots, he was eating at the best restaurants in Little Rock. Frank had only one thing in mind that year: managing in the Majors. Dick Allen had only one thing in mind: playing in the Majors. Lucchesi may not have liked the fact that I was going to get there before him. [29]

Allen was not quite twenty years old when he arrived in Little Rock. He was not familiar with southern culture or the manner by which the town's blacks navigated the racial discrimination they experienced on a daily basis. He was an angry young man, left on his own without any support from an organization that simply didn't know how, or refused, to protect him.

"There were fans in Little Rock who truly loved the game," admitted Allen.

For some of them, color didn't matter. I gathered my strength from them. But there were others who got off on racial intimidation. Between innings, coming in from the outfield to the dugout I would hear the voices – "Hey, Chocolate Drop" or "Watch your back, nigger." I would look up, but I could never find the guy who made the remark. Racist fans have a way of hissing and mumbling under their breath that makes them hard to locate. Black players know this and after a while learn not to look up. I would have loved to go a round with any one of them. I think a one-on-one slugfest with one of those racist cowards would have given me the release I needed. [30]

Still, Allen managed to do more than survive.

He compiled a .289 average, leading the International League in home runs (33), RBIs (97), and triples (12). The Phillies called him up in September, and he proceeded to hit Major League pitching at a .292 clip. After the season was over Allen declared that he was "ready for the Majors," explaining that he "started out the season by pressing because I was the first colored player Little Rock ever had." But the September call-up and the experience he had that month showed him that "baseball is baseball, regardless of the level of competition" and that he "had the ability to move up."[31] Despite the fact that the Travelers fans voted Allen the team's MVP, the discrimination he experienced at Little Rock left him bitter and distrustful of the Phillies organization.

Rookie of the Year, 1964

The next season Allen had to deal with the pressure of a summer-long pennant race while playing third base, a new position. With Covington, Gonzalez, and Callison fixed in the outfield, there was no place for him at that position. But there was room in the infield. The Phillies had traded an experienced third baseman in Don Demeter to Detroit for Jim Bunning, a side-arming righthander who they hoped would provide some sorely needed pitching. Mauch believed that he could fill the void with Allen. "He can play third good enough to get by," insisted the Phils skipper. "He has good reactions and good hands and third isn't as demanding a spot as short or second where he began his career." "Besides," he added, "I know that Allen's bat has to help us. He can drive the ball a mile to right center."[32]

Mauch's prediction proved to be correct. Allen carried the Phillies from the very beginning of the season. Throughout April the team found itself in first place with their rookie third baseman leading them in every major offensive category: .431 average, 6 home runs, 13 RBIs. "There's just no telling how good this kid can be," Mauch boasted. "He's got great hands, and a very quick, very short swing. But what impresses me most about him is his professional approach to the game. He doesn't get way up when things are going good or way down when things are going bad. And that's the best approach to any professional sport."[33]

By midseason Allen's swing was being compared to Cincinnati's Frank Robinson's, and his hitting to Hank Aaron's of the Milwaukee Braves. Sportswriter Larry Merchant of the *Philadelphia Daily News* predicted that Allen would "hit around .300, drive in and score 100 runs, get 190 to 200 base hits, with 30 to 35 homers, 35 to 40 doubles, and 10 triples; and he'll strike out 160 times. There is no way he can have anything but a big, big year."[34] Never before had the Phillies or their fans seen the kind of offensive production that Allen was giving them at third base. They reveled in his Rookie-of-the-Year performance, secretly hoping that he would help the team capture the pennant that seemed to have eluded them since 1950.

When asked about all the hoopla surrounding his performance, Allen replied: "I'm not surprised by anything. It's a game up here, just like anywhere else. It's a game I love to play and I want to be the best at it. Not one of the best. The best."[35] And he was, for 150 games that season. So were the Phillies.

Bunning gave the team the ace they needed to become a consistent winner. He chalked up nineteen wins, including a perfect game against the New York Mets on Father's Day that year. His 2.63 ERA and 219 strike-outs kept the Phillies in the chase for most of the season. Chris Short added another seventeen victories and 181 strikeouts, while posting a 2.20 ERA. Art Mahaffey (12–9, 80 K) and Dennis Bennett (12–14, 125 K, 3.68 ERA) added depth to the pitching. The Phillies also had a potent offense. Allen hit .318 with 29 homers and 91 RBIS. Callison hit .274 with 31 homers and 104 RBIS. Frank Thomas, a veteran power hitter, added to the offensive production when he was acquired from the Mets in August. In thirty-four games as the Phillies first baseman Thomas collected 26 RBIS before a thumb injury ended his season on September 8. Defensively, the infield was strong through the middle with second baseman Tony Taylor, and Ruben Amaro Sr. and Bobby Wine splitting the duties at shortstop. Clay Dalrymple and Gus Triandos were experienced catchers with exceptionally strong throwing arms. Even Allen's League-leading forty-one errors at third didn't seem to cost the club too many games, until the final two weeks of the season.[36]

With twelve games remaining the Phils had a six-and-a-half-game lead and looked to be a sure bet to capture the NL flag. Over the next week they lost every game they played while the Cardinals and Reds won all of theirs, and the Giants, the Phils' closest competitors for most of the season, won seven of nine games. Mauch began to panic, relying on Bunning and Short to get them out of the fix. Though he did not use them exclusively down the stretch (of which he has been unfairly accused), Mauch did pitch his two top hurlers on three different occasions, each with only two days' rest. It didn't help. The Reds moved into first place on September 27 by sweeping two games from the Mets. With one game remaining in the season they were tied with the Cards for first place, the Phillies being one game behind. If the Phils beat the Reds and the Cardinals lost to the Mets there would have been a three-way tie, forcing a playoff. The Phillies finally won, defeating the Reds 10–0. But the Cardinals also beat the Mets 11–5, winning their first pennant since 1946.[37]

Watching the pennant slip through their grasp was devastating for the Phillies. The organization had already printed World Series programs and tickets. In the minds of the players, the fans, and the front office the pennant had already been clinched. "It was such a heartbreaking experience for so many of us," said shortstop Ruben Amaro Sr. "That team had lived through the good and the bad together. It was the same nucleus of players that had suffered through the twenty-three game losing streak three seasons earlier. A trying experience like that gives you a certain resolve to win, and I think we all felt we deserved that pennant in '64."[38]

Callison agreed. "The players had to live with it," he said. "It was just a damn shame. We had battled so hard all year and I didn't remember any easy series. They all threw the best pitchers at us. Then, at the end, this lousy thing happens. The long summer's effort left a sad, painful anger on that team."[39]

To be sure, the '64 Phillies were a close-knit team, composed of young players who genuinely liked each other on and off the field. "Between the Hispanic, black, and white players there was an outstanding chemistry on that team," recalled second baseman Tony Taylor. "Most of the players were young and had come up together, plus we had a young manager in Gene Mauch. He kept everybody together. He had come up through the Dodgers' organization during the Jackie Robinson years, he had played baseball in Cuba, so he knew how important it was to build a good chemistry on an integrated team."[40]

Unfortunately, Mauch seemed to destroy the very chemistry he had worked so hard to build the longer his team was mired in its slump. "Mauch was only thirty-eight years old and he wanted to win so badly," Allen explained.

He would have done anything to win. But somewhere along the line in '64, he forgot the most elementary rule of baseball: to have fun. Once we started to skid, he'd become a wild man. After losses, he would close the clubhouse door and start dressing us down, throwing things around. All we really needed was for him to pat us on the fanny and say, "Thanks fellas, good effort, we'll get 'em tomorrow." Instead we got ranting and raving and all that did was make us feel more tired than we already were.[41]

Ironically, Mauch could not discipline himself to do the very thing he admired so much about Allen – keep an even temper, regardless of the fortunes of the team. Perhaps his inability to do so was a result of his own frustrating career as a ballplayer. He was never part of a winner. Nor did he possess the talent to carry a team. In 1964 Mauch had come the closest he had ever been to being a winner and he watched the pennant slip away before his eyes. He would become more distant from his players after that season. His relationship with Allen vacillated between being a protector and an antagonist. Mauch was, at the same time, jealous and respectful of his young slugger's exceptional talent; something that was recognized by the baseball writers who voted Allen the NL's Rookie of the Year in '64.

The Thomas Incident, July 1965

In 1965 the Phillies were determined to clinch the pennant that had eluded them the season before. Desperate to land the veterans who could make the difference, Quinn acquired Dick Stuart, a power-hitting first baseman, and pitcher Bo Belinsky, a free-spirited pitcher with a lively arm. But it didn't work. Stuart proved to be inconsistent at the plate and his wacky defense earned him the nickname "Dr. Strangeglove." Belinsky's social life was livelier than his pitching. He won only four of thirteen decisions and argued constantly with Mauch. Nor was the Phillies' pitching nearly as good as the previous season's. Not surprisingly, the Phils struggled to play .500 ball for most of the season. Allen, on the other hand, picked up where he had left off in '64. By the end of June he was hitting .348 and had been named to the NL All-Star Team. Then, on July 3 things began to deteriorate.

Allen was taking ground balls at third base before that night's game against the Cincinnati Reds while Frank Thomas was taking his cuts in the cage. Johnny Callison, who stopped by to visit with Allen, suggested that they taunt Thomas for his poor showing at the plate during the previous night's game against the Giants. (With runners on first and third and one out, Thomas had tried to avoid hitting into a double play by bunting the ball. After three failed attempts the thirty-six-year-old slugger struck out, setting off uproarious laughter from his own teammates.) Allen and Callison – both of whom had been the object of Thomas's own ridicule several times before – were ready to get even.

Down in the cage Thomas took a big swing and missed. "Hey Donkey!" yelled Callison, referring to the veteran by his nickname, "Why don't you try bunting?" Instead of responding to Callison, Thomas glared down the third base line at Allen and shouted: "What are you trying to be, another Muhammad Clay, always running your mouth off?" Insulted by the comparison to Cassius Clay, the colorful but controversial heavyweight boxing champion who had recently changed his name to Muhammad Ali, Allen charged the cage and the two players went at each other. Allen hit Thomas with a left hook to the jaw, sending him to the ground. When he got to his feet Thomas was wielding his bat and connected with Allen's left shoulder. By now the rest of the team was at home plate trying to restrain the two players.

According to Allen, Thomas "knew it was Callison who had taunted him." But Thomas's response was, once again, directed at Allen. "The 'Muhammad Clay' remark was meant to say a lot," insists Allen.

> It reminded me of how Frank would pretend to offer his hand in a soul shake to a young black player on the team. When the player would offer his hand in return, Thomas would grab his thumb and bend it back. To him, it was a big joke. But I saw too many brothers on the team with swollen thumbs to get any laughs. So I popped him. I just wanted to teach him a lesson. But after he hit me with the bat, I wanted to kill him. [42]

One of those "young black players" to whom Allen referred was his best friend on the team, twenty-one-year-old outfielder Johnny Briggs. Like Allen, Briggs experienced the same alienation playing for the Arkansas Travelers. A speedy base runner who played the outfield with an exceptional instinct, the Phillies expected too much too soon from Briggs. After an impressive start at Class A Bakersfield, where he hit .297 with 21 homers and 83 RBIs, the Phillies rushed him through the farm system. With less than two hundred games' experience in the Minors, the Phils promoted Briggs to the Majors for the pennant race in '64. He played the outfield so effectively for twenty games, they decided to keep him on the roster in '65. It was a mistake.

Briggs platooned center field with Tony Gonzalez and was made the lead-off hitter as well. He struggled to hit .230 for most of the season and never really felt comfortable with his role on the team, even stating that he would have preferred being sent back to Little Rock just to play on an everyday basis. [43] Ironically, the Phillies found themselves in a no-win situation with Briggs. While Briggs was a part of their earnest attempt to integrate the team, the Phillies only damaged his self-confidence by not sending him back to the Minors. Perhaps their decision was based on potential, or simply on a genuine desire to protect a young black player from even more discrimination at the hands of the Little Rock fans. Whatever the case might have been, the Phillies failed on both counts. And Thomas only made matters worse for Briggs in Philadelphia.

According to Pat Corrales, the Phillies' reserve catcher, Thomas "had been picking on Johnny Briggs all season, saying 'Boy this' and 'Boy that.'" Allen "didn't go for that." He came to Briggs's defense time and again. Finally, Thomas turned on Allen and it culminated in the fight. [44] Callison agreed, stating that the hard feelings had been building between the two players for quite some time. "I knew that Thomas had been riding Richie and that a fight was only a matter of time," he said. "Richie was under control until Thomas took that swing at him with the bat. After that, it took five guys to keep Allen off Thomas. Our shortstop, Ruben Amaro, took a shot in the chops trying to restrain Richie." [45]

Amaro, who found himself in the middle of the brawl, also called it "a racial situation." But he remembered it a bit differently than either Allen or Callison had. Thomas liked to intimidate his teammates, especially the young players, who called him "Donkey" because he had a knack for saying the wrong thing at the wrong time. But Allen wasn't completely innocent either. He was taking ground balls at third before the game and started taunting Thomas, saying, "Hey Donkey, you can't hit a ball past me!" Thomas yelled back: "Okay Richie X, see if you can catch this one!" Of course, Thomas was referring to Malcolm X, a very controversial black leader at the time. Allen got mad. He went over to the cage and told Thomas: "I won't call you Donkey anymore and you better not call me Richie X." Allen returned to third base and Thomas hits a screaming line drive in his direction that goes all the way down the line. Before you know it, Thomas is yelling at him: "Hey Richie X, how come you didn't catch that one?" That did it. Allen stormed the cage and the fight began. [46]

The Phillies went on to lose to the Reds that night, 10–8. Allen hit two triples, one a 400-foot shot off the Ballantine Beer scoreboard in right-center field in the seventh. Thomas followed it with a pinch-hit home run an inning later. After the game Thomas was waived to Houston and Mauch threatened Allen with a $2,000 fine if he discussed the incident with the press. [47] Allen pleaded with Mauch to spare Thomas, who had a large family to support. But the Phillies skipper refused to listen. [48] When the press asked about the decision, Mauch replied: "I had to choose between a 36-year-old veteran who was hitting .250 and a 23-year-old power hitter who was hitting .348, the kind of player you see once in a lifetime."[49] It was the worst thing he could have said.

Thomas took his case to the press, exploiting the role of a victim. "I've always liked Richie," he insisted. "I've always tried to help him. I guess certain guys can dish it out, but can't take it." [50] Fans began to blame Allen for the fight, booing him unmercifully. Allen took it in stride. "The fans are not the ones I want to beat," he stated. "If I paid my money to see a ball game, I guess I'd raise a little hell, too."[51] But years later he would admit that all the abuse took its toll. "After the Thomas fight, I started playing angry baseball," Allen confessed. "It seemed the whole city of Philadelphia blamed me for what happened. They hung banners from the bleachers at Connie Mack Stadium in support of Thomas. I began getting hate mail and lots of it. Most of the letters I got started off with "Nigger." None of them were ever signed. Racists are cowards. After a while, I just dumped the mail in the trash, unopened."[52]

The rest of the season proved to be a nightmare. Allen vividly recalls being "sucker punched" by one fan, others screaming "darkie" or "monkey" at him, and one especially painful memory of a man "holding his little boy up in the air with one hand and pointing at me with the other, teaching his son to boo." There were times he admitted to "feeling the anger at the plate, ripping through [his] veins." He would go to bat, hit the ball out of the park, and see "40,000 Philadelphians giving me a standing ovation. Thirty seconds earlier I was a 'monkey.' Now, I'm a hero. It was the ultimate mind game, and it was my mind they were playing with."[53]

The "mind game" inevitably affected Allen's performance, along with the badly bruised shoulder he had suffered from the fight with Thomas. After the incident he hit only .271, refusing to be taken out of the lineup. Still he finished the '65 season with a very respectable .302 average, 20 home runs, and 85 RBIS.[54]

Internalizing the Stereotype

The Thomas incident marked the turning point in Allen's relationship with Philadelphia. The fight reinforced, in the minds of white Philadelphians, the negative racial stereotyping of blacks. Regardless of Allen's response, the fans and the press labeled him a "troublemaker" and scrutinized his every act. He eventually began to internalize the stereotype.

Mauch later admitted that both he and the Phillies mishandled the situation. "Thomas was going to go anyway," he conceded. "I should have shipped him sooner. Instead the town came down on Richie's head. If he did one little thing wrong, they would see it as so much worse because, in their heads, he was a bad guy." [55] At times the press was even more malicious than the fans. According to Tony Taylor, Allen's roommate, the press "never knew Dick Allen. They made a much bigger thing out of the fight than it really was. They knew that Thomas liked to intimidate young players, but he was also a popular veteran who was brought over here to Philadelphia to help win the pennant. Dick, on the other hand, was still a young player making his name. Everybody on the team liked him. But the press gave him the label of a 'troublemaker.' It wasn't fair." [56]

Playing in Philadelphia became an increasingly hellish experience for Allen. The fans booed him every night, throwing pennies, bolts, or beer bottles at him whenever he played the outfield. He began wearing a batting helmet just to protect himself from the projectiles. Off the field Allen received hate mail regularly. The front lawn of his home was strewn with trash, compliments of the neighborhood's disgruntled fans. The abuse became so bad that some of his friends even urged him to hire a bodyguard. But Allen persevered. In '66 he still managed to post an impressive .317 average with 40 home runs and 110 RBIs for a team that finished in fourth place. But the negative treatment began to take its toll the following season.

On July 8, 1967, Allen arrived at the ballpark unable to walk a straight line or talk without slurring his words and was sent home by Coach George Myatt. Mauch awkwardly announced a "late fine," claiming that Allen went home because he was "too late to play." Eleven days later he was given another late fine, this time because his "car broke down." [57] In fact, Allen's drinking was becoming a serious problem.

"Before ball games, instead of going straight to the ballpark, I started making regular stops at watering holes along the way," he admitted. I had a regular route from my home in northwest Philadelphia to the ballpark in the inner city. Whenever Mauch would smell booze on my breath, he'd throw a tantrum and then fine me. I told 'em, I expect to pay when I mess up. Let him put an envelope in my box, but don't call me in for no lectures." [58]

To be sure, Mauch was trying to protect his prized power hitter, but Allen made it increasingly difficult to do so. The press had already labeled him "lazy" and a "troublemaker." [59] Even honest mistakes were treated with deep cynicism. On August 24, for example, Allen sustained a career-threatening injury while trying to push his stalled car up the driveway. In the process, his right hand slipped and went through the headlight. After a five-hour operation to repair the severed tendons and nerves, doctors gave him a fifty-fifty chance of making a comeback. Immediately rumors spread that Allen's story of an accident was a cover-up, that he had actually been knifed in a bar fight or jumped through a window after being caught sleeping with a teammate's wife.[60] Now, some members of the Phillies brain trust were beginning to turn on him.

Oppositional Identity

Allen developed an "oppositional identity" to protect himself. The anger and resentment he felt eventually took over. As he put it, "I'd been hearing I was a bum for so long that I began to think maybe that's just what I was." Allen adopted the identity of a rebel. His "in-your-face" behavior only served to threaten teammates as well as the front office. No longer was he the victim of racism but rather a manipulator of it. His repeated requests for a trade were always dismissed. So Allen responded with a litany of curfew violations, beer-drinking episodes, and excessive lateness to games. Fines were no deterrent. Allen paid them, realizing that his lucrative contracts would more than make up for it. In the process, Allen and the Phillies developed a mutual distrust of each other that was colored by the specter of racism.

The strained relationship began after the '67 season when Allen's contract came up for negotiation. Because of the severe injury to his hand, General Manager John Quinn attempted to sign him to a conditional pact. Allen refused to deal with him and took his case directly to owner Bob Carpenter. It was the first of many times Allen manipulated racism for his own benefit. He even said as much in his autobiography:

> Baseball owners know that black players come from unstable backgrounds, and either consciously or not – and in the case of Bob Carpenter, I truly believe it was unconscious – they often use that insecurity against them at contract time. Their standard line was to "pay your dues first and the real dust will come later." It's a lie. In baseball, as in life, you've got to get what's coming to you while you're producing because the day you stop – it's "later, Baby." In my case, having grown up in western Pennsylvania among white people, I could walk that walk, talk that talk. Contract time I had my act together. A jacket and tie, always. I would state clearly what I

had done the season before. Front office types weren't use to dealing with black players who could talk their game. When I came in for meetings at contract time, the boss men would perspire right through their jackets.[61]

Allen walked into Carpenter's office, reminded the owner that he had hit .307 with 23 home runs and 77 RBIS in an abbreviated season, and that he wanted $100,000 to play for the Phillies in 1968. Carpenter, realizing that Allen was the key to his club's success and that he wouldn't think twice about holding out, talked him down to $85,000. It was still the highest salary in the game for a fourth-year player. Allen had been successful at his ploy.[62] Over the next two years he would play the race card time and again.

With free agency not yet a viable option, Allen in 1968 launched a campaign of minor transgressions in the hope of forcing a trade. On March 8 he left spring training in Clearwater, Florida, without permission, only to be fined upon his return two days later. While Mauch berated him in the clubhouse office, he told the press that Allen was "very worried about his injured hand" and had gone to see a doctor in Philadelphia.[63] Allen paid the fine and dismissed his manager's lecture. On April 30 he had another run-in with Mauch.

    *

Driving his own car from Philadelphia for an afternoon game against the Mets at New York's Shea Stadium, Allen arrived twenty minutes before game time, insisting that he was "stuck in a traffic jam" on the Long Island Expressway. Mauch exploded at him for refusing to ask permission to drive to the game. Scratching his star player from the lineup, the Little General slapped him with another fine while also revoking permission for players to drive to New York in the future.

The Phillies went on to drop the game, 1–0. Afterward, when asked by the press how he planned to handle Allen's violation, Mauch again protected his star. "If the rest of my players produced the way he does, they [could] be late, too. Besides, whatever's going to be done has been done."[64] But the conflict only continued to escalate.

On May 26 Mauch fined Allen for his failure to hustle on the base paths, and the following night Allen reported to the ballpark drunk. Mauch sent him home, telling the press that his slugger was out with a groin injury. In fact, Allen was hit with a two-week suspension. Allen would manipulate the situation to his own advantage, or so he thought.

When he finally returned to the team in early June, Allen announced a "sit-down strike" and refused to play. "Hell, how can they suspend me until they hear my side of the story?" he asked the Philadelphia press. Shortly after, he was given that opportunity by sportscaster Al Meltzer in a candid television interview. Registering his "deep disappointment with the behavior of the fans," Allen insisted that he be "left alone off the field" and be "judged solely on his playing abilities." Owner Bob Carpenter had heard enough. In a closed-door meeting Allen agreed to a truce, telling the owner that he had been "ready to play all along." When Mauch was informed of the response, he supposedly gave Carpenter a "me-or-him" ultimatum, asking, "Do you want me to call him a liar?" Finally, on June 15 the Phillies skipper was dismissed.[65] Allen's plan had backfired.

To be sure, Allen wasn't the only reason for Mauch's firing. The Phillies were going nowhere in 1968. Having traded the 36-year-old Bunning to Pittsburgh, they had pinned their hopes on a new ace, Chris Short, and on Larry Jackson, a 37-year-old veteran acquired from the Cubs. Short missed several stretches early in the season because of a knee injury, and Jackson was ineffective. Youngsters Rick Wise and Grant Jackson were too inexperienced to pick up the slack and the pitching staff collapsed, ending the season with a 3.36 team ERA, third worst in the NL. Worse, the team's top two hitters were trying to recover from serious injuries. Allen was still hampered by the damaged nerves in his right hand and the aging first baseman Bill White, acquired from the St. Louis Cardinals, was recovering from a severed Achilles tendon.[66]

As long as the Phils fielded a contender, Mauch's job was safe. The Little General didn't have the patience to wait for younger players to develop. Besides, he only had a year left on his contract. Quinn was just as impatient. He was so driven for immediate success he acquired Larry Jackson from the Cubs by trading away a promising hurler in Fergie Jenkins, who went on to have a Hall-of-Fame career with Chicago.[67] But as the Phils dropped lower in the standings, it became clear that a change had to be made.

While Quinn admitted that the "Allen problem was a factor" in the decision to fire Mauch, he insisted that it was not the "entire reason."[68] Mauch's wife had recently been hospitalized with a serious illness and the Phillies questioned whether he would be able to manage with the added pressure. Four days after his firing Mauch absolved Carpenter and Quinn for the decision. "Something had to be done," he admitted. "They made the best decision under the circumstances. They couldn't foresee Nina Lee getting sick. It was a terribly tough situation for them. Besides, if someone had told me I'd be here nine years, I'd have said they were nuts. I didn't get a raw deal." When asked about the difficulty of managing Allen, Mauch refused to go into any detail. "I'm not going to knock Richie Allen," he replied, dismissing the question. "That son-of-a-gun gave me many a thrill. There was nothing personal in my handling of Allen. It was objective. When I jump on a player, it is to make him better."[69]

Mauch's response was a calculated one. He knew that Major League Baseball was expanding to Montreal the next season and that he would be the most eligible candidate for a managerial post there, as long as he took the moral high ground. The press would do the rest. And they did.

News of Mauch's firing played just as big in New York as in Philadelphia. Arthur Daley of the *New York Times* made Mauch into a martyr, attributing his dismissal almost solely to "disciplinary problems with Richie Allen, a superstar with a built-in distaste for discipline." Daley registered his admiration for the Little General's repeated public defenses of Allen whenever Allen broke team policy. "But no manager can permit an athlete to erode the morale of an entire ball club by disregarding the rules that others faithfully observe," he added. Comparing the Mauch-Allen situation to Yankee manager Miller Huggins's ongoing conflict with Babe Ruth, Daley pointed out that Huggins "was deemed a joke manager until he finally brought Ruth into line. That's when he gained the respect of all his players, including a contrite Babe. Through it all, Ruth was a joyous character, the pet of his teammates. Allen is not. Whereas the Babe's shenanigans were known only to a few insiders, if that, Richie has done the damnedest things. Yet Gene might have survived if he had bowed his neck ever so slightly to Allen, another guy with an unbowable neck."[70]

Daley confirmed what every Philadelphia sportswriter believed. The game was changing and Allen was a catalyst for that change. Prior to Mauch's firing, a manager could threaten a player with a demotion, no matter how talented he was. But Allen was a high-priced superstar and one who was coveted by the owner. Mauch could demean him, fine him, and suspend him. Carpenter, however, certainly would not allow Allen to be demoted or traded. Ultimately, Allen's differences with Mauch determined the 42-year-old manager's employment. Allen didn't see it that way, though:

Hell, I didn't want Mauch fired. I liked him. He was tough, but mostly he was fair. I wanted to get myself traded instead. I'd gone to Bob Carpenter four or five times and asked to be traded. He refused. He kept telling me that things would turn around. I didn't believe it. The fans were no longer just booing, it was open warfare. My family was scared and unhappy. And the Phillies were a lousy team. I had my mind on only one thing: getting the hell out of Philadelphia. That's when I began to act the role that Philadelphia had carved out for me. . . . By the second month of the '68 season, Mauch and I were no longer communicating. By that time he was fining me every week: $1,000 for drinking, $500 for missing batting practice, $1,500 for showing up late for a game. My weekly fines were the equal of some players' paychecks. We were coming to a showdown.[71]

Ironically, Allen's ploy to force a trade resulted in Mauch's firing. But it also seemed to improve his situation with management.

The Phillies replaced Mauch with Bob Skinner, a soft-spoken 36-year-old who managed San Diego of the Pacific Coast League. When asked about the possibility of having one set of rules for the Phillies superstar and another for the other twenty-four players, Skinner told the press that he "anticipated no trouble" with Allen and that he would have "one set of rules" for all the players.[72] Allen responded to Skinner's hiring by going on a tear. After the All-Star Game he led the Phils to a seven-game winning streak, banging out 15 hits in 30 trips to the plate, including 5 homers and 15 RBIS. By mid-July he was hitting at a .314 clip. While he finished the season with a .263 average, Allen was among the NL's leaders in home runs (33) and RBIS (90).[73] Still the Phillies finished in seventh place with a record of 76–86, twenty-one games behind the pennant-wining Cardinals. It was their worst performance since 1961 and the fans had registered their disapproval. Only 664,546 turned out to see the Phillies that season, though it would have taken about 950,000 to break even at the gate.[74]

"One way or another, you'll see a new team on the field in 1969," vowed Bob Carpenter, who planned to rebuild. "I feel we'll bounce back next year with four or five kids to excite people. Even Allen's not untouchable. I'm disappointed in his production. I think he should give us a .300 average and 120 RBIS."[75] It appeared as if Allen would get his wish to be traded. In fact, Carpenter even directed Quinn to explore possibilities to trade Allen to the New York Mets or Cleveland Indians during the off-season. But the Phillies' asking price proved to be too high in both cases.[76]

Allen begrudgingly returned to the Phillies in '69, this time as a full-time first baseman. But he was more intent than ever to force a trade.

In early May he missed a flight to St. Louis, then missed the same flight the next morning. As a result he missed one complete game and part of another against the Cardinals. Skinner was furious and fined him $1,000. "I definitely need to get out of Philadelphia," he told the press. "Bob Carpenter has been real good to me, but I've got to play somewhere else." When asked to explain the reasons for his frustration with Philadelphia, Allen pointed to the press. "I have no trouble with the other players," he insisted. "I get along great with my teammates. But you fellas have created an atmosphere where people who have never met me hate me. You can knock me and say 'I'm a no good black so-and-so' and I can still be your friend. But if you don't ask me about something and take someone else's word for it and write it as fact, then I got to cut you loose. Sometimes I get so disgusted. I really do love to play the game, but the writers take all the fun out of it."[77]

Again, Allen brought the issue of race into the conflict. His choice of words – "I'm a no good black so-and-so" – suggested that the press was treating him poorly because of the color of his skin. It was part of his own manipulation and it was beginning to wear on his teammates as well, whether he realized it or not.

In late June reserve infielder Cookie Rojas called a clubhouse meeting and tore into Allen. Rojas told him that the team "resented his coming and going as he pleased," as well as his "lack of hustle on the field." The team, which had previously been supportive, was now divided in its opinion toward Allen. "When Carpenter gave him that $80,000 contract everybody lost authority over him," said one disgruntled white veteran. "Nobody that age deserves that kind of money. He doesn't hustle all the time and he has his own set of rules. He's letting us down." But another white player suggested that it "might just look like he doesn't care, the way he never changes his expression when he strikes out. Maybe we're jealous of his talent and expect too much of him." Allen's manipulation had caught up with him. "It hurt me," he said of his teammates' remarks. "I just started to say, 'The hell with it.' "[78]

Predictably, on June 24 Allen missed a twinight doubleheader at Shea Stadium, choosing instead to stay at a horse race in New Jersey. He claimed that he tried to phone Skinner when he realized that he would be late. On his way to the stadium he learned, over the radio, that Skinner had suspended him. Instead of going to the game, Allen went to his hotel room. "I sat there all night and got madder and madder. I really thought Skinner had been treating me fairly. He said he'd never take any action until he heard my side of the story." While the suspension was indefinite and Allen could have returned at any time, he chose to stay away from the game for twenty-six days, claiming that he would "never again play for the Phillies."[79]

At the urging of owner Bob Carpenter and Clem Cappozoli, a sales manager for the American Baking Company who served as Allen's agent, Allen agreed to be reinstated on the condition that the Phillies would trade him at the end of the year. [80] Now the fans would register their disapproval even more forcefully. Not only did Allen fail to make the All-Star Team in 1969 – a clear rejection of his behavior by the fans in so far as he was among the NL leaders in home runs and batting average – but the Philadelphia faithful also refused to name the slugger to the organization's All-Time Team as part of baseball's centennial celebration. Instead they named Eddie Waitkus as their first baseman, a popular Whiz Kid of the 1950 pennant-winning Phillies. When Willie Mays, the San Francisco Giants' future Hall of Famer, learned of the choice, he was incredulous: "It's stupid! How could Richie Allen not be on that team? He's the best hitter they've had since I've been around. None of those Whiz Kids could carry his bat."[81]

By now Allen's behavior was a regular topic of discussion across the nation. At a White House press reception before the All-Star Game, President Richard Nixon, an avid baseball fan, approached the Phillies' lone representative on the team, pitcher Grant Jackson, and said, "You tell Richie Allen to get back on the job. You tell him he's not going to get as good a job if he quits baseball. You tell Richie it's not for the good of the Phillies, or the good of the fans, but for the good of Richie Allen that he get back. 'I'll tell him, sir,' replied Jackson courteously, not having the heart to tell the president that Allen had already been reinstated."[82]

A week before he was to play his first postsuspension game, Allen removed his belongings from the clubhouse and set up his own private dressing room in a storage area near the manager's office at Connie Mack Stadium. When the press asked why he had moved his belongings, Allen said, only half in jest: "To keep the writers away."[83] In fact, Allen had told Skinner that "he just wanted to be left alone" and that "something might happen" if he remained in the clubhouse.

"I don't want any trouble," he insisted. "I really don't care if my team-mates dislike me. I've got some friends on this team, and there really isn't anyone I dislike. But baseball is an individual game. What I do doesn't hurt them. When I've done wrong, I've paid for it, and the only one who is hurt is Dick Allen himself." [84] Years later Allen would admit that his action was taken to "keep my teammates from getting into trouble." He recognized that his reputation as "baseball's bad boy, the bad ass of the National League" could have a negative effect on his closest friends, like Johnny Briggs. [85] Whatever the case might have been, the action infuriated Skinner, who ordered Allen's belongings returned to the clubhouse. "I don't care if he sits in that closet," Skinner told the press, "but he'll dress with everyone else!" Allen continued to dress in his private locker room for the next two weeks. Skinner kept ordering the clubhouse attendants to return his things to the locker room. Finally, the Phillies skipper gave up. [86] On August 7 he announced his resignation in a conference room at Reading Municipal Stadium, where the Phillies were scheduled to play their Double A club that night.

According to Skinner, the "straw that broke the camel's back" occurred earlier in the day when Allen came to him and said he refused to play at Reading because his "deal with Mr. Carpenter didn't include playing in exhibition games." When Skinner confronted both Carpenter and Quinn on the issue, they defended Allen's position. "I have too much pride to stay without support from the front office, particularly in my handling of Richie Allen," Skinner told the press. "Now I know what Gene Mauch went through. I feel like I've done a great job. I am a winner and I want to be a winner and you can't win this way. Not with Allen, who's been a big factor in our losing. There is very definitely disharmony on our club because he's been spoiled to the point where no manager can handle him." [87] Skinner also intimated that Carpenter and Quinn had been returning fines to Allen, which only served to undermine his authority even more. [88] Carpenter immediately rejected the notion.

Expressing his regret at Skinner's decision to resign, the Phillies owner admitted that he "interceded on occasion to mediate problems with Allen." "Whatever I did," he said, "was, in my opinion, in the best in-terests of the team." At the same time, Carpenter insisted that he never "interfered with the operation of the team on the field" or returned fine money. [89]

After the resignation Allen claimed that he was being made a scapegoat. Referring to his former manager, Allen stated:

He don't show me any guts by quitting like that and laying it in my lap. He's got a team that's twenty-one games under .500, and it's all my fault. Besides, I never told him I could go over his head. What did I ever do to him? I resent being made a scapegoat in another managerial move. If it boiled down to him or me, he didn't have to go. He can't put all the blame on me. He can't blame me for a 44–64 record. Nor have I ever seen a cent of the money Skinner said was returned to me by the front office. They say I call my own shots. How can they say that when all I want to do is get the hell out of Philadelphia?"[90]

There was some truth to Allen's statement. He had already missed forty-four games at that point in the season, and in spite of it Allen still led the team in batting average, home runs, and RBIs. With the exception of prospects like center fielder Larry Hisle and pitcher Rick Wise, the team was a collection of journeyman players and aging veterans. There wasn't much talent left. Then, again, Skinner wasn't referring to Allen's playing performance but his divisive behavior, which seemed to put the club in almost constant turmoil. The *Sporting News* registered that point in a very biting editorial on August 23:

If ever a young man needed some counseling and guidance, that man is Richie Allen. The Phillies slugger has $1,000,000 worth of talent and 10¢ worth of ability to understand what his role is with a team that has 24 other players besides himself. Unless a firm hand is taken with Allen, he'll go through more managers than Bluebeard does wives. Allen has just disposed of his second manager, Bob Skinner, who resigned in disgust, and there's no reason to believe that he won't dispense with others unless owner Bob Carpenter takes a firm hand. Just what Allen's problem is in Philadelphia is unclear. He says he's unhappy there, but would he be happier someplace else? There are a lot of club owners who aren't willing to find out. Allen's value keeps diminishing as his propensity for showing up late or not at all keeps rising. . . . More severe penalties against Allen might be the answer, but if Carpenter keeps refunding the fines, what's the purpose of assessing them in the first place? Skinner underwent the same harassment as his predecessor, Gene Mauch. But Skinner brought to light something that many had suggested but didn't know for sure. Allen's rebellious attitude had caused disharmony on the club, an intolerable situation, said Skinner. It might pay Carpenter to realize that he has a team to consider – and it isn't composed of one man.[91]

When Quinn handed over the interim manager's position to George Myatt, the press asked him how he would handle Allen. "I believe God Almighty hisself would have trouble handling Richie Allen," remarked the Phillies long-time coach. To be sure, Myatt refused to become embroiled in more controversy. He suspended most of the club's rules for the remaining games and humored Allen's behavior, which now included scratching messages to the fans in the dirt around first base. On August 9 Allen scratched "Oct. 2" – the last day of the regular season and his date of liberation from the Phillies. Quinn phoned NL president Warren Giles for a ruling on the action and Giles told him that it was "inappropriate." Quinn had the grounds crew erase the message. But Allen would not be deterred. The following night he scratched "Coke" onto the first base cutout, later explaining that the fans were "getting on me and I wanted to hit a home run over the Coca Cola sign to shut them up." The next night he wrote "Boo" – and the fans happily obliged him.[92]

Allen continued scratching messages over the next six days, a span in which he hit five home runs. "I kept it up 'cause everyone made such a fuss over it," he admitted. Shortly after, Commissioner Bowie Kuhn attended a doubleheader, witnessed Allen's artwork, and ordered him to stop. Allen responded to Kuhn's edit during the second game by writing "No" and "Why?". Finally, the home plate umpire called time out, went over to Allen and told him that Quinn had called to complain. Begrudgingly Allen erased the words. His final message came the next night when he scratched "Mom" into the dirt. It was a reference to his mother who Allen claimed was "the only one who can tell me what to do."[93]

The Phillies sputtered to a fifth-place finish in 1969, thirty-seven games out. Shortly after, Allen was traded to the St. Louis Cardinals in a seven-player deal that would later go down in the annals of baseball history. The Phillies sent Allen, Cookie Rojas, and pitcher Jerry Johnson to St. Louis for Curt Flood, a Gold Glove centerfielder, Byron Browne, a young outfield prospect, catcher Tim McCarver, and reliever Joe Hoerner.[94] The irony in this deal was that Flood, who was black, refused to report to the Phillies. Instead he challenged baseball's reserve clause, setting in motion a chain of events that would result in free agency.

Allen was overjoyed by the news. "You don't know how good it feels to get out of Philadelphia," he said. "They treat you like cattle. It was like a form of slavery. Once you step out of bounds they'll do everything possible to destroy your soul."[95]

Interlude, 1970–74

Allen would continue his impressive hitting in St. Louis, but the Cards had acquired him to make them a contender. Instead, they finished thirteen games out of first, just as they had the previous season without him. Stating that their "needs had changed" and that they were "looking for defense and speed rather than power hitting," the Cardinals traded Allen to the Los Angeles Dodgers in 1971.[96] There he was a large part of the team's success. His .295 average, 23 homers, and 90 RBIs propelled the Dodgers into the thick of a pennant race. But Allen refused to cater to the fans and repeatedly rejected Dodger president Walter O'Malley's requests to make public appearances. Again he was traded, this time to the Chicago White Sox, where he spent the happiest three years of his baseball career.

When playing for Chuck Tanner, a neighbor from Wampum, Allen excelled, turning a mediocre team into a contender. In '72 he was named the AL's MVP. His 37 home runs that season set a franchise record, and his 113 RBIs led the League. The following season he was hitting .310 until he broke his leg in a collision at first base and missed the remainder of the season. In '74 he was having another remarkable year, hitting at a .310 clip, when chronic shoulder pain convinced him to take an early retirement.[97]

Craig Wright points to Allen's success in other cities to debunk all the criticism of the Phillies' first black superstar. Quoting the favorable impressions of Allen's managers from the Cardinals, Dodgers, and White Sox, Wright notes that they all considered him "a good teammate and a team player." While those sentiments were voiced by men who were managing pennant contenders and were made nearly two decades after Allen's career had ended, they should still be taken seriously. In fact, Wright insists that had Allen "started off with another team, in another city, or just at a later time," the sportswriters' "attitudes towards him and our perceptions about him would be entirely different." Instead Wright dismisses the "troublemaker attitude" by stating that Allen was "not interested in being known," that he was "content to present a blank canvas to the media and fans," and that the writers "took that opportunity to paint our archetype of the disruptive player."[98] But there are too many coincidences between Allen's "individualism" and the turmoil that visited the Phillies' clubhouse to dismiss his manipulative behavior. That became clear, once again, in the mid-1970s, when Allen returned to Philadelphia.

Return to Philadelphia, 1975–76

When Allen returned to Philadelphia in 1975, he had a genuine desire to become a constructive member of the organization. His five years away seemed to have given him the necessary time and distance to put his earlier years with the team in perspective. Changes within the Phillies organization also made the opportunity an attractive one for him.

By the mid-1970s the Philadelphia Phillies were building another contender. Danny Ozark, who Allen had come to admire during his year in the Dodgers organization, was now the manager. Ozark was a fatherly type, ideally suited for the talented young team the Phillies were putting together. Under the direction of General Manager Paul Owens and Director of Player Development Dallas Green, the team's farm system had produced some impressive young talent. Among the budding stars were shortstop Larry Bowa, outfielder Greg Luzinski, catcher Bob Boone, first baseman Willie Montanez, and third baseman Mike Schmidt. They had also engineered some trades that paid off immediately. Steve Carlton, acquired from the Cardinals in 1972, was establishing himself as one of the finest pitchers in the game. He was joined by another former Cy Young Award–winner, former BoSox hurler Jim Lonborg. Other trades brought veterans such as Bill Robinson, an outfielder once touted by the Yankees as the "next Mickey Mantle," Del Unser, a steady hitter who platooned in the Indians' outfield, and Dave Cash, a scrappy veteran second baseman who was instrumental in Pittsburgh's three division titles and a world championship. The experience, enthusiasm, and aggressive play of these veterans were just what the young Phillies needed to win. But they were still missing that veteran power hitter who could put them over the top. Owens believed that Dick Allen was the player who could do it.

After retiring in September of 1974, Allen returned to his farm in Perkasie, Pennsylvania, intending to pursue his "other" passion – raising thoroughbred horses. But the Phillies believed that Allen still had a lot of baseball left in him. The .302 average and 32 homers he compiled in '74 certainly seemed to reinforce that feeling. The following April, a small contingent of Phillies – Schmidt, Cash, and broadcaster Rich Ashburn – paid the recently retired slugger a visit.

"It was a conversation I wouldn't forget," said Allen.

Schmidt was talking about the Phils needing some additional clout, a big stick in the lineup to go with his and Luzinski's. He said something about "Schmidt-Luzinski-Allen firepower." Cash was rapping about the brothers on the Phils team and how they could use a veteran to inspire them. And ol' Richie Ashburn was telling tales about how much the city of Philadelphia had changed for the better. That was as specific as it got, but I got the message: "Come home, Dick. We love you. They're gonna love you!"

At first I figured it had to be a joke. It's not my style to return to the scene of the crime. But I had to admit the idea of coming home did fire me up a bit. I always did like surprises – even when the surprises were on me. When they left the farm that day, I hugged them all. I was touched to feel wanted by guys who played for the Phillies.[99]

That visit was followed by another. This one from Ashburn and Hall-of-Famer Robin Roberts. Again, the Phillies attempted to reconcile with their one-time Rookie of the Year. "No specific requests were made and no promises given," insisted Allen.[100] A few days later the *Philadelphia Inquirer* reported that Commissioner Bowie Kuhn was investigating the Phillies for tampering with the retired slugger. Almost immediately the White Sox sold Allen to the Atlanta Braves. Of course, Allen had no intention of playing for Atlanta, not after the painful experience of playing in the South at the start of his career. The Braves quickly realized that fact and, after Kuhn dismissed the tampering charges, dealt him to the Phillies.[101] To make room for Allen, Owens traded first baseman Willie Montanez to the San Francisco Giants for centerfielder Garry Maddox, an excellent defensive centerfielder.

Allen's decision to return to the Phillies shocked the baseball world. To those who really knew him, though, it was consistent with his approach to the game itself. Allen's career had always been distinguished by predictable unpredictability. Depending upon the observer's point of view, that could be a wonderful asset or a dismantling liability. But two things were certain: Allen was blessed with the hugely exceptional talent of a superstar and, at the age of thirty-three, he still had not realized his full potential. He knew it, too. Allen understood that he had not fulfilled anybody's expectations – the fans', the baseball world's, or, sadly, his own. In eleven previous seasons he had hit 40 home runs once, drove in 100 runs three times, and never had the experience of being on a pennant winner.

Only twice did he match the offensive productivity of his 1964 Rookie-of-the-Year season – in 1966 when he belted 40 homers, and in '72 when he batted .308, hit 37 home runs, and drove in 113 RBIS to win the AL's MVP Award. Instead, his career was troubled by an odd assortment of injuries and an inability to cope with people who had difficulty understanding him.[102] Perhaps a second chance in Philadelphia was what he needed. He got it.

Ashburn was correct. Phillies baseball had changed in the six years since Allen had last played for the team. There was no more Connie Mack Stadium. Instead, the Phillies played in the brand new Veterans Stadium. The crowds were suburban and white. There was a new owner in Ruly Carpenter, who seemed more compassionate and more approachable than his sterile, ultraconservative father. Conditions seemed right for a reconciliation and, with a little luck, that pennant that Allen desired. He was excited to return to his old team which, as he put it, "finally entered the twentieth century in terms of race." In the 1960s Allen believed that he represented "a threat to white people in Philadelphia. I wore my hair in an Afro," he recalled.

> I said what was on my mind. I didn't take shit. But now Philadelphia and its fans seemed to have changed. The brothers on the team represented a new generation of black ballplayers. They were talented and proud of it and didn't take a back seat to anybody. In terms of pure baseball, I looked around that clubhouse and liked what I saw. We had Schmidty at third base and there's no telling what he could do, Cash at second, Bowa at short, Bob Boone behind the plate, me at first. Pretty tough infield. We had Luzinski and Maddox in the outfield, and platooners Ollie Brown and Mike Anderson to round it out. We had pitchers like Steve Carlton and Jim Lonborg, and Tug McGraw in the bullpen. I remember thinking that maybe with this bunch I could get myself a World Series ring after all.[103]

Allen returned to the Phillies' lineup against the Cincinnati Reds in mid-May. It was a hero's homecoming. His new teammates openly embraced him. The energy level on the club seemed to soar. The fans were even more receptive, even patronizing. If Allen made a miscue during those first few games back – as he did several times, having missed all of spring training – it was excused. He was cheered constantly for routine plays. Perhaps the most paternalistic expression of fan appreciation came in a game against San Francisco. After struggling all evening against the

Giants' pitching, in the tenth inning Allen hit a sharp liner down the left field line that dribbled through the third baseman's legs. When the winning run scored on the error, the Phillies' faithful erupted with applause and demanded a curtain call from their new hero.[104] Even the press was friendly.

Allen found himself glibly answering the questions of sportswriters he had refused to talk to six years earlier. Now they followed the fans' lead, a band of admirers toting pads and pens, hanging on his every word. Six years before, the press had run Allen out of town, steadfastly continuing to call him "Richie," knowing fully that he found the name denigrating because it sounded like a boy's name and whites tended to think of blacks as "boys." He had requested time and again that he be referred to as "Dick Allen." Now they graciously deferred to his request.[105] While all the media hype unfolded, Ruly Carpenter, who understood the fickle nature of the local press, stood by watching, concerned that they wouldn't run his new slugger out of town again. "I hope to hell they leave him alone," he said quietly. "I could never understand why they got on him so when he was here before. He's a serious, dedicated athlete, he's a great team player, and really, he never did anything you could consider bad for the game of baseball. Hell, Babe Ruth was drunk all the time, whored around like mad, set a lousy example for kids, and there was never a bad word written about him. Allen would show up late for a practice once and they'd crucify him. How do you explain it?"[106]

Carpenter seemed to forget that Ruth was white and played in New York, a melting pot for different ethnic and racial groups. Allen was black and was playing in Philadelphia, a city with a reputation for racism.

Initially Allen picked up where he had left off in Chicago, serving as a good teammate. He took a young Mike Schmidt under his wing. There was a natural affinity between the two men. Like Allen, Schmidt in 1975 had superstar potential and an extremely sensitive ego. Both men were natural athletes in the truest sense of the term. Both were blessed with tall, muscular, athletic builds. Both were power hitters with high strikeout ratios. Both had to labor under the unrealistic expectations of the Philadelphia fans and the local media. What had been said about Allen was said about Schmidt in 1975: "The only thing that can keep Mike Schmidt from being a superstar is Mike Schmidt. He has all the tools and it is only a matter of applying himself and not getting fatheaded."[107] It was almost as if Schmidt had inherited Allen's legacy. In that sense it was

Schmidt's good fortune that the Phillies acquired the enigmatic slugger when his own career was at a critical juncture.

"Growing up," said Schmidt, "I admired Dick Allen. I pretended I was like him when I was up at bat playing Legion ball in Ohio. I was fortunate that we became good friends on the Phillies and that I learned a lot from him."[108] Allen would help Schmidt learn to cope with the press, the boo-birds, the fickleness of Philadelphia baseball itself. He was really the only person who could help, having experienced it himself six years earlier.

"Schmidt had as much talent as anybody I've ever seen play the game," said Allen of his younger teammate.

> Quick wrists. Strong. Perfect baseball body. But he was trying to hit every pitch out of the park, and when he didn't, he'd sulk about it. When I got to Philly in '75 he didn't seem to be playing the game. I talked to him about swinging down on the ball. The downswing is the ticket. Schmidt picked up on it pretty quick. The other thing about him was his attitude. He was moody and if he had a bad game, he'd take it home with him. I used to take him out after a game for a couple of beers and we'd talk about things, have a few laughs, put the ballyard behind us. I used to tell Schmidty to pretend he was back in the sandlots of Ohio where he grew up. Get out there and bang that ball like you did in high school. He began to get the message. He hit 38 homers in '75 but struggled with his average. He still had some work to do.[109]

While Allen's mentoring of Schmidt was useful to the young power hitter, the former certainly didn't contribute much to the offense. By early September he was hitting an anemic .230 with only 12 home runs and 62 RBIS, and the Phillies found themselves floundering in a two-week slump. Manager Danny Ozark was understandably frustrated. He had an awesome team that featured both 1974 home run champions (Schmidt and Allen), two former Cy Young Award–winners (Carlton and Lonborg), the best second base-shortstop combination in the game (Cash and Bowa), a top-notch bullpen led by Tug McGraw (who was acquired from the New York Mets), and a quality bench. Of the twenty-four Major League teams, only Cincinnati and Oakland could match the Phillies in terms of all-around talent. Yet the Phils couldn't put it all together and finished in second place, six-and-a-half games behind the Pittsburgh Pirates in the NL East.

Although the second-place finish was a tremendous disappointment, there were some bright spots. Cash, Bowa, and Garry Maddox gave the

Phils an excellent defense up the middle. Cash also contributed mightily to the offense, topping the NL in hits with 213, scoring 111 runs, and batting .305. In addition to Schmidt's 38 homers and 95 RBIS, Luzinski, who was rebounding from his injury of the previous season, contributed some formidable power with 34 homers and a league-leading 120 RBIS. McGraw went 9–16 with 14 saves out of the bullpen, establishing his role as closer. Journeyman outfielder Jay Johnstone found a home in Philadelphia's outfield as a platoon player with a reputation as a solid contact hitter who rarely struck out. What's more, the Phillies had a good mix of young ballplayers and seasoned veterans, all of whom were returning the following season.

Pitchers Tom Underwood and Larry Christenson were, at twenty-two years old, the youngest players on the team. Cash (28), Bowa (30), Luzinski (26), Schmidt (26), Maddox (26), and Boone (28) had not yet reached their prime. Allen (35), Lonborg (33), Carlton (32), and McGraw (30) had had enough experience with winning to provide the kind of leadership necessary for a contender. The Phillies' exceptional combination of age, talent, speed, defense, and power allowed them to dominate the NL in 1976, at least through the first half of the season.[110]

The Phillies didn't seem to lose during the first four months of the '76 campaign. At the All-Star break they held a commanding ten-game lead over the second-place Pirates. They had been playing .800 baseball since the beginning of June. Eleven of the Phils were hitting .300 or better. Carlton, who had been considered by many sportswriters as "washed up" after a 44–47 three-year slump, was 5–2, rejuvenated by the return of his close friend and personal catcher, Tim McCarver. Jim Lonborg, another former Cy Young Award–winner who also suffered the same criticism, was 8–0 at midseason, which included a near-perfect game against the Dodgers. Together with Larry Christenson, Carlton and Lonborg combined to win eighteen consecutive decisions. Not surprisingly, the Phils increased their lead to fifteen-and-a-half games by August 1. Thomas Boswell of the *Washington Post*, one of the more astute baseball writers, stated that the Phils were "on the sort of natural, unrealistic high that blesses a team perhaps once every 20 years. They can beat you every way: power, hitting [for average], speed, defense, and brains."[111]

The Phils were coasting along through the '76 season until September. Then they went into a three-week tailspin. They lost 10 of their last 11 games, while the second-place Pirates won 12 of their last 13. Their lead had dwindled to just 3 games by late September.[112] "It was a nightmare," said Schmidt. "The hate mail, the letters saying we were choking, the abuse. I'd be out there trying to catch a tough grounder, thinking that what I did would decide whether we'd be 2 1/2 in front the next day or 4 1/2. Blow this one, I'd think, and I'll need cops to guard my house."[113] Finally, on September 26 in the first game of a doubleheader against Montreal, Jim Lonborg pitched the Phillies past the Expos for a 4–1 victory to clinch the division.[114] It was the first time the Phils would go to postseason play in twenty-six years. Unfortunately, they would go on to lose to Cincinnati's "Big Red Machine" in four straight games.

Despite the Phillies' success on the playing field, there were signs of racial turmoil in the clubhouse. Once again the controversy seemed to center on Dick Allen. Bowa constantly criticized his inability to dig balls out of the dirt at first base, something Allen's predecessor Willie Montanez could do with great skill. Allen confronted the antagonistic shortstop, telling him to make more accurate throws. At the same time, Allen by early August had begun to question the equity of Ozark's platoon system in the outfield. He believed that the black players Ollie Brown and Bobby Tolan were not "getting the shot they deserved" and that the Phillies were "working a quota system."[115]

Matters became worse as the Phillies' losing streak mounted in September. It almost appeared as if they were two teams – one white, the other black. Just before the Phillies clinched their division, management announced that they had to cut the postseason squad to twenty-five players and that veteran Tony Taylor would probably not be eligible for the playoffs. Taylor, a scrappy Cuban-born infielder and a fan favorite, had played with the Phillies for fifteen seasons and had never made it to the playoffs. "I was disappointed," admitted Taylor years later. "I was 42 years old at the time and realized that they wanted to keep the younger players on the roster. But I had also played all those years in Philadelphia and would have liked the chance to play in the playoffs. Still, I realized I had no control over the situation."[116] Allen, on the other hand, was furious.

He and Taylor had been roommates when they came up together in the Phillies organization in the 1960s.

To my way of thinking, nothing could be more unfair than for the Phillies to take Tony Taylor's uniform. . . . He played 19 seasons in the big leagues,

but never in a World Series. He was a model player in the Phillies' organization, mostly through the club's worst times. He was the one guy that
would walk to the box seats and sign autographs before every game. He
was the one guy who would volunteer to do a postgame interview when
the rest of us were turning our backs on the press. In all his years, he never
complained. Tony Taylor was Philadelphia Phillies baseball.[117]

Allen took the snub personally, and he gave the Phillies an ultimatum:
unless Taylor was made eligible he would refuse to play in the postseason.
"With God as my witness," he told the front office, "if you take Tony
Taylor's uniform off his back, you'll have to take mine, too."[118] It was
no idle threat. The Phillies eventually agreed to keep Taylor in uniform
for the playoffs, but placed him on the roster as a coach.

After the Phils clinched their division in Montreal, Allen, Cash, Maddox, and Schmidt gathered in an equipment room near the visitors'
locker room while the rest of the team celebrated. Allen offered a prayer
of thanks that the four players had shared the season together and then
they joined their teammates' celebration. Some of the other players noticed their absence and made a remark about their "attitude."[119] Dave
Cash insists that "there was nothing racial about that meeting. Something
like that should have never been written by the press," he added.

> To set the record straight – yes, we did have a meeting in the back of the
> clubhouse after the first game of the doubleheader. It was 9:30 at night
> and it was about 35 degrees outside, too cold to hang out in the dugout.
> All the starting players were in that room, not just Dick Allen, Dave Cash,
> Garry Maddox, and Mike Schmidt. That small group of us just wanted to
> get together to thank the good Lord that He had taken us that far. But the
> press purposefully misinterpreted the remarks of one teammate, which
> was meant to be taken humorously, and made a racial thing out of it.[120]

Again, Allen was at the center of the controversy.

Afterward, the Phillies headed to St. Louis for their final regular-season
series and Allen returned to Philadelphia. He was mired in a slump and
Ozark agreed to let him have the time off. When the press reported these
events they were less than complimentary to Allen. "To them, it was the
reemergence of 'Richie' Allen," said the Phils' first baseman. "I began to
get booed, and the threats started coming to me in the mail. It was the
1960s all over again."[121]

Not surprisingly, Allen was released by the Phillies shortly after the playoffs. His final statistics for the season (.268 avg, 15 home runs, 49 RBIS) confirmed the fact that his best days were already behind him. He would return to the American League with the Oakland A's for one last season before retiring in 1977. Dave Cash, who asked for and failed to receive a long-term contract, became a free agent and was eventually signed by the Montreal Expos. "I don't know whether those actions were racially motivated or not," said Cash years later, "and I really didn't care because I thought I could play with any team and so could Dick Allen. I can't speak for Dick, but I certainly didn't look upon the situation as a racial one. When a club gives you your release or fails to sign you to a contract, it's usually because they have someone else to replace you."[122]

Schmidt agreed. While the press interpreted his friendship with Allen as well as the perm hair style he wore during the mid-1970s as a rejection of the organization's poor treatment of its black players, Schmidt denies that he was making any political statement. "Sure, I may have confided in Dick Allen," he admitted looking back on the early part of his career.

> I respected his playing abilities, just as I did those of my other teammates. But that doesn't mean I was making a statement about race relations on the Phillies. Sure, I heard Dick talk about his experience in the Minor Leagues and having to stay in a separate hotel. Like anybody else – white or black – I felt badly for him that he had to deal with that kind of discrimination. But I never donned a curled hair style – or what some called a "red afro" – to show my sympathy for him or any of the other blacks on the team. In fact, many white players wore that kind of hair style in the '70s. It was a practical thing to do. You didn't need to blowdry your hair after a shower! It had nothing to do with the black athletes on the team.[123]

Like Cash, it is still difficult for Schmidt to understand why the press always seemed to misinterpret Allen's behavior as racially motivated. "The baseball writers used to claim that Dick would divide the clubhouse along racial lines," said Schmidt. "That was a lie. You walk into any Major League clubhouse today and you'll see the white guys at one end listening to their music and the black players listening theirs. It was that way in Dick Allen's era, and it's that way today. In all my years, I've never seen it different. The truth is that Dick never divided any clubhouse. He just got guys thinking."[124]

*

Dick Allen played fifteen seasons in the Major Leagues. During that span he hit 351 home runs and posted a career batting average of .292. A six-time All-Star, he was also the NL's Rookie of the Year in 1964 and the AL's Most Valuable Player in 1972. While that kind of career is worthy of Hall-of-Fame consideration, Allen has never come close because of his controversial reputation as a "troublemaker."

When he first came to the Phillies in the early 1960s, Allen was a naive teenager from rural Pennsylvania who "never wanted to be a superstar" but simply "play a good game of baseball" without being scrutinized by the fans or the press.[125] Victimized by racial prejudice and the distortions of the media, Allen panicked. He wanted out of Philadelphia, but he was too valuable to the organization to let go. So he rebelled, manipulating race and the Phillies' own double standard for him as the means by which to force a trade. In the process Dick Allen could be defensive in his attitude toward others, erratic in his behavior, and overly absorbed with the problems that surrounded him, many of his own creation. What he really wanted, though, was to be liked. That is why he returned to Philadelphia in 1975 and why he continues to work for the Phillies public relations department today. Sadly, the turmoil has cost him a bronze plaque in Cooperstown.

Sadder still is Allen's own epitaph, which he wrote in his 1989 autobiography, *Crash*: "I was labeled an outlaw, and after a while that's what I became. Still I wonder how good I could have been."[126]

NOTES

1. B. James, *The Politics of Glory: How Baseball's Hall of Fame Really Works* (New York: Macmillan, 1994), 322–25.

2. D. Wellman, *Portraits of White Racism* (Cambridge: Cambridge University Press, 1977), chap. 1.

3. K. L. Shropshire, *In Black and White: Race and Sports in America* (New York: New York University Press, 1996), 7–11.

4. See B. D. Tatum, *"Why Are All the Black Kids Sitting Together In the Cafeteria?" and Other Conversations about Race* (New York: Basic Books, 1999), 7–12.

5. W. E. Cross Jr., *Shades of Black: Diversity in African-American Identity* (Philadelphia: Temple University Press, 1991).

6. See J. Robinson, *I Never Had It Made* (New York: Putnam, 1972), 71–76; D. Falkner, *Great Time Coming: The Life of Jackie Robinson from Baseball to*

Birmingham (New York: Simon and Schuster, 1995), 163–64; and T. McGrath, "Color Me Badd," *Fan* (September 1996): 39.

7. McGrath, "Color Me Badd," 39; and M. Sokolove, "Nice Is Not Enough," *Philadelphia Inquirer Magazine*, March 30, 1997, 21. For more on John Kennedy see *Philadelphia Inquirer*, February 9, 14, 23, 25, 27, 1957; March 23, 27, 1957; May 6, 1957; and April 30, 1998.

8. For urban history of Philadelphia see E. Wold II, *Philadelphia: Portrait of an American City* (Philadelphia: Camino Books, 1990), 320–47; and R. F. Weigley, *Philadelphia: A 300-Year History* (New York: W. W. Norton, 1982), 704–27. For an analysis of the social problems confronting Philadelphia in the 1960s see J. A. Michener, *The Quality of Life* (Philadelphia: The Girard Company, 1970).

9. See Weigley, *Philadelphia*, 661–63; and S. A. Paolantonio, *Frank Rizzo: The Last Big Man in Big City America* (Philadelphia: Camino Books, 1993).

10. R. Westcott and F. Bilovsky, *The Phillies' Encyclopedia* (Philadelphia: Temple University Press, 1993), 479–83.

11. Westcott and Bilovsky, *Phillies' Encyclopedia*, 452–54.

12. Mauch quoted in R. Kelly, "Mauch Cracks Down on Phillies," *Philadelphia Evening Bulletin*, May 12, 1960.

13. See "Robert M. Carpenter Papers, Philadelphia Baseball Club – National League," manuscript box #1: Player Development Papers, 1957–64, Manuscript Collection, Hagley Library, Wilmington DE (hereafter, "Carpenter Papers"). Approximately twenty players were on the roster of each team in the Phillies' Minor League system during the period 1957–64. Those teams were: Buffalo (AAA), Indianapolis (AAA), Chattanooga (AA), Asheville (A), Williamsport (A), Des Moines (B), Bakersfield (C), Tampa (D), Elmira (D), and Johnson City (D).

14. See "Player Signings, 1958–64," Carpenter Papers.

15. See "Player Signings, 1958–64," Carpenter Papers.

16. See "Player Development Papers, 1957–62," Carpenter Papers.

17. Tatum, *Conversations about Race*, 133–36. The U.S. Bureau of the Census defines "Hispanic" as an ethnic label that includes those Latinos who trace their family background to Mexico, Puerto Rico, Cuba, the Dominican Republic, Colombia, Ecuador, El Salvador, Guatemala, Peru, or Nicaragua.

18. Westcott and Bilovsky, *Phillies' Encyclopedia*, 490–91. It is important to note that the Phillies' first regular minority player was not John Kennedy but rather Chico Fernandez, who was acquired from the Brooklyn Dodgers in the spring of 1957 to fill the team's need at shortstop. He was the Phils' regular shortstop for two years, hitting .260 in 1957 and .230 in 1958 before losing the starting job. Although he had good range as a fielder, he also committed a fair amount of errors. In 1959 he was traded to the Detroit Tigers and became

their regular shortstop for the next three years. See R. Kelly, "Phils' Deal for Fernandez Shapes Up as a Wise Move," *Philadelphia Evening Bulletin*, April 6, 1957; idem, "Fernandez Has Jittery Debut," *Philadelphia Evening Bulletin*, April 8, 1957; and Westcott and Bilovsky, *Phillies' Encyclopedia*, 234–35.

19. R. Allen and T. Whitaker, *Crash: The Life and Times of Dick Allen* (New York: Ticknor and Fields, 1989), 47–52.

20. Allen and Whitaker, *Crash*, 35–36.

21. Allen and Whitaker, *Crash*, 37.

22. Allen and Whitaker, *Crash*, 36.

23. Allen and Whitaker, *Crash*, 47–48.

24. Westcott and Bilovsky, *Phillies' Encyclopedia*, 117–21.

25. Allen and Whitaker, *Crash*, 14; and C. Nesfield, "New Team. New Town: New Richie?" *Black Sports* (July 1971): 31.

26. Allen and Whitaker, *Crash*, 11.

27. Allen and Whitaker, *Crash*, 14.

28. In 1970, after Lucchesi had been named Phillies manager and Allen was gone from the organization, he was asked about his former players' contention of racist treatment by the Little Rock fans. Lucchesi replied: "I dispute that claim. He [Allen] was voted the club's most valuable player by the fans. Do fans who hate a player give him a new suit?" See Lucchesi as quoted by B. Conlin, "Richie Is Beautiful: He Don't Give a Damn for Nobody," *Jock* 2 (January 1970): 94.

29. Conlin, "Richie Is Beautiful," 13–15, 21.

30. Conlin, "Richie Is Beautiful," 20.

31. Allen quoted by A. Lewis, "Phils May Transplant Speedy Gardener Allen at Hot Corner," *Sporting News*, October 26, 1963.

32. Mauch quoted in Lewis, "Phils May Transplant Allen."

33. Mauch quoted in A. Lewis, "Phils Get Rich with Wampum Whiz," *Sporting News*, May 23, 1964.

34. *Philadelphia Daily News*, July 13, 1964.

35. *Philadelphia Daily News*, July 13, 1964.

36. Westcott and Bilovsky, *Phillies' Encyclopedia*, 122.

37. Westcott and Bilovsky, *Phillies' Encyclopedia*, 121–23; and D. Anderson, "1964: The Phillies' Phlop," in *Pennant Races* (New York: Doubleday, 1994), 255–88.

38. Interview with Ruben Amaro Sr. at Lackawanna County Stadium, Scranton PA, August 11, 1999.

39. J. Callison, *The Johnny Callison Story* (New York: Vantage Press, 1991), 125.

40. Interview with Tony Taylor at Veterans Stadium, Philadelphia, July 27, 1999.

41. Allen and Whitaker, *Crash*, 54–55.

42. Allen and Whitaker, *Crash*, 4–7.

43. A. Lewis, "Briggs Came to Play and Phils Are Glad They Gave Him a Break," *Philadelphia Evening Bulletin*, July 31, 1965; and idem, "Phils Eye Briggs as Stu's Successor," *Sporting News*, October 30, 1965.

44. Pat Corrales as quoted by C. R. Wright, "Another View of Dick Allen," SABR's *Baseball Research Journal* 24 (1995): 4.

45. Callison quoted in Allen and Whitaker, *Crash*, 7.

46. Amaro interview, August 11, 1999.

47. R. Kelly, "Reds Snap Phils' six game Streak, 10–8," *Philadelphia Evening Bulletin*, July 4, 1965.

48. Conlin, "Richie Is Beautiful," 91; and Allen and Whitaker, *Crash*, 8.

49. Mauch quoted in D. Wolf, "Let's Everybody Boo Rich Allen!" *Life Magazine* (August 1969): 51; and Allen and Whitaker, *Crash*, 9.

50. Thomas quoted in *Philadelphia Evening Bulletin*, July 5, 1965.

51. R. Kelly, "37,110 Watch Allen Slam Phils to Split with Giants," *Philadelphia Evening Bulletin*, July 9, 1965.

52. Allen and Whitaker, *Crash*, 58.

53. Allen and Whitaker, *Crash*, 58–59.

54. Wright, "Another View of Allen," 4.

55. Mauch quoted in Wright, "Another View of Allen"; and Mauch quoted in Conlin, "Richie Is Beautiful," 91.

56. Taylor interview, July 27, 1999.

57. Conlin, "Richie Is Beautiful," 91.

58. Conlin, "Richie Is Beautiful," 91; and Allen and Whitaker, *Crash*, 71–72.

59. Allen and Whitaker, *Crash*, 37.

60. Allen and Whitaker, *Crash*, 65; and Wright, "Another View of Allen," 5.

61. Allen and Whitaker, *Crash*, 62–63.

62. Conlin, "Richie Is Beautiful," 92; and Wolf, "Let's Everybody Boo Allen," 51.

63. Conlin, "Richie Is Beautiful," 91; and R. Young, "Mauch's Firing Proves Players Call Shots," *New York Daily News*, June 20, 1968.

64. A. Lewis, "'Traffic Jam' Late Arrive Richie Tells Grim Mauch," *Sporting News*, May 18, 1968; and Young, "Mauch's Firing."

65. Conlin, "Richie Is Beautiful," 91–92.

66. A. Lewis, "Lots of 'Ifs' in Mauch Sizeup of Phils," *Sporting News*, February 17, 1968.

67. S. Grady, "Phillies Too Impatient to Start Rebuilding Now," *Philadelphia Evening Bulletin*, December 31, 1967.

68. Quinn quoted in A. Lewis, "Allen Rift Called 'Factor' in Mauch's Firing," *Sporting News*, June 29, 1968.

69. Mauch quoted in A. Lewis, "Mauch Absolves Phillies in Firing Snafu," *Philadelphia Inquirer*, July 6, 1968; and Mauch in R. Young, "Gene Takes Phillies Off Hook," *New York Daily News*, June 20, 1968.

70. A. Daley, "Sports of the Times," *New York Times*, June 25, 1968.

71. Allen and Whitaker, *Crash*, 70–73; and Wolf, "Let's Boo Allen," 52.

72. Skinner quoted in A. Lewis, " 'Many Pilots Would Like Rich – I'm One of 'Em': Skinner," *Sporting News*, June 29, 1968.

73. A. Lewis, "Plate Skid Adds to Allen's Philly Enigma," *Sporting News*, September 28, 1968.

74. A. Lewis, "Carpenter Planning Shakeup of Phillies," *Sporting News*, October 19, 1968.

75. Carpenter quoted in Lewis, "Carpenter Planning Shakeup."

76. See A. Lewis, "Phils Put Callison, Rojas, and Allen on the Trading Block," *Sporting News*, October 26, 1968; and R. Schneider, "Tribe Dickering for Allen, Shudders at Hefty Price," *Sporting News*, November 30, 1968.

77. Allen quoted in "Richie Allen Is Not All Bad Boy," *New York Times*, May 18, 1969.

78. Allen and Rojas quoted in Wolf, "Let's Boo Allen," 53.

79. Wolf, "Let's Boo Allen," 54.

80. Conlin, "Richie Is Beautiful," 93–94; and R. Young, "Allen Forgiving Philly Fans? Not Yet He Ain't," *New York Daily News*, April 16, 1969.

81. Conlin, "Richie Is Beautiful," 88.

82. Conlin, "Richie Is Beautiful," 88.

83. Conlin, "Richie Is Beautiful," 94.

84. Allen quoted in *Philadelphia Inquirer*, July 31, 1969.

85. Allen and Whitaker, *Crash*, 79.

86. Wolf, "Let's Boo Allen," 53.

87. Skinner quoted in A. Lewis, "Skinner Quits – Had His Phil of Richie," *Philadelphia Inquirer*, August 8, 1969.

88. Conlin, "Richie Is Beautiful," 93

89. Carpenter quoted in Lewis, "Skinner Quits"; and Carpenter quoted in idem, "No Quaker Meeting When Skinner Made His Exit," *Sporting News*, August 23, 1969.

90. Allen quoted in A. Lewis, " 'Skinner Pushed Panic Button . . . So Did I,' says Richie," *Philadelphia Inquirer*, August 9, 1969; Conlin, "Richie Is Beautiful," 93; and Allen quoted in Wolf, "Let's Boo Allen," 53.

91. "Who's In Charge Around Here?" *Sporting News*, August 23, 1969.

92. Myatt quoted in Conlin, "Richie Is Beautiful," 93, 111.

93. Allen and Whitaker, *Crash*, 78; Wolf, "Let's Boo Allen," 51–53; and Conlin, "Richie Is Beautiful," 93.

94. "Phils Trade Allen to St. Louis. Phila. Gets Hoerner and Browne – Flood Plans to Retire as Player," *New York Times*, October 9, 1969.

95. "Phils Trade Allen," *New York Times*, October 9, 1969; and Allen quoted in W. B. Mead, *The Explosive Sixties: Baseball's Decade of Expansion* (Alexandria va: Redefinition, 1989).

96. Nesfield, "New Team, New Town," 63; and G. Kiseda, "For the Record: Allen Didn't Hurt Cardinals' Morale," *Philadelphia Evening Bulletin*, October 8, 1970.

97. Wright, "Another View of Allen," 8–10.

98. Wright, "Another View of Allen," 14.

99. Allen and Whitaker, *Crash*, 153.

100. Allen and Whitaker, *Crash*, 153.

101. Allen and Whitaker, *Crash*, 156–58.

102. For Allen's statistics see Wolff, *Baseball Encyclopedia*, 625; and B. Rosenberg, "Two for the See-Saw," *Philadelphia Magazine* (September 1975): 130–44.

103. Allen and Whitaker, *Crash*, 159–60.

104. Rosenberg, "Two for the See-Saw," 138.

105. Rosenberg, "Two for the See-Saw," 131–32.

106. Carpenter quoted in Rosenberg, "Two for the See-Saw," 135.

107. R. Kelly, "Schmidt Star Still Is Rising, Phillies Assert," *Sporting News*, February 22, 1975.

108. Interview with Mike Schmidt at Jupiter fl, October 8, 1998.

109. Allen and Whitaker, *Crash*, 161.

110. Westcott and Bilovsky, *Phillies' Encyclopedia*, 139, 204.

111. T. Boswell, "Cast Offs, Stars – They Do It for the Phillies," *Washington Post*, July 15, 1976.

112. Westcott and Bilovsky, *Phillies' Encyclopedia*, 138.

113. Schmidt quoted in R. Smith, "The Unmaking of a Reds' Fan," *New York Times*, October 9, 1976.

114. *Philadelphia Inquirer*, September 27, 1976.

115. Allen and Whitaker, *Crash*, 163.

116. Taylor interview, July 27, 1999.

117. Allen and Whitaker, *Crash*, 164.

118. Allen and Whitaker, *Crash*, 165.

119. Allen and Whitaker, *Crash*, 166.

120. Interview with Dave Cash at Lackawanna County Stadium, Scranton pa, August 11, 1999.

121. Allen and Whitaker, *Crash*, 167.

122. Cash interview, August 11, 1999.
123. Schmidt interview, October 8, 1998.
124. Schmidt interview, October 8, 1998.
125. Conlin, "Richie Is Beautiful," 90.
126. Allen and Whitaker, *Crash*, 34.

ANTHONY R. PRATKANIS & MARLENE E. TURNER

Nine Principles of Successful Affirmative Action

Mr. Branch Rickey, Mr. Jackie Robinson, and the Integration of Baseball

FOR MOST AMERICANS, April 10, 1947, began just like any other Thursday. Commuters went off to work; shopkeepers opened their stores for business; farmers planted their spring crops; children went off to school perhaps dreaming of playing Major League Baseball or, at least, of playing a little ball at recess. The news of the day was just like the news of any other – a border dispute in Poland, geologists claiming that Antarctica was gradually warming, a world trade conference in Geneva, and a telephone operator strike in New Jersey. The weather forecast called for a sunny day with highs in the upper 50s in Brooklyn, New York.

Around 11:00 a.m., a crowd of baseball fans began to gather on the steep cobblestone slope of Bedford Avenue just outside of Ebbets Field in Brooklyn. Later, the biggest crowd of the spring – 14,282 paying fans, plus a few youngsters looking in through a gap under the metal gate in right-center field – would be on hand to see the Brooklyn Dodgers play their top Minor League ball club, the Montreal Royals (the 1946 champions of the International League), in one of the last exhibition games of the preseason. The crowd was abuzz with the big sports story of the day: Major League Baseball Commissioner Happy Chandler had announced a one-year suspension of Dodger manager Leo Durocher for "accumulation of unpleasant incidents which can be construed as detrimental to baseball". Dodger fans commiserated about the injustice of the action. Perhaps a few fans were discussing a short article in the *New York Times* reporting that "of particular interest would be the performance of Jackie Robinson, Negro star, who is expected to play first base for the International league champion Royals. Dodger officials are considering whether to shift Robinson's contract to the Brooklyn club."[1] No black individual had played white Major League Baseball since 1887.

The game began at 2:00 p.m. with the playing of the National Anthem. Robinson's first at bat in Ebbets Field came in the top of the first; he received what the *New York Times* called a "warm and pleasant reception" from the fans. As Robinson was batting in the top of the fifth, Mr. Branch Rickey, president of the Dodger ball club, gave his assistant Arthur Mann a note to take up to the press box. At the top of the sixth, Red Barber, the Dodger announcer, read the statement for the fans listening to the game on the radio: "The Brooklyn Dodgers today purchased the contract of Jackie Roosevelt Robinson from the Montreal Royals. He will report immediately – Branch Rickey."

With these nineteen words, Mr. Rickey announced to the public what historian Jules Tygiel has called "baseball's great experiment" and what we view as the first, largely successful, affirmative action program in human history.[2] We define affirmative action as the proactive removal of discriminatory barriers and the promotion of institutions leading to integration of in- and out-groups. In other words, affirmative action is the inclusion of an out-group in an activity or institution that has a history of exclusion (such as black Americans and baseball) and the promotion of positive relations between the members of the groups.[3] In our previous essay (reprinted elsewhere in the present volume), we reviewed the history of black American exclusion from the game of baseball and looked at some of the reasons why Mr. Rickey and Mr. Robinson inaugurated history's first affirmative action program.[4] In this essay, we look at just how they did it and why their efforts were such a success.

How did Mr. Rickey integrate his Brooklyn Dodger ball club?[5] For over forty years, social psychologists have been studying how best to implement desegregation programs. This research has taught us that the best way to accomplish the goal of integration is to change directly the institutions and social patterns that support discrimination; attitude change will follow from the resulting behavior change. Our thesis is that many of the principles discovered by social psychologists are illustrated in Mr. Rickey's hiring of Jackie Robinson. We have identified nine principles used to integrate the '47 Dodgers – principles that can still be used today to improve the effectiveness of affirmative action programs.

1. *Create the Psychology of Inevitable Change*

One factor that increases the likelihood of successful integration is the feeling that change is inevitable – the out-group member (in this case, black Americans) will be joining the in-group members (white Major League Baseball) in the very near future and there is nothing that can be done to prevent it. This principle was identified by social psychologists studying the desegregation efforts of the 1950s and 1960s. For example, in a case analysis of communities implementing school desegregation, Thomas Pettigrew found that violence often occurred in cities (for example, Little Rock and Clinton ARK) where authorities hinted that deseg-regation was reversible; peaceful integration generally occurred in towns (such as Norfolk and Winston-Salem) where leaders made it clear that the decision was irreversible.[6]

How does the psychology of the inevitable work to reduce prejudices? In 1944 Gunnar Myrdal argued that race relations in America are guided by a moral dilemma: on the one hand the American Creed demands that all people be treated as equals, but, on the other hand, cultural mores and norms prescribe that some people should receive inferior treatment.[7] For in-group members, this dilemma results in a sense of moral uneasiness and ambivalence or what can be termed "cognitive dissonance." In every-day life, this dissonance can be reduced by avoiding the issue, avoiding the out-group, denigrating the out-group (stereotyping), adopting sym-bols of the American Creed, and politely deferring to local norms and the "way things are done."

Myrdal's moral dilemma, however, cannot be avoided when changes in the norms supporting prejudice are enacted; it must be faced squarely. There are two routes for resolving the dissonance: increased prejudice and resistance to change (leading to violence) or reduced prejudice and rejection of the norm of prejudice. The position of leaders is the key to determining which route will be taken. When leaders openly oppose or halfheartedly support affirmative action, then opposition and even violence can result. In contrast, support for affirmative action closes off this route; to reduce dissonance, the in-group member is motivated to scrutinize his or her prejudice and to alter negative stereotypes. The inevitability of change encourages in-group members to bring their at-titudes in line with the new reality.

The psychology of the inevitable can be seen in how Red Barber came to terms with a Negro player coming to the Dodgers. As the official voice of the Brooklyn Dodgers, Mr. Rickey required the full support of Barber. He took Barber into his confidence early in March of 1945. According to Barber, Rickey broke the news during lunch at Joe's Restaurant; after some small talk, Rickey's voice grew serious, "I'm going to tell you something only the board of directors of the Brooklyn ball club and my family knows." He looked Barber straight in the eyes and fixed his attention. "I'm going to bring a Negro to the Brooklyn Dodgers. I've got my best scouts searching for the best Negro players. They think they are searching for the Brown Dodgers. They don't know that what they are really searching for is the first black player I can put on the white Dodgers. I don't know who he is or where he is, but he is coming."[8] Barber recalls that Rickey spoke those last words very slowly, very intently, very positively.

Red Barber was stunned by the announcement. He was born in Mississippi, raised in Florida, and had been taught a strict code by which to navigate relationships with black Americans. His first words to his wife when he got home were, "I'm going to quit." Red Barber felt he could not work with a team where one or more of the players were black. After his initial anger, however, Barber began to think. As he put it:

> There is a force on this earth called economic determinism. That force whispered to me that at Brooklyn I had the best sports announcing job not only in the country, but in the world. If I threw it away, what would I do? I didn't quit. I made myself realize that I had no choice in the parents I was born to, no choice in the place of my birth or the time of it. I was born white just as a Negro was born black. I had been given a fortunate set of circumstances, none of which I had done anything to merit, and therefore I had best be careful about being puffed up over my color.[9]

Mr. Rickey also used the psychology of the inevitable to help change the attitudes of the Dodgers players. One of the more colorful stories involved then Dodger manager, Leo Durocher. During spring training of 1947, Durocher found out that some Dodger players – Dixie Walker, Eddie Stanky, Kirby Higbe, Bobby Bragan, and others – were drawing up a petition to warn that they would never play with Robinson. At first Durocher decided to wait until Mr. Rickey returned from a trip; however, the idea of a petition gnawed at Durocher. Tossing and turning in bed, unable to sleep, Durocher resolved to take action. He told his coaches to round everyone up for a team meeting in his kitchen. Once the team had assembled, Durocher came in in his pajamas and bright yellow bathrobe – his words were quick and to the point:

> I hear some of you fellows don't want to play with Robinson and that you have a petition drawn up that you are going to sign. Well, boys, you know what you can do with that petition. You can wipe your ass with it. I hear Dixie Walker is going to send Mr. Rickey a letter asking to be traded. Just hand him the letter, Dixie, and you're gone. GONE! I don't care if a guy is yellow or black or if he has stripes like a fuckin' zebra. I am the manager, and I say he plays. [10]

(Little wonder that Rickey was disturbed when Durocher was suspended just before the start of the '47 season. He was ably replaced by Burt Shotton. Durocher returned to the helm in '48).

The next night, Mr. Rickey called the players to his hotel suite. He began the meeting with a lecture on Americanism. Several of the players felt ashamed and gave ground. Others did not. Mr. Rickey then offered to trade any player who didn't want to be on the team with Robinson. Dixie Walker sent a letter to Rickey asking for a trade. (At the time, Walker was one of the most popular Dodgers and was nicknamed "The People's Cherce"). True to his words, Rickey worked out a deal with Pittsburgh. But, Walker, realizing the inevitable, reversed his decision and asked for his letter back. Rickey canceled the trade (see Principle 7, below). Kirby Higbe also wanted to be traded and persisted in his opposition to Robinson. Rickey sent Higbe to the last-place Pirates for close to $200,000 in cash. (As late as 1967, Higbe continued to believe what he did was right.) Mr. Rickey dragged his heels on a third trade involving Bobby Bragan; he felt that Bragan was working through emotional difficulties. Events would prove him correct (again, see Principle 7, below). In 1965, Bobby Bragan sat next to Jackie Robinson at the funeral of Mr. Rickey. As Bragan puts it: "We shook hands warmly. I don't think either of us thought anything about it, or of the past. It was a new time. I changed. Jackie changed. The world changed." [11]

The spring-training petition was not to be the last attempt to ban Robinson. In early May of 1947, three players from the St. Louis Cardinals began to organize a strike. They would not take the field against the Dodgers when they came to St. Louis with Jackie Robinson; further the Cardinal players were trying to enlist the support of players on other teams. When NL President Ford Frick found out about the plan, he issued the following statement to the players:

> If you do this you will be suspended from the League. You will find that the friends you think you have in the press box will not support you, that you will be outcasts. I do not care if half the League strikes. Those who do will encounter quick retribution. All will be suspended and I don't care if it wrecks the National League for five years. This is the United States of America and one citizen has as much right to play as another. The National League will go down the line with Robinson no matter the consequences. You will find, if you go through with your intentions, that you have been guilty of complete madness.[12]

President Frick's statement put a quick end to the strike.

Many of the participants in baseball's great experiment understood the power of authority to create the psychology of the inevitable. Often in this paper we refer to Branch Rickey as Mr. Rickey. In a 1946 interview, Rachel Robinson, Jackie's wife, noted: "We always called him *Mr.* Rickey. Everyone did. I think we wanted to hold him in that position of respect and honor. Part of his power was maintaining that mystique about himself."[13]

2. *Establish Equal-Status Contact with a Superordinate Goal*

At the time Rickey was making the final plans to bring a black American to baseball, some were of the opinion that blacks and whites could not get along in close interpersonal relationships. Intergroup contact would inevitably result in strife – the races just could not get along. Casual observation may lead some to believe that conflict between races must occur.

Conflict need not inevitably result, however. In the early 1950s, social psychologists and sociologists identified what has been termed "the equal-status contact" hypothesis. Gordon Allport stated it as follows: positive intergroup relations are most likely to occur when members from the two groups (a) possess equal status, (b) seek common goals, (c) are cooperatively dependent on each other, and (d) interact with positive support of authorities, laws, or customs.[14]

There is much support for this equal-status contact hypothesis. For example, Morton Deutsch and Mary Evans Collins found that white attitudes toward blacks showed less prejudice if blacks and whites were assigned to share the same building in a public housing complex; such positive attitudes did not occur if buildings were segregated.[15] In a dramatic experiment, Muzafer Sherif first created social conflict among boys attending a summer camp merely by creating artificial groups (Rattlers and Eagles) and placing them in competition. The conflict was reduced by giving the groups a superordinate goal (i.e., joining together to bring water to the camp, to rent a movie, and to start a stalled truck).[16]

Research leading to the equal-status contact hypothesis was begun in the 1940s. Branch Rickey was privy to the thinking of social scientists of the time. Dan Dodson – a New York University sociologist and a member of the Mayor's Committee on Unity – became a Rickey confidant. He gave Rickey the following advice: "Don't worry about the attitudes of people who are asked to accept new members. When relationships are predicated on the basis of goals other than integration – in the Dodgers' case, winning the pennant – the people involved [will] adjust appropriately."[17]

In Rickey's mind, baseball offered the unique opportunity to test out social scientists' theories about integration. In many ways, the typical ball club does or (more often) can meet Gordon Allport's four conditions. Each playing position has more or less equal status; teams seek a common goal (the pennant); each player is mutually dependent on teammates to reach the goal (it is easier to score an RBI with runners in scoring position; put-outs require a coordinated infield); and Rickey's managers could provide the positive support of authority (see Principle 1, above).

The task of Dodger management was to keep the team on track toward its superordinate goal – a task that should be routinely performed by every manager. Dodger management reminded the white players of how close they came in 1946 to going to the World Series (losing out to the Cardinals in the final week of the season) and that the missing component just might be Robinson's speed on the base paths. As Durocher repeatedly told the white players in spring training, "He'll put money in your pocket, boys. Money in your pocket." In other words, the chances of going to the Series were much improved with Robinson.

The results of equal-status contact can be seen in the behavior of Dixie Walker (a leader of the petition drive). A short time into the 1947 season, Walker approached Robinson in the batting cage and spoke his first words to him in a deep southern accent, "Ah think you'd be better able to handle that curve ball if you didn't stride so far."[18] That afternoon,

Robinson, taking the advice, hit a line drive double, a bunt single, and a single up the middle. He thanked Walker quietly in the clubhouse. Walker later showed the rookie Robinson how to hit behind the runner. When asked why he did it, he replied, "I saw things in this light. When you're on a team, you got to pull together to win."[19] At the end of the 1947 season, Walker commented that it was Robinson that had put the Dodgers in the race.

3. *The "Pee Wee" Reese Principle: Puncture the Norm of Prejudice*

One factor that maintains and perpetuates prejudice is norms. A norm is a rule or expectation used to guide and direct social behavior (e.g., whites don't play baseball with blacks; women can't handle top management positions, and so forth). Norms can prescribe what "ought" to happen in a social situation and can describe how most people will act in a setting. Norms gain their power from the belief (often mistaken) that everyone else believes and performs the norm (pluralistic ignorance) and from the belief that social sanctions will result if the norm is transgressed.[20]

Numerous sociopsychological studies have demonstrated the importance of social norms in maintaining prejudice. For example, Thomas Pettigrew found that conformity to social pressures was a key determinant of prejudice in the South.[21] Ralph Minard documents a case where black and white coal miners followed a pattern of complete integration below ground, but were almost completely segregated above ground where the norms were different.[22]

The power of social norms can be illustrated in Clay Hopper's (manager of the International League Montreal Royals) reaction upon learning that Jackie Robinson was being assigned to his club for the '46 season. Hopper did not protest because Robinson couldn't play or because he hated blacks or because he felt he couldn't manage what might be a racially charged situation. Instead, he pleaded with Mr. Rickey: "Please don't do this to me. I'm white and I've lived in Mississippi all my life. If you're going to do this, you're going to force me to move my family and home out of Mississippi."[23] A year later, we might add, it was Clay Hopper who urged Mr. Rickey to promote Robinson to the Majors; in Hopper's mind, Robinson was ready and had proved all he could prove in the Minors.

Although norms are powerful and persistent, they can be changed. A series of classic studies by Solomon Asch illustrates how the presence of even one dissenter can shatter the power of group pressure and norms.[24] In his studies, a group of seven "subjects" were shown sets of three lines differing in length and were asked to choose the one line that was the same length as a standard. Unbeknownst to the real subject (who always selected last), the other "subjects" were really confederates of Asch and were instructed to unanimously pick a wrong line on key trials. The results showed that the real subject yielded to the group influence in a substantial number of trials. When, however, Asch gave the real subject a partner – either another naive subject or a confederate instructed to pick the correct line – conformity was reduced by 75 percent.

When Rickey hired Robinson he took the first step toward breaking the norms of prejudice. Others also displayed their support for the hiring. For example, Brooklyn fans began wearing "I'm for Robinson" buttons around Ebbets Field. Sportswriters such as Louis Effrat and Arthur Daley wrote sympathetic articles for the *New York Times*. Pirate Hank Greenberg supported Robinson when Pittsburgh fans began to verbally abuse Jackie. (Greenberg – a Jewish American – had received similar treatment a few seasons earlier.) Boxing's heavyweight champion, Joe Louis, came to a Dodger game to shake Jackie's hand.

One Dodger stands out, however, in his actions to break the norms of prejudice – Harold "Pee Wee" Reese. A ten-time NL All-Star, Reese had a career .269 batting average and often lead the League in fielding at his shortstop position. When Robinson was moved to second, they made an unbeatable double play team. Many may consider "Pee Wee" Reese as an odd choice to be a civil rights leader. Reese, born in Ekron, Kentucky, was a southerner who learned the racial code of conduct at quite an early age.

In spring training, Reese refused to sign the petition against Robinson. His actions surprised teammates and petition organizers; they expected that a southern boy would know better. Perhaps Bobby Bragan (a petition-organizer) best understood what Reese's actions meant:

> Those early days were awfully tough on Jackie. I remember times on the train when nobody would sit with him or talk with him. Pee Wee always seemed to be the first to break the tension. He kidded Jackie before anybody else did and made him a part of the team. He was probably the first Dodger to have a meal with him off the field. Pee Wee was a real leader on our club, and when he started being friendly with Jackie, everybody started being friendly. In the beginning Jackie was alone at the dining

table. By the middle of the year you couldn't get a seat at the dining table with him, there were so many guys.[25]

One incident involving Reese and Robinson has achieved the status of legend. Early in the 1947 season, the Dodgers traveled to Crosley Field in Cincinnati, Ohio, to play the Reds. (Robinson later describes the incident as happening in Boston; Reese doesn't even remember the event, though he does recall Robinson saying that it took place in Cincinnati; Reese also remembers that such incidents were quite common, especially in that first year.) The ballpark was jammed with thousands coming up from Reese's boyhood home of Kentucky. Many of Reese's friends and relatives despised him for playing on a team with a black man. The crowd hurled racial slurs – "get the nigger off the field"; "watermelon eater"; "Reese, the nigger lover." The hatemongering continued into the bottom of the first when the Dodgers took the field. Mr. Reese left his shortstop position and walked the 120 feet over to first base where Robinson stood. He smiled at Robinson; Robinson smiled back. Tapping his glove, Reese spoke a few words to Robinson. All eyes were on the pair at first base. "Pee Wee" then placed his right arm around Robinson's shoulder as chums often do. There was absolute silence in the stands. Mr. Reese's action not only punctured the norm of antiblack racism, but also broke another common myth: that all whites are racists and incapable of change.

In 1984, Harold "Pee Wee" Reese was elected into the National Baseball Hall of Fame. The last line of his Hall-of-Fame plaque lists this accomplishment: "Instrumental in easing acceptance of Jackie Robinson as baseball's first black performer."

4. *Practice Nonviolent Resistance*

The story of the first meeting between Robinson and Rickey has been told many times. Clyde Sukeforth, one of Rickey's most trusted assistants, had been scouting Negro League talent under the guise that Mr. Rickey planned to form the Brown Dodgers in a new Negro League. Mr. Rickey kept his true intentions secret because of considerable opposition in the past to hiring black Americans to play baseball. When, however, Mr. Rickey asked him to bring Robinson to Brooklyn and then added the comment, "If he can't come to New York, arrange a time for me to go out to the Midwest to meet him," Sukeforth realized that this would be no routine meeting.

Jackie Robinson met Mr. Rickey for the first time on August 28, 1945, in Rickey's Brooklyn office. Branch Rickey stared intently at Robinson, studying his every movement. Robinson recalls the moment, "His piercing eyes roamed over me with such meticulous care I almost felt naked." Robinson stared back as if he were trying to get inside the man. Rickey broke the ice with a question about Robinson's family. Jackie responded that he was planning to marry his girlfriend, Rachel. Rickey was pleased because he knew Robinson would need all the family support he could get. Then Rickey broke the news, "The truth is you are not a candidate for the Brooklyn Brown Dodgers. I've sent for you because I'm interested in you as a candidate for the Brooklyn National League club. I think you can play in the Major Leagues. How do you feel about it?" Robinson was skeptical; black Americans had been led on before. Indeed, in April of 1945, Jackie Robinson, along with black Americans Sam Jethroe and Marvin Williams, had participated in a sham tryout with the Boston Red Sox.

Rickey continued, "I know you're a good ballplayer. My scouts have told me this. What I don't know is whether you have the guts." Robinson bristled at the implication that he was a coward. Rickey told him that he wished that all that mattered was the box score – that maybe someday that would be all that counted. Right now, however, that wasn't all that mattered. For the next three hours, he described the situations that Robinson would face as a black man entering an all-white league. He told him about the segregated hotels and restaurants; he told him what his wife would hear in the stands; he told him the abuse he would take on the field. Rickey, always the actor, would get up into Robinson's face and yell insults and racial slurs. Robinson recalled, "His acting was so convincing that I found myself chain-gripping my fingers behind my back." Rickey brought the tension to a climax: "Suppose a player comes down from first base – you are the shortstop – the player slides, spikes you high, and cuts you on the leg. As you feel the blood running down your leg, the white player laughs in your face, and sneers, 'How do you like that, nigger boy?'" Robinson asked, "Mr. Rickey do you want a Negro who's afraid to fight back?" Rickey's answer, "I want a ballplayer with guts enough not to fight back." Rickey then reached into a desk drawer and pulled out a copy of Giovanni Papini's *The Life of Christ* and read a section on nonviolent resistance. He told Robinson there was only one way to break the color barrier, "You can not retaliate; you can not answer a blow with a blow; you can not echo a curse with a curse." He looked Robinson straight in the eye and asked, "Can you do it?" Robinson stared straight back and answered, "Mr. Rickey, I've got to do it."

When Mr. Robinson left the office that day, he had made two commitments to Branch Rickey: (a) for three years he would not return violence with violence; and (b) that he would play for the Dodgers' top farm club in Montreal. Robinson honored both commitments. The color barrier was officially broken.

Branch Rickey's nickname was "Mahatma," after the Indian civil rights leader Mahatma Gandhi. Nonviolence was a guiding principle of Rickey's life. For example, just before the start of the 1947 season, Rickey met with black civic leaders and impressed upon them that any violence would set back race relations. The motto became, "Don't spoil Jackie's chances." Why did Mr. Rickey place so much emphasis on nonviolent resistance? Branch Rickey was afraid of a spiral of violence. A white person would attack a black; the black person would respond; then more white persons would attack until a full-scale riot broke out. Black Americans would inevitably take the blame – "See, they can't get along."

Branch Rickey had every reason to expect a spiral of violence. Between 1900 and 1949, there were thirty-three major race riots in the United States – most in the North and many near baseball towns. At least two of these riots must have stuck out in Rickey's mind. On July 2, 1917, the second worst race riot in American history occurred in East St. Louis, Illinois. Nine whites and at least thirty-nine blacks died in the violence; estimates of the number of blacks who died varies because the bodies of many black Americans were mutilated and burned beyond recognition, making an exact count difficult. Seeking refuge, thousands of black Americans crossed one of the three bridges over the Mississippi River into St. Louis, Missouri. Mr. Rickey had just begun his managerial career with the St. Louis Cardinals. In 1943, the fourth-worst race riot in American history took place in Detroit, Michigan (with nine whites and twenty-five blacks killed). One of the triggering events for this riot was the promotion of three black assembly line workers. Coming just as he was making plans to hire a black American, the location of (a baseball town) and the reason for (black employment) the Detroit riot were probably not lost on Mr. Rickey. Nonviolence was one way that Mr. Rickey saw to prevent a spiral of violence.

But nonviolence is more than just breaking the spiral; it changes the dynamics of social interaction. Nonviolent resistance is not just passive acceptance of the status quo. Rather, it shows an irrevocable commitment to a course of action and to change. Nonviolent action says, "No matter what you do to me, I will not hurt you; I will, however, continue to move to the new goal ." Nonviolent resistance also switches the locus of responsibility for what happens to others. Robinson was not to blame for any incidents. When Robinson was mistreated, it became the responsibility of the Dodger team to stand up for him. Finally, nonviolence (compared to violence) made it easier for the "enemy" to be converted to the cause (see Principle 7, below).

The value of nonviolent resistance can be seen in a study by Morton Deutsch. [26] In his study, an accomplice of the experimenter and a real subject played a two-person game that permitted altruistic, cooperative, individualistic, defensive, and aggressive behaviors. Subjects won varying amounts of money by cooperating, attacking, or ignoring the other player. The results showed that when the accomplice played a nonviolent-resistance strategy (i.e., cooperate if the other player cooperated and play defensively when attacked) both players gained more money compared to other possible strategies (i.e., passivity, deterrence, et al.). Further, practicing nonviolent resistance resulted in the accomplice being perceived as fair and cooperative.

The value of Mr. Rickey's nonviolent resistance can also be observed on the playing field. Perhaps the most dramatic event occurred late in the season on August 20 when the Dodgers were playing the fourth game of a series with the Cardinals. In the opening game, Joe Medwick had spiked Robinson's left foot. Two games later, Robinson barely removed his leg in time to avoid an Enos Slaughter spike. In the top of the seventh of game four, Slaughter – a man known for his opposition to blacks in baseball – hit a grounder that was tossed to Robinson at first. Robinson took the throw with his foot on the inside of the bag. This time Slaughter's spike came down hard on the back of Jackie's leg, missing the Achilles tendon (and thus an injury that would likely have ended Robinson's career) by an inch. The cut on Robinson's leg was eight inches above the ankle – a location that made it hard to argue that it was an accidental spiking. Robinson's Dodger teammates, lead by Hugh Casey, came out en masse to protest. Several Dodger players threatened the Cardinals with "dire consequences" if the attacks continued. Nonviolent resistance by Robinson had changed the social dynamics, preventing a spiral of violence and increasing the cohesion of the Dodger ball club.

For a long time, the principle of nonviolent resistance stirred not only Robinson's teammates to action, but sportswriters, as well. Red Barber is of the opinion that Enos Slaughter's entrance into the Hall of Fame was delayed by this spiking incident because many sportswriters (including himself), knowing what he had done to Robinson, could not bring themselves to cast a vote for Slaughter. (Slaughter, it may be noted, agrees with Barber's assessment.)

5. *Create Empathy*

One effective means of achieving attitudinal change is to reverse perceptions and present the world through another's point of view. The ability to experience empathy – the ability to feel the emotions of others – is perhaps a uniquely human trait. Seeing the world as another sees it provides an opportunity to receive new information and to challenge old ways of viewing matters. Observing another's pain often results in empathy, which predisposes the observer to take altruistic action.[27] (Relatedly, it has been shown that when whites have black friends, they are more likely to support affirmative action.)[28] Part of Mr. Rickey's success was his ability to get the Dodgers to see the world through Robinson's eyes and to feel his pain.

The Dodgers' baptism by fire occurred on April 22 when the Philadelphia Phillies came to town for a three-game series. It was a very cold day in Brooklyn, with highs only in the low 40s; the fans sat chilled in their seats. On the field, things were quite a bit hotter. Ben Chapman (manager of the Phillies) started screaming out racial slurs at Robinson.[29] "Hey nigger, why don't you go pickin' cotton?" Soon his team joined in: "Hey, coon, do you always smell so bad?" and then they would flap their hands as if something stunk. The slurs continued inning after inning and into the second game of the series. "Hey, darkie, you shouldn't be here in the big leagues – they need you back home to clean out the latrines." Robinson called it the worst experience of his life; he cursed Mr. Rickey and his experiment under his breath. But Robinson stood firm and took the abuse. And the attack continued. "If that black-lipped nigger was a white boy, he'd been sent to Newport News a long time ago." Feelings on the Dodger bench were tense. Imagine what it must have been like for the white Dodger players that day. Most likely, they had never experienced prejudice directly before and now they were getting the full treatment. "Hey nigger lovers, they are waiting for your black boy back in the jungle." "Hey snowflake, which one of the white boys' wives you shacking' up with tonight?" "Hey, you carpetbaggers, how's your little reconstruction period getting along?"

Toward the end of the second game, the white Dodgers could not continue to take the pressure, and they exploded with rage. Eddie Stanky was the first off the bench; he screamed at the Phillie bench, "What kind of men are you anyway? You're all chicken! Why the hell don't you pick on someone who can fight back? You know Robinson can't fight back – knock it off and just play ball!" Dixie Walker joined in. Yes, this was the same Eddie Stanky and the same Dixie Walker who two months earlier were heading a petition drive against Robinson. It was the same Eddie Stanky who told Robinson on his first day of work, "I don't like you, but we'll play together and get along because you're my teammate." Stanky's support of Robinson diminished the intensity of the Phillies attack, although it still continued over the next few years. Unfortunately, after this blatant racial attack, death threats directed at Mr. Rickey and Mr. Robinson increased; many commentators link the two events.

For the record, it should be noted that Robinson was not completely silent during the series; he spoke the language every baseball fan understands – that of his bat. In game one, Robinson broke the ice with a hit in the bottom of the sixth. With the score tied 0–0 in the bottom of the eighth, Robinson reached first on an infield hit. As Pete Reiser was striking out, Robinson stole second and reached third on a throwing error by the catcher. Dixie Walker then walked. Gene Hermanski took an 0–2 count to 3–2 and then lined a drive to center. Brooklyn won, 1–0, with Robinson scoring the lone run. In game two, Robinson walked and then scored on a Reiser double. Robinson bunted, then scored on a bases-loaded single by Carl Furillo: the Dodgers won 5–2. In game three, Robinson reached first on an error; he scored the go-ahead run on a Dixie Walker hit: the Dodgers won, 2–0. The Brooklyn fans brought out their brooms; the Dodgers swept the three-game series from the Phillies.

Branch Rickey was beside himself with glee and could not resist the opportunity to gloat over the win and to lecture Ben Chapman. As he himself acknowledged, the Chapman incident did more than anything else to make the other Dodgers speak up in Robinson's behalf. When Chapman and the others poured out that string of unconscionable abuse, he inadvertently solidified and unified thirty men, not one of whom was willing to see someone kick around a man who had his hands tied behind his back. Chapman created on Robinson's behalf what is called "sympathy," the most unifying word in the world. The word has a Greek origin – it means "to suffer." To say "I sympathize with you" means "I suffer with you." And that is what Chapman did. He caused men like Stanky to suffer with Robinson, and he made this Negro a real member of the Dodgers. [30]

6. *Individuate the New Group Member*

One problem that occurs when an out-group member joins an in-group is the continued categorization of the new member in terms of out-group stereotypes – the person is not "Jackie Robinson," but rather a Negro ballplayer. The continued use of such labels and categories can pose a number of problems for integration. [31] It is easier to attack a vague category (especially one that has been denigrated) than it is to hurt a real flesh-and-blood human being. When group identities are salient, in-group favoritism (perceiving the in-group to be better than the out-group; rewarding the in-group over the out-group) is common. [32] The stereotype serves to organize perceptions about the out-group member in what is termed an "attribution error": negative acts by out-group members are seen as caused by permanent dispositions whereas positive acts are attributed to situational factors or luck. [33]

One special problem for the first in-group members entering a newly desegregated setting is their solo or token status. Rosabeth Kanter has marshaled considerable evidence to show that tokenism is a particularly painful psychological state. [34] The solo receives close scrutiny and attention by the in-group members. In-group members have a tendency to exaggerate evaluations of the performance of the solo and to see the solo as playing a special, often stereotypic, role in the group. [35]

One way to reduce categorization and token effects is to encourage the treatment of the new group member as an individual. For example, researchers have found that typical in-group favoritism was reduced when members of an out-group acted as individuals and signed their names in notes sent to members of the in-group. [36] Similarly, other researchers have reduced prejudice in children by having them learn and memorize the names of out-group members and by having the children make judgments on how out-group members were similar and different from each other. [37]

Rickey felt that through the "intimacy" of baseball and the heat of competition, the white Dodgers would come to know and like Robinson. (Dixie Walker's remarks to Robinson on his batting stance demonstrate this point.) Baseball fans would not, however, have the opportunity to interact personally with Robinson. Rickey called on his friends in the media to "introduce" Robinson to the fans. Stories by Arthur Mann and *New York Times* writers Louis Effrat and Arthur Daley portrayed Robinson as an individual of accomplishment. (Of course, not all sportswriters were connected to Rickey and not all followed suit; even a supporter of Rickey, such as Mann, was not above poking fun in private circles at the effort by Rickey to hire Robinson.)[38]

Here is how Effrat first described Robinson to the Brooklyn fans: "A native of Georgia, Robinson won fame in baseball, football, basketball, and track at the University of California at Los Angeles before entering the army as a private. He emerged a lieutenant in 1945 and in October of that year was signed to a Montreal contract. Robinson's performance in the International League, which he led in batting last season with an average of .349, prompted President Branch Rickey of the Dodgers to promote Jackie."[39]

The article was accompanied by a picture of Clay Hopper congratulating a smiling Jackie Robinson. Indeed, after the early months of the 1947 season, sportswriters often failed to mention Robinson's race as well as the race of other black stars, such as Larry Doby and Roy Campanella. Interestingly, sportswriters continued to mention the race of black pitchers such as Don Newcombe, perhaps because "pitcher" is a leadership position (see Guy Waterman's contribution elsewhere in the present volume).[40]

In 1950 Jackie Robinson contributed greatly to the individuation effort by personally starring in the film, "The Jackie Robinson Story."[41] The film features a likable and determined Jackie Robinson facing the torrent of racism in his first years in the League. We see the young Jackie develop his love of baseball, his first meeting with Mr. Rickey, Robinson's exclusion from facilities during spring training, how he learned the new position of first base, as well as the unwavering strength of character of his mother, Mallie Robinson. Even the most casual of viewers would likely have been left with two impressions: (1) Jackie Robinson is truly a great American hero; and (2) it would be nice to have the Robinsons – Rachel and Jackie – over for a barbeque this weekend.

7. Offer Forgiveness and Redemption

In many ways, Mr. Rickey's introduction of Jackie Robinson to the Dodgers and white America can be viewed as one elaborate cognitive dissonance experiment – white Americans were forced to confront Myrdal's dilemma. First, through the psychology of the inevitable, he placed pressure on white Americans to change their prejudices. Next, he blocked off negative, but typical, routes for dealing with Myrdal's dilemma, such as derogating Robinson, bolstering negative stereotypes, and hatemongering. Finally, he needed to provide a positive means of coming to terms with racism. Mr. Rickey's devotion to Christ provided just such a mechanism: forgiveness and redemption.

In Mr. Rickey's Methodist theology, redemption meant the renewal and transformation of the person; you loved the sinner, but hated the sin. Forgiveness meant more than just a formal apology; indeed, it often did not involve an apology. When Mr. Rickey saw signs that an oppositional white player was "coming around" he would immediately place that player in a new role of authority – a position that would involve interacting with and serving black Americans. Social scientists refer to this process as "cooptation."[42] Cooptation provides the opponent with a new role, complete with new information, role expectations, and social pressures that increase identification with the organization's goals.

A case in point is Bobby Bragan. A lifetime .240 hitter over seven seasons, Bragan was the Dodger's second-string catcher and considered expendable. Mr. Rickey could have easily gotten rid of him after Bragan's participation in the petition drive. According to Rickey's confidant, Arthur Mann, Mr. Rickey recognized unusual courage in the man; he felt Bragan needed time to think and that someday he would learn that he was wrong. Bragan remained a Dodger for the 1947 season (although he spent some time in the Minors). In 1948, Mr. Rickey appointed Bragan manager of the Dodger farm club in Fort Worth. The Bragan-led club won the pennant in 1948 and again in 1949. Mr. Rickey's confidence was not lost on Bragan. As he put it, "Mr. Rickey paid me the ultimate compliment when he hired me after my playing days were over to work in the Dodger farm system."[43] Bragan also took great pride in his coaching of black ball players. "When I was a manager in the Dodger organization, I helped Tommy Davis, and later on I really worked hard with Maury Wills. I made him into a switch hitter, and he got to the Majors and became the great base stealer and fine player he was. I'm very proud of that."[44]

Hank Aaron acknowledges that Bobby Bragan made him a complete player by encouraging him to steal. Hall-of-Famer Monte Irvin, one of the first black Americans to play for the New York Giants, described it this way: "After a year or so, Bragan realized how wrong his attitude was. Later he went out of his way to help black ballplayers."[45]

Mr. Rickey was not above using even the bitter Chapman incident to promote his cause. After the Phillies attacked Robinson and the other Dodgers, there was a public outcry against Chapman. Fans seated near the Phillies' dugout wrote protest leaders to Baseball Commissioner Happy Chandler. Chapman's actions were deplored in the black press and by some white sportswriters. Walter Winchell attacked Chapman on his national Sunday radio broadcast. Worried about his and the Phillies' image, Chapman issued a statement that he was riding Robinson just like he would any rookie. Few believed him. Mr. Rickey then took the opportunity to stage a photo of Chapman with Robinson. The photo of both men in uniform holding a bat appeared in the sports section of every major paper. There is little doubt that Chapman's "apology" lacked sincerity. (Robinson considered it one of the most difficult things he had ever done.) Nevertheless, Chapman had once again served Mr. Rickey's purposes; Chapman's photo with Robinson demonstrated to a nation that even the most hardened can change.

8. *Undo the Perception of Preferential Selection*

Many white Americans doubted Jackie Robinson's ability to make it into the NL. The pitcher Bob Feller stated, "If he were a white man, I doubt they would even consider him big-league material." When Robinson had a day off because of a sore shoulder, a reporter commented, "Had he been white, the Royals would have dropped him immediately." Larry McPhail – Rickey's nemesis as general manager of the New York Yankees – stated in 1946 that the level of Robinson's ability, "were he white, would make him eligible for a trial with, let us say, the Brooklyn Dodgers' Class B farm [club] at Newport News." McPhail also believed blacks, in general, could not make it in the white Major Leagues without considerable training. As he put it, "A Major League player must have something besides natural ability. He must also have a competitive attitude and discipline," implying that blacks lacked these latter abilities.

The fact that Jackie Robinson was perceived as preferentially selected for the Dodgers should alert us to one potential problem of affirmative action – it can lead to the (mis)perception that the recipient was hired just because he or she was black (or a woman, and so forth) and therefore can't do the job. The perception that Robinson was preferentially hired is ridiculous. In 1946 with the Montreal Royals of the International League (the top farm league), Robinson won the batting championship with a .349 average, was a terror on the base paths, scored 113 runs, was selected league MVP, and went on to lead the club to the League pennant and victory in the Little World Series. If Robinson was not qualified for his chance in the Majors, then no other Minor League player that year was qualified.

Social psychologists have identified three general reasons why affirmative action can be (mis)perceived as preferential selection. The first is racism. As the quote from McPhail indicates, some believed that blacks lacked certain abilities to play baseball (they were inferior in some dimension). If they lacked the ability, then why did they get the job? The answer: it must be preferential selection. Audrey Murrell and her colleagues have found that whites are more accepting of affirmative action for the elderly and for the handicapped than for blacks;[46] second, that some affirmative action procedures may be seen to violate the norms of universality and procedural justice or fairness;[47] and finally, that white resistance to affirmative action is higher among those whites who feel relatively deprived or perceive that they have not gotten all that they deserve from life.[48] In such cases, attitudes toward affirmative action serve a self-protective or scapegoating function – the dissatisfied white individual comes to blame blacks for his or her problems.[49]

The perception of affirmative action as preferential selection can have negative consequences for the recipient of affirmative action. Considerable research has shown that women who feel they were preferentially selected for a desired position gave lower self-evaluations of their abilities and skills and that, under certain conditions, preferential selection can result in poorer performance.[50] It should be noted that Robinson was particularly sensitive to racial slurs that attacked his ability – that is, implied he was preferentially selected. As if to stress the point, he titled his autobiography, *I Never Had It Made*.

To account for the negative consequences of preferential selection, we have developed a model of affirmative action as help.[51] Sometimes help can be supportive and result in positive consequences for the recipient – for example, when the help conforms to social norms and removes barriers to success that have been erected through no fault of the recipient. On the other hand, help can be self-threatening – for example, when the help conveys to the recipient that he or she lacks ability or that the help was unfairly awarded. In such cases, the help results in negative self-evaluations and defensive behavior.

We have used this model to generate a number of specific actions that can be taken to reduce and eliminate the negative consequences of the perception of preferential selection. Many of these actions were intuitively taken by Branch Rickey and his assistants. Some of these measures include: (a) Establish unambiguous, explicit, and focused qualification criteria to be used in the selection decision (the baseball box score); (b) be certain that selection procedures are perceived as fair (Robinson has paid his dues in the Minors); (c) provide specific information testifying to the competencies of the new hire (Rickey's and Durocher's confidence in Robinson's ability; Robinson's season with Montreal); (d) emphasize the recipient's contributions to the team (Durocher's claim that Robinson would get the Dodgers into the pennant race); (e) develop socialization strategies that deter feelings of helplessness (the Minor Leagues and Dodgertown); (f) reinforce the fact that affirmative action is not preferential selection (Rickey repeatedly telling Robinson that he would have to make it own his own – in the box score and with his teammates – and not to be dependent on Rickey for help); and (g) refocus the helping effort away from the recipient by identifying and communicating the social barriers preventing integration (everyone knows about the color barrier).

9. *Identify and Remove Institutional Barriers*

Out-groups are excluded from the in-group by more than just interpersonal prejudice; certain institutional practices can also operate to restrict the choices and rights of an out-group.[52] Such practices can be subtle and unintended or blatant and intentional. For example, institutional barriers can include such things as inferior schools in areas populated by minorities; the lack of day care for working parents; limited job opportunities in poor areas; a heavy reliance on standardized tests for admissions decisions; laws restricting new housing; insisting on traditional career paths; the flow of information in "old boy" networks; and tracking out-groups into certain careers, among other practices.

One institution that posed a particular problem for Mr. Rickey was the segregated housing and dining facilities in many towns. Black ballplayers were not allowed to stay in many hotels or eat in many restaurants. Some clubs attempted to solve this problem by serving players box lunches on the team bus; others moved their spring training from Florida to Arizona, which, though still segregated, was so to a somewhat lesser extent.

Mr. Rickey adopted a more radical solution. In 1947, the Dodgers held spring training in Havana, Cuba – a racially desegregated country. Given the cost of hotels and transportation, this was an expensive move on the part of the Dodgers. Ironically, Kirby Higbe – one of the petition-drive organizers – made a major contribution to Mr. Rickey's effort; the money Mr. Rickey received from the sale of Higbe went to pay for the extra cost of holding spring camp in Cuba.

In 1948, Rickey opened "Dodgertown," fulfilling his dream of a college of baseball that provided a safe haven from segregation. In Dodgertown, black and white players could room together, eat together, and train together without the pressure of local segregation laws.[53] Of course, when the players stepped out of Dodgertown into the surrounding Vero Beach, Florida, community, they still felt the sting of racism. Complete integration could only occur with the full dismantling of the Jim Crow laws of segregation. It is interesting to note that long after the repeal of segregation, Dodgertown and its many imitators are still in operation because such camps were found to be useful in creating team cohesion. There is a lesson to be learned: the creative removal of institutions serving as barriers for the out-group can also improve the lot of the in-group.

Concluding Remarks: A Final Box score

What did Mr. Rickey and Mr. Robinson accomplish? Today, roughly 18 percent of all professional baseball players are black (this is down from a high of 30 percent in 1975).[54] Many of the game's greatest stars are black Americans.[55] It would be wrong, however, to conclude that Mr. Rickey and Mr. Robinson eliminated racism from baseball. Even superstar players such as Hank Aaron have been routinely subjected to both subtle and blatant racial abuse, and black Americans are still frequently excluded from the ranks of managers and baseball's front offices.[56] Mr. Rickey and Mr. Robinson have, however, left us a legacy for addressing the racism we still encounter today; they gave us nine principles of successful affirmative action.

Jackie Robinson played for the Brooklyn Dodgers for ten years – a period baseball writers call the Golden Decade. In that ten-year period, the Dodgers won the NL pennant six times, the World Series in 1955, took opponents to the wire in two races, and only once finished as low as third. In 1948, black Americans Roy Campanella and Don Newcombe joined the Dodgers. Together with Jackie Robinson, Gil Hodges, "Pee Wee" Reese, "Preacher" Roe, and Duke Snider, they formed the nucleus of one of baseball's greatest teams.

Mr. Rickey stayed with the Dodgers for three more seasons after 1947. After building dynasties in St. Louis and Brooklyn, Rickey moved to Pittsburgh in 1951 to become the Pirates' general manager and vice-president. Rickey built an outstanding farm system at Pittsburgh, which would later win the World Series in 1960. In October 1955, he retired from baseball at the age of seventy-three. Ever the innovator (and perhaps inspired by his years of watching Robinson get beaned), Rickey developed the modern batting helmet, which became standard Major League equipment in 1957. Despite poor health, Rickey continued to study America's race relations and to speak out for integration. On one occasion in late 1956, Mr. Rickey was speaking to an audience in Washington DC when he felt faint and lost his vision. He clutched the podium for three minutes until his vision returned, apologized to his audience for the embarrassing silence, and then continued with his plea for the integration of America. In 1957, he was appointed chair of a presidential commission to promote racial harmony and justice (a precursor to the Equal Opportunity Employment Commission [EOEC]). As he was receiving an award, Mr. Branch Rickey had a heart attack; he died a short time later on December 9, 1965, at the age of eighty-three. Two years later Rickey received baseball's highest honor. His plaque in the National Baseball Hall of Fame reads:

Wesley Branch Rickey

St. Louis AL 1905–1906, 1914

New York AL 1907

Founder of farm system which he developed for St. Louis Cardinals and Brooklyn Dodgers. Copied by all other Major League teams. Served as executive for Browns, Cardinals, Dodgers, and Pirates. Brought Jackie Robinson to Brooklyn in 1947.

Mr. Jackie Robinson was named Rookie of the Year in 1947 and NL MVP in 1949. He stole home an exciting nineteen times (and five times in one season). He was named to the NL All-Star Team for six consecutive years. In the fall of 1947, he finished second to Bing Crosby in a poll as the most popular man in America. Robinson retired from baseball after the 1956 season and before the club moved to Los Angeles. He became vice-president of Chock Full O' Nuts, a fast food chain that employed many black Americans. Despite his bout with diabetes, Jackie Robinson also continued his struggle for civil rights. He was active in the Harlem YMCA, he promoted black capitalism through the Freedom National Bank, he refused a token membership at an exclusive "white" golf club (preferring to wait two hours for a time at the public course), and he continued to speak out against racism through his column in the *New York Post* as well as in other forums. In 1962, Mr. Jackie Robinson received baseball's highest honor, election to the National Baseball Hall of Fame. When he received his award, he asked three persons to stand beside him: his mother, Mallie; his wife, Rachel; and his friend, Branch Rickey. The plaque in Cooperstown reads:

Jack Roosevelt Robinson
Brooklyn NL 1947–1956
Leading NL batter in 1949. Holds fielding mark for second baseman playing 150 or more games at .992. Led NL in stolen bases in 1947 and 1949. Most Valuable Player in 1949. Lifetime batting average .311. Joint record holder for most double plays by second baseman, 137 in 1951. Led second basemen in double plays 1949–50-51–52.

Fittingly, the plaque does not mention the achievement for which Mr. Jackie Robinson is most remembered.

NOTES

Portions of this paper were presented at the National Baseball Hall of Fame's Fifth Cooperstown Symposium on Baseball and American Culture, June 10, 1993, in Cooperstown, New York. We thank Elliot Aronson, Susan Finnemore Brennan, Nancy Carlson, Jonathan Cobb, Ken Fuld, David Morishige, T. Douglass Wuggazer, and Dan Ziniuk for helpful comments and discussion.

1. "Dodgers to Play Royals," *New York Times*, April 10, 1947, 32.

2. J. Tygiel, *Baseball's Great Experiment: Jackie Robinson and His Legacy* (New York: Vintage, 1983).

3. T. F. Pettigrew, *Racially Separate or Together?* (New York: McGraw-Hill, 1971).

4. A. R. Pratkanis and M. E. Turner, "The Year 'Cool Papa' Bell Lost the Batting Title: I. Mr. Branch Rickey and Mr. Jackie Robinson's Plea for Affir-

mative Action," NINE: *A Journal of Baseball History and Social Policy Perspectives* 2 (1994): 260–76.

5. We base our account on the following excellent descriptions of Robinson's introduction to the white Major Leagues: M. Allen, *Jackie Robinson: A Life Remembered* (New York: Franklin Watts, 1987); M. Alvarez, *The Official Baseball Hall of Fame Story of Jackie Robinson* (New York: Simon and Schuster, 1990); R. Barber, *1947: When All Hell Broke Loose in Baseball* (New York: De Capo, 1982); L. Durocher, *Nice Guys Finish Last* (New York: Pocket Books, 1976); G. Eskenazi, *The Lip: A Biography of Leo Durocher* (New York: William Marrow, 1993); H. Frommer, *Rickey and Robinson: The Men Who Broke Baseball's Color Barrier* (New York: MacMillian, 1982); P. Golenbock and P. Bacon, *Teammates* (San Diego: Harcourt Brace Jovanovich, 1990); A. E. Green (Director), *The Jackie Robinson Story Starring Jackie Robinson* [Film] (New York: Goodtimes Home Video Corp., 1950); R. Kahn, *The Boys of Summer* (New York: Harper and Row, 1972); A. Mann, *Branch Rickey: American in Action* (Boston: Houghton Mifflin, 1957); J. R. Robinson, *I Never Had it Made* (New York: G. P. Putnam and Sons, 1972); J. R. Robinson and C. Dexter, *Baseball has Done It* (Philadelphia: J. B. Lippincott, 1964); F. Sabin, *Jackie Robinson* (Mahwah NJ: Troll, 1985); G. Schoor, *The Leo Durocher Story* (New York: Julian Messner, 1955); R. Scott, *Jackie Robinson* (New York: Chelsea House, 1987); M. J. Shapiro, *Jackie Robinson of the Brooklyn Dodgers* (New York: Pocket Books, 1967); D. Snider, *The Duke of Flatbush* (New York: Zebra Books, 1988); J. Thorn and J. Tygiel, "Jackie Robinson's Signing: The Real, Untold Story," in J. Thorn and P. Palmer, eds., *Total Baseball: The Ultimate Encyclopedia of Baseball* 3d ed. (New York: HarperCollins, 1993), 148–53; and especially Tygiel, *Baseball's Great Experiment*.

6. T. F. Pettigrew, "Social Psychology and Desegregation Research," *American Psychologist* 16 (1961): 1045–1112; for a review see E. Aronson, *The Social Animal*, 6th ed. (New York: W. H. Freeman, 1992).

7. G. Myrdal, *An American Dilemma* (New York: Harper and Row, 1944).

8. Barber, *1947*, 50–52.

9. Barber, *1947*, 63–64.

10. For details see Barber, *1947*; Tygiel, *Baseball's Great Experiment*.

11. Quoted in Allen, *Jackie Robinson*, 103.

12. Quoted in Barber, *1947*, 175.

13. Quoted in Tygiel, *Baseball's Great Experiment*, 48.

14. G. W. Allport, *The Nature of Prejudice* (Reading MA: Addison-Wesley, 1954).

15. M. Deutsch and M. E. Collins, *Interracial Housing: A Psychological Evaluation of a Social Experiment* (Minneapolis: University of Minnesota Press, 1951).

16. M. Sherif, "Experiments in Group Conflict," *Scientific American* 195 (1956): 54–58.

17. Quoted in Tygiel, *Baseball's Great Experiment*, 195.

18. Quoted in Allen, *Jackie Robinson*, 132.

19. Quoted in Tygiel, Baseball's Great Experiment, 195.

20. R. B. Cialdini, C. A. Kallgren, and R. R. Reno, "A Focus Theory of Normative Conduct," in M. P. Zanna, ed., *Advances in Experimental Social Psychology*, Vol. 24 (San Diego: Academic Press, 1991), 201–34; T. F. Pettigrew, "Normative Theory in Intergroup Relations: Explaining Both Harmony and Conflict," *Psychology and Developing Societies* 3 (1991): 3–16.

21. T. F. Pettigrew, "Regional Differences in Anti-Negro Prejudice," *Journal of Abnormal and Social Psychology* 59 (1950): 28–36. See also idem, "Personality and Sociocultural Factors in Intergroup Attitudes: A Cross-National Comparison," *Journal of Conflict Resolution* 2 (1959): 29–42.

22. R. D. Minard, "Race Relations in the Pocahontas Coal Field," *Journal of Social Issues* 8 (1952): 29–44.

23. For more discussion see Tygiel, *Baseball's Great Experiment*, 103–4.

24. S. E. Asch, "Opinions and Social Pressure," *Scientific American* 193 (1955): 31–35.

25. Quoted in Allen, *Jackie Robinson*, 102–3.

26. M. Deutsch, *The Resolution of Conflict* (New Haven: Yale University Press, 1973).

27. M. D. Storms, "Videotape and the Attribution Process: Reversing Actors' and Observers' Points of View," *Journal of Personality and Social Psychology* 27 (1973): 165–75; C. D. Batson, *The Altruism Question: Toward a Social-Psychological Answer* (Hillsdale NJ: Lawrence Erlbaum, 1991); M. L. Hoffman, "Moral Internalization: Current Theory and Research," in L. Berkowitz, ed., *Advances in Experimental Social Psychology*, Vol. 10 (New York: Academic Press, 1977), 86–133.

28. M. R. Jackman and M. Crane, "Some of My Best Friends are Black . . . : Interracial Friendships and Whites' Racial Attitudes," *Public Opinion Quarterly* 50 (1986): 459–86.

29. We compiled this list of racial slurs hurled at Robinson from sources listed in note 5, above. Most observers of the incident comment that published accounts do not adequately describe the abuse and have been edited to remove the more offensive remarks.

30. Quoted in Frommer, *Rickey and Robinson*, 137.

31. D. A. Wilder, "Social Categorization: Implications for Creation and Reduction of Intergroup Bias," in L. Berkowitz, ed., *Advances in Experimental Social Psychology*, Vol. 19 (New York Academic Press, 1986), 291–355.

32. M. B. Brewer, "In-Group Bias in the Minimal Intergroup Situation," *Psychological Bulletin* 86 (1979): 307–24; H. Tajfel, "Experiments in Intergroup Discrimination," *Scientific American* 223 (1970): 96–102.

33. T. F. Pettigrew, "The Ultimate Attribution Error: Extending Allport's Cognitive Analysis of Prejudice," *Personality and Social Psychology Bulletin* 5 (1979): 461–76.

34. R. M. Kanter, *Men and Women of the Corporation* (New York: Basic Books, 1977). See also S. E. Taylor, "A Categorization Approach to Stereotyping," in D. L. Hamilton, ed., *Cognitive Processes in Stereotyping and Intergroup Behavior* (Hillsdale NJ: Lawrence Erlbaum, 1981), 83–114.

35. Of course, one way to reduce solo effects is to hire more members of the out-group. This is not always possible if the out-group is a numerical minority. An unpublished 1945 manuscript by Arthur Mann and some lost photos of Robinson with other black players to accompany the piece in *Look* magazine indicate that Rickey had planned to bring more black Americans to the Dodgers. Rickey rushed the news of the Robinson hiring before signing other black stars because he felt that political pressures were mounting to sign a black American. He thought the integration of baseball would run more smoothly if it were perceived to be a voluntary effort. For an intriguing account see Thorn and Tygiel, "Jackie Robinson's Signing."

36. D. A. Wilder, "Reduction of Intergroup Discrimination Through Individuation of the Out-Group," *Journal of Personality and Social Psychology* 36 (1978): 1361–74.

37. P. A. Katz, "Stimulus Predifferentiation and Modification of Children's Racial Attitudes," *Child Development* 44 (1973): 232–37.

38. See Tygiel, *Baseball's Great Experiment*, 92–93.

39. L. Effrat, "Royals' Star Signs With Brooks Today," *New York Times*, April 11, 1947, 20.

40. G. Waterman, "Racial Pioneering on the Mound: Don Newcombe's Social and Psychological Ordeal," NINE: *A Journal of Baseball History and Social Policy Perspectives* 1 (1993): 185–95 (reprinted elsewhere in the present volume).

41. Green, *The Jackie Robinson Story*.

42. J. Pfeffer, *Power in Organizations* (Boston: Pitman, 1981).

43. Quoted in Allen, *Jackie Robinson*, 102.

44. Quoted in Allen, *Jackie Robinson*, 103.

45. Quoted in Frommer, *Rickey and Robinson*, 127–28.

46. A. J. Murrell, B. L. Dietz, J. F. Dovidio, S. L. Gaertner, and C. Drout, "Aversive Racism and Resistance to Affirmative Action: Perceptions of Justice are Not Necessarily Color Blind," *Basic and Applied Social Psychology*, in press. See also J. F. Dovidio, J. A. Mann, and S. L. Gaertner, "Resistance to Affirmative Action:

The Implications of Aversive Racism," in F. A. Blanchard and F. J. Crosby, eds., *Affirmative Action in Perspective* (New York: Springer-Verlag, 1989) 83–102.

47. R. Barnes Nacoste, "If Empowerment is the Goal . . . : Affirmative Action and Social Interaction," *Basic and Applied Social Psychology*, in press. L. Sigelman and S. Welch, *Black Americans' Views of Racial Inequality: The Dream Deferred* (Cambridge: Cambridge University Press, 1991).

48. J. R. Kluegel and E. R. Smith, *Beliefs About Inequality* (Hawthorne NY: Aldine de Gruyter, 1986).

49. A. R. Pratkanis and A. G. Greenwald, "A Socio-Cognitive Model of Attitude Structure and Function," in L. Berkowitz, ed., *Advances in Experimental Social Psychology*, Vol. 22 (New York: Academic Press, 1989), 245–85.

50. M. E. Heilman, M. C. Simon, and D. P. Repper, "Intentionally Favored, Unintentionally Harmed? Impact of Sex-Based Preferential Selection on Self-Perceptions and Self-Evaluations," *Journal of Applied Psychology* 72 (1987): 62–66; T. F. Pettigrew and J. Martin, "Shaping the Organizational Context for Black American Inclusion," *Journal of Social Issues* 43 (1987): 41–78; M. E. Turner, A. R. Pratkanis, and T. J. Hardaway, "Sex Differences in Reactions to Preferential Selection: Towards a Model of Preferential Selection as Help," *Journal of Social Behavior and Personality* 6 (1991): 797–814; M. E. Turner and A. R. Pratkanis, "Effects of Preferential and Meritorious Selection on Performance: An Examination of Intuitive and Self-handicapping Perspectives," *Personality and Social Psychology Bulletin* 19 (1993): 47–58. For a review see M. E. Turner and A. R. Pratkanis, "Affirmative Action as Help: A Review of Recipient Reactions to Preferential Selection and Affirmative Action," *Basic and Applied Social Psychology*, in press.

51. See Turner and Pratkanis, *Basic and Applied Social Psychology*.

52. J. M. Jones, *Prejudice and Racism* (Reading MA: Addison-Wesley, 1972); idem, "Racism in Black and White: A Bicultural Model of Reaction and Evolution," in P. A. Katz and D. A. Taylor, eds., *Eliminating Racism* (New York: Plenum, 1988), 117–35.

53. For a discussion see Tygiel, *Baseball's Great Experiment*, 315–18.

54. D. E. Albrecht, "An Inquiry Into the Decline of Baseball in Black America: Some Answers – More Questions," NINE: *A Journal of Baseball History and Social Policy Perspectives* 1 (1992): 31–41.

55. For a listing of the accomplishments of black baseball players see A. Rust, *Get That Nigger Off the Field: The Oral History of the Negro Leagues* (Brooklyn NY: Book Mail Services, 1992).

56. H. Aaron, *I Had a Hammer: The Hank Aaron Story* (New York: Harper-Paperbacks, 1991).

Contributors

JEAN HASTINGS ARDELL lives in Corona del Mar, California, where she works as a freelance writer. Her presentation on the career of left-hander Ila Borders earned the 1999 *USA Today Baseball Weekly*/SABR Award for Research. Her book *Breaking into Baseball: Women and the National Pastime* was published by Southern Illinois University Press in 2005.

GAI INGHAM BERLAGE is a professor of sociology at Iona College. She is the author of *Women in Baseball: The Forgotten History* and coauthor of *Understanding Social Issues: Critical Thinking and Analysis*.

WILLIAM C. KASHATUS is a professional historian for the Chester County Historical Society. He is the author or coauthor of several books, including *One-Armed Wonder: Pete Gray, Wartime Baseball and the American Dream, September Swoon: Richie Allen, the '64 Phillies, and Racial Integration*, and *Connie Mack's '29 Triumph: The Rise and Fall of the Philadelphia Athletics Dynasty*.

LEE LOWENFISH is a freelance writer and the author of several books, including *The Imperfect Diamond: The Story of Baseball's Reserve System and the Men Who Fought to Change It* and *The Art of Pitching*

The late JERRY MALLOY was considered by many to be the most knowledgeable authority on nineteenth-century black baseball.

ANTHONY R. PRATKANIS is a professor of psychology at the University of California–Santa Cruz. He has authored many articles and books, including *Age of Propaganda: The Everyday Use and Abuse of Persuasion*.

SCOTT ROPER is an assistant professor of geography at West Texas A & M University in Canyon, Texas.

ROB RUCK is a senior lecturer of history at the University of Pittsburgh. He has written several books on sport, including *The Tropic of Baseball: Baseball in the Dominican Republic* and *Sandlot Seasons: Sport in Black Pittsburgh*.

MARLENE E. TURNER is a professor of organization and management at San Jose State University. She is the author of *Groups at Work: Theory and Research*.

GUY WATERMAN died suddenly in 2000. He was a frequent contributor to *NINE* and many other publications. With his wife, he also coauthored four books on nature.

JERRY JAYE WRIGHT is a professor of physical education at Penn State University in Altoona, Pennsylvania, and the former book review editor of *NINE*.

Source Acknowledgments

"The Birth of the Cuban Giants: The Origins of Black Professional Baseball" by Jerry Malloy. Originally published in *NINE* 2, no. 2.

"When All Heaven Rejoiced: Branch Rickey and the Origins of the Breaking of the Color Line" by Lee Lowenfish. Originally published in *NINE* 11, no. 1.

"The Year 'Cool Papa' Bell Lost the Batting Title: Mr. Branch Rickey and Mr. Jackie Robinson's Plea for Affirmative Action" by Anthony R. Pratkanis and Marlene E. Turner. Originally published in *NINE* 2, no. 2.

"Baseball and Community: From Pittsburgh's Hill to San Pedro's Canefields" by Rob Ruck. Originally published in *NINE* 7, no. 1.

"The Strange Career of Sol. White, Black Baseball's First Historian" by Jerry Malloy. Originally published in *NINE* 4, no. 2.

"'Another Chink in Jim Crow'? Race and Baseball on the Northern Plains, 1900–1935" by Scott Roper. Originally published in *NINE* 2, no. 1.

"From Giants to Monarchs: The 1890 Season of the Colored Monarchs of York, Pennsylvania" by Jerry Jaye Wright. Originally published in *NINE* 2, no. 2.

"Racial Pioneering on the Mound: Don Newcombe's Social and Psychological Ordeal" by Guy Waterman. Originally published in *NINE* 1, no. 2.

"Mamie 'Peanut' Johnson: The Last Female Voice of the Negro Leagues" by Jean Hastings Ardell. Originally published in *NINE* 10, no. 1.

"Effa Manley, A Major Force in Negro Baseball in the 1930s and 1940s" by Gai Ingham Berlage. Originally published in *NINE* 1, no. 2.

"Dick Allen, the Phillies, and Racism" by William C. Kashatus. Originally published in *NINE* 9, no. 2.

"Nine Principles of Successful Affirmative Action: Mr. Branch Rickey, Mr. Jackie Robinson, and the Integration of Baseball" by Anthony R. Pratkanis and Marlene E. Turner. Originally published in *NINE* 3, no. 1.